In the Rapids of Revolution

JOHN MACLEAN
In the Rapids of Revolution

Essays, articles and letters 1902-23

Edited with an introduction
and commentaries by
Nan Milton

Allison & Busby/London

First published in Great Britain 1978
by Allison & Busby Limited
6a Noel Street, London W1V 3RB

This selection copyright © Nan Milton and
Allison & Busby Ltd. 1978

ISBN 0 85031 153 3 (hardback)
ISBN 0 85031 175 6 (paperback)

Library of Congress Catalog Card Number: 78-000-340

Set in 10pt Lectura and 8pt Univers and printed by
Villiers Publications Ltd, Ingestre Road, London NW5

Contents

Biographical Introduction/9

I PRE-WAR SOCIAL DEMOCRACY/27

1: Marxism, marxist economics and the Labour Party
Wage slavery (1902)/30
Time-saving and Karl Marx (1907)/32
Böhm-Bawerk's theory of interest (1909)/34
Karl Marx and the Labour Party (1909)/35
Why a Labour Party? Come out! (1910)/36
My objections (1910)/37
Why a Labour Party? (1910)/39
A workers' party necessary, but Labour Party useless (1910)/40
Finale (1910)/41
The Labour Party muddle (1910)/42
Inflation (1910)/43
The rise in prices (1911)/45

2: Aspects of social democratic activity
Municipal housing (1904)/50
Socialism and the land question (1906)/51
A farm colony for Renfrewshire (1910)/51
Public health (1907)/52
Democracy and the coming coronation (1911)/55
The strike at Singer's (1911)/56
The end of the Singer's strike (1911)/58
The Scottish Co-operative Conference (1911)/60
Co-operation and the rise in prices (1911)/62
The foundation of the British Socialist Party (1911)/68

II WARTIME AND REVOLUTION/71

3: The anti-war struggle and the Russian revolution
War and robbery (1914)/76
The war: its cause and cure (1914)/77
Scottish chivalry and freedom in Pollokshaws (1915)/79
Our freedom is going (1915)/81
The fight for freedom in Glasgow (1915)/83
The Clyde unrest (1915)/84
Rent victories (1915)/85
The conscription menace (1915)/87
German industrial development (1915)/89
Zimmerwald (1915)/91
Speech from the dock (1915)/93
Peter Petroff (1915)/94
Speech from the dock (1916)/95
Miners' historic protest against profiteers (1917)/97
Russian distress fund (1918)/98
Correspondence on the Russian Consulate (1918)/99

4: "Unconstitutional action"
Speech from the dock (1918)/100
Letter from MacLean's wife to editor of "The Call" (1918)/115

5: Working-class education and the Scottish Labour College
A plea for a Labour College for Scotland (1916)/116
Independence in working-class education (1917)/122
The war after the war (1917)/124

III THE POST-WAR STRUGGLE/137

6: Revolutionary struggle in Britain
Now's the day and now's the hour (1919)/148
Rumblings of the revolution (1919)/150
Sack Dalrymple, sack Stevenson: the forty-hour strike
  (1919)/151
Onward, ever onward (1919)/153
The miners' next move (1919)/156
Labour's commissariat department (1919)/157

7: Ireland
The James Connolly birthday celebrations (1919)/160
Impressions of Dublin (1919)/161
The Irish fight for freedom (1920)/163
The Irish tragedy: Scotland's disgrace (1920)/165
Scotsmen, stand by Ireland! (1920)/175
Up, India! (1920)/177
Stray straws (1920)/179
The Irish tragedy (1920)/179

8: American imperialism
War on socialism! Which? (1919)/181
The coming war with America (1919)/182
America's shame (1919)/191

9: Capitalist crisis, inflation and unemployment
Will capitalism collapse? (1919)/193
Capitalists everywhere accept marxism (1919)/196
Away with the idle rich (1920)/200
"Burn Bradbury and down with prices" (1919)/202
The unemployed (1920)/204
Unemployment (1920)/206
The unemployed: will there be a general strike? (1921)/207
Speech from the dock (October 1921)/209

10: World revolution
Foreword to "The Class Struggle" (1919)/211
On with the revolution! (1919)/211
May Day (1920)/214
"The Vanguard' resurrected (1920)/215

11: The Scottish workers' republic
All hail, the Scottish Workers' Republic (1920)/217
Irish stew (1920)/218
Scotch broth (1920)/219
The Irish tragedy: up Scottish revolutionists (1920)/220
Literary note (1920)/221
The Highland land seizures (1920)/221
Stray straws: the defeat of the raiders (1920)/224
A Scottish Communist Party (1920)/224
Open letter to Lenin (1921)/226
Scottish history in the making (1921)/229
Account of speech from the dock (May 1921)/232
Speech from the dock (October 1921)/233
Election address (1922)/234
Red flag flutters (1922)/238

Explanation of election address (1922)/240
Municipal election address (February 1923)/242
Municipal election address (November 1923)/244
General election address (1923)/246

12: Letters
Letter to James Clunie from Barlinnie Prison (1922)/249
Letter to his daughters (1922)/250
Letters to James Clunie from Glasgow (1923)/251

Index/254

In memory of John MacLean
Born in Pollokshaws on 24 August, 1879,
And died there on 30 November, 1923.
Famous pioneer of working class education,
He forged the Scottish link in the
Golden Chain of World Socialism.

On 2 December 1973, a large crowd gathered in the modern shopping precinct of a very up-to-date and (to me) unfamiliar Pollokshaws, dotted here and there with high-rise flats and brand-new council houses. There a cairn, built to commemorate the fiftieth anniversary of John MacLean's death and bearing the above inscription, was unveiled by myself, my sister, and Glasgow's Lord Provost.

This was the culmination of a long campaign by the John MacLean Society — a campaign which involved not only the collection of the necessary finance, but also the widespread dissemination of information about MacLean's life and work. As a result, I do not think there would be many onlookers who did not understand why MacLean, rather than any of the other almost forgotten Red Clydesiders, was being honoured.

Nan Milton, 1977

8

Biographical Introduction

John MacLean's parents had both been victims of the Highland clearances, when the crofters had been evicted from their land to make way for sheep, often under conditions of terrible brutality. As Marx stated in **Capital:**

"But what 'clearing of estates' really and properly signifies, we learn only in the promised land of modern romance, the Highlands of Scotland. There the process is distinguished by its systematic character, by the magnitude of the scale on which it is carried out at one blow (in Ireland landlords have gone to the length of sweeping away several villages at once; in Scotland areas as large as German principalities are dealt with)."

His father Daniel was born in 1845 on the island of Mull on the west coast of Scotland, the traditional home of the Clan Mac-Lean. He had been forced to make his way to the mainland when still a youth, and eventually became a potter. His mother, Anne MacPhee, was born in 1846 in Corpach, a village situated at the foot of Ben Nevis. When, as a young child, she accompanied her parents on their forced migration to the south, she could not speak a word of English. So John MacLean had every right to use the pseudonym "Gael" when he wrote "Scottish Notes" every week in the British Socialist Party paper **Justice** from 1911 to 1914.

Daniel in due course obtained employment in Lockhart's Pottery in Pollokshaws, and in 1867 married Anne, who lived with her parents in the neighbouring village of Nitshill, where she worked as a weaver in a local mill. John was the sixth of seven children, but only four survived. Early in their married life Daniel developed the "Potters' disease", which nowadays would be called silicosis, and was often unable to work at his trade. Life was hard: he died in 1887, when John was only eight years of age, and Anne was left in those days of unbridled capitalism, when there were no widows' pensions, to bring up her four children as best she could. With the help of her own mother she went back to work as a weaver, and before her death in 1914 she saw both her sons become graduates of Glasgow University and school teachers, and both her daughters "respectably" married to well-doing young men. This real triumph was not achieved without tremendous sacrifices by all concerned, the greatest sacrifice being made by the older son Daniel, who died prematurely from tuberculosis. It was the knowledge of all this which spurred John into making up his mind to use his own education in the service of the working class.

John MacLean was already an enthusiastic socialist when he began his teaching career in 1900, and it is obvious from the letters he wrote to **The Pollokshaws News** at this period that he was also a convinced marxist. He joined the Social Democratic Federation at the end of 1903, and from that time onwards his life was completely dedicated to the socialist movement.

At this point it should be clearly understood that at that time a "social democrat" meant a revolutionary socialist, not a believer in the mixed economy as it does today. In the introduction to her brilliant pamphlet **Reform or Revolution,** written in 1899, Rosa Luxemburg explained concisely one important aspect of social democracy:

> "The daily struggle for reforms, for the amelioration of the condition of the workers within the framework of the existing social order, and for democratic institutions, offers to Social Democracy the only means of engaging in the proletarian class war and working in the direction of the final goal — the conquest of political power and the suppression of wage-labour. Between social reforms and revolution there exists for Social Democracy an indissoluble tie. The struggle for reforms is its means; the social revolution, its aim."

The SDF had been formed by H. M. Hyndman in 1881, and in 1883 it adopted a foundation of marxism. The Fabian Society was formed soon afterwards, explicitly to drive marxism out of the British labour movement. The Fabians were the first "revisionists", and Eduard Bernstein very quickly followed their example. It was to refute his ideas, including the notorious "The final goal, no matter what it is, is nothing; the movement is everything", that Rosa Luxemburg wrote **Reform or Revolution.**

The Independent Labour Party (that is to say, independent of the Liberal Party), formed by Keir Hardie in 1893, was also anti-marxist. It was customary for its leaders to insist that it was more important to obtain independent working-class representation than to emphasise the end and aim of socialism. In Scotland ILPers would assert that their socialism was derived from the New Testament and Robert Burns, not Karl Marx. Nevertheless, the anti-marxist feeling could not have been so strong in Scotland by 1911; the claim by Thomas Johnston,[1] editor of the Scottish ILP weekly **Forward,** that the Labour Party was "the heir of the marxist tradition", seems to demonstrate this. This claim precipitated a long controversy in the columns of **Forward,** excerpts from which are of such historical interest that they have been included here.

Seventy-one years ago, in the autumn of 1906, MacLean founded the Pollokshaws branch of the SDF at an open-air meeting by the old Townshouse, not more than fifty yards from the memorial cairn. Propaganda meetings were held there, or at the nearby Shawbrig, every week for many years.

MacLean took a weekly evening class, from 1908 until his first imprisonment in 1915, at the Sir John Stirling-Maxwell School (named after the local landowner). The subjects taught at this class were industrial history from the standpoint of the materialist conception of history, marxist economics, and the histories of the trade union and co-operative movements. The main textbook was **Capital,** and MacLean was paid the full rate for the job by the Education Authority, Eastwood School Board (of which Sir John Stirling-Maxwell was a leading member).

Among the pupils at this class were engineers from Weir's Works, Cathcart, the cradle of the famous Clyde Workers' Committee, which blazed the trail for the revolutionary shop stewards' movement that developed in Britain during the first world war. One of MacLean's assistants at this class was James D. MacDougall, the teenage son of the Tory provost, who became MacLean's most important assistant in the herculean task of pioneering scientific socialism in Scotland. Occasionally MacLean was also assisted by another young teacher, James Maxton, also a native of Pollokshaws, who had been converted to socialism by MacLean, and who became probably the most famous of all the Red Clydesiders.

MacLean trained other tutors, and when war broke out in 1914 regular classes in marxism were being held by the British Socialist Party (successor to the SDF) in all the strategic centres of industrial Scotland — classes which became the storm centres of the anti-war struggle. This was especially true of the huge Glasgow class, which most of the leading shop stewards attended. During the winter of 1915, when the rent strikes and the fights against dilution of labour and conscription were making Glasgow a thorn in the side of the government, this class had a regular weekly attendance of 493. At that time the Greenock class had a regular attendance of 121.

Of course this educational work was only one of the many activities undertaken by MacLean and the members of the BSP. Nevertheless marxists, and MacLean was no exception, always laid great stress on educational work, which had to consist to a large extent in counteracting the brainwashing carried out by the capitalist state through the state educational machine, the churches, the mass media, etc. In an advanced capitalist country with a long tradition of democracy, the ideological battle was considered of the first importance.

It is obvious that the "working-class education" recorded on the cairn was not the kind of orthodox adult education provided by, for example, the Workers' Educational Association. It was primarily concerned with schooling masses of workers in the basic principles of marxism, which MacLean at one time defined as "the science of society in its evolution and functioning". He was quite certain that "the very antagonisms in society that called into being the co-operative organisation in production and distribution, the trade union movement, socialist parties and the Labour Party, make it equally urgent that the workers should forge their own educational machine for their own class ends".

11

The "educational machine" referred to was the Labour College Movement, of which one of the favourite slogans was "Rise with your class, not out of your class", and one of MacLean's most cherished ambitions was soon to be realised when a committee elected from the Glasgow class set about organising a conference to found a Scottish Labour College, after the style of the Central Labour College in London, now suspended for the duration of the war. The purpose was quite explicit:

"The universities and other institutions for higher education have for their objective the training of men and women to run capitalist society in the interests of the wealthy. We think the time has come for an independent college, financed and controlled by the working class, in which workers might be trained for the battle against the masters. Such a college could be conveniently established in Glasgow."

MacLean was not present at the founding conference, which was held on 12 February 1916 and attended by about five hundred delegates from every section of the labour movement. He was lying in Edinburgh Castle as a prisoner-of-war, charged with sedition. He himself was convinced that his chief crime in the eyes of the authorities was the successful teaching of marxism to the Scottish workers. In his autobiography **Revolt on the Clyde**, William Gallacher described the dynamic effect of this teaching:

"MacLean never dealt in 'abstract' marxism of the Kautsky variety. He applied his marxist knowledge to the events round him and used all that was happening to show the truth of marxism. He demonstrated in the clearest manner that the war was a war for trade and brought out into full relief the sinister robber forces behind it. He gave example after example of the financiers and the big employers pointing a gun at the head of the government and demanding increased profits, and of other firms selling war material to neutrals with the full knowledge that they were being resold to Germany. . . . These examples were carried day after day into the factories."

In this passage Gallacher made handsome amends for his earlier hostility to marxist economics classes.[2] Although he had been a product of MacLean's teaching and a member of the BSP, he had spent 1913 in Chicago and had come home imbued with the syndicalist and anti-parliamentarian ideas of the Industrial Workers of the World,[3] whose headquarters were in Chicago. He was already clashing with MacLean when, at the end of 1914, both attended a conference of the Renfrewshire Co-operative Society, at which MacLean delivered the main speech on "The War: Its Cause and Cure", giving the classical marxist analysis. During discussion time, he was immediately challenged by Gallacher, whose contribution was reported as follows:

"The discussion was opened by Mr Gallacher (Paisley Trades Council) who did not agree with Mr MacLean. He argued that this war could have been stopped if the workers, instead of

12

trusting to political action by Liberalism, Toryism, and Labourism, had had an intelligent working-class organisation, organised on the lines of syndicalism, and prepared to throw down their tools. This was the only force that could prevent war. The capitalists did not have any parties; and, while he had heard a lot about taking over the instruments of production by political action, he had never heard any man explain how it was to be done. The capitalists could bring about such a dislocation of business as would discredit any party which did not do as they told it."[4]

Later on in 1917 Gallacher, along with John Paton, produced a pamphlet (published by Paisley Trades and Labour Council) which ignored the war altogether. It was along the lines of Guild socialism, akin to syndicalism, which advocated a system of peaceful "encroaching" control, in which workshop organisations could gradually take over, control and administer the factory system. This was continuing the tendency towards "economism" which MacLean had objected to in the Clyde Workers' Committee, of which Gallacher was chairman. This difference between the two revolutionary leaders did not come to a head until 1920. Gallacher ignored this rift in Revolt on the Clyde, and tried to explain it by asserting that imprisonments, hunger-strikes, and forcible feeding had undermined MacLean's health, and that he had become mentally unbalanced.

By 1920 MacLean had developed a political strategy for social revolution based on the break-up of the British empire. At that time Gallacher was still concentrating on the home industrial base of capitalism and underestimating the importance of its imperialist extension. MacLean did not need Lenin to teach him that imperialism was the "highest stage of capitalism", but he failed to do what Lenin did — convert Gallacher to classical marxism. But in 1920 MacLean was correct when he described Gallacher as a "self-confessed anarchist". Although Gallacher, once he met Lenin, became a model of orthodoxy (his "gramophone", according to MacLean) the conversion process was in fact gradual.

Another brand of syndicalism had come into Scotland with the formation in 1903 of the Socialist Labour Party, a breakaway from the SDF which took away the majority of the Scottish branches. Syndicalism was basically a plan for turning trade unions from organs of defence into organs of attack on capitalism. The trade unions were to take over industry and run it themselves in the interests of the workers, by-passing orthodox political action, which was regarded as worse than useless. The SLP, however, believed in a certain amount of political action, but only as a subsidiary to industrial action. It was also hostile to trade or craft unions, and wanted the workers to organise in industrial unions, ultimately to be joined together in one big union, which would be the instrument of the social revolution. Members were forbidden to take office in trade unions or take part in the "day-to-day" struggle for reforms, and regarded all who did so as "labour fakirs".

13

John MacLean supported industrial unionism in the sense of the amalgamation of existing trade unions, and later on he also advocated "one big union". But he was almost as impatient with those who wanted to limit activity to the industrial sphere as he was with those who, like the ILPers, wanted to limit it to the political sphere and leave industrial activity to the trade unions. MacLean put this quite clearly in his October 1921 trial speech, when he said:

"I argued that the workers should not confine themselves to industrial action, but should take political action as well. Neither political nor industrial action would do separately, and I pointed out in that direction the need for education."

After his marriage at the end of 1909, MacLean had gone to live in Langside, a Glasgow suburb, and during the war most of his political activity was concentrated in Glasgow and the surrounding mining areas. Glasgow had been for more than thirty years the second city of the British empire, and the centre of the world's shipbuilding industry. Indeed at that time the Clyde Valley was "one of the greatest centres of capital investment and industrial concentration in the world".[5] This tremendous industrial achievement depended on wave after wave of cheap, forced labour, as the populations of the Scottish Highlands and of rural Ireland were driven by economic necessity to Scotland's industrial belt.

As the war advanced, one hundred thousand people came to Clydeside, and sixty thousand of these came to Glasgow itself to work in the shipyards and munition factories. As the city came more and more under the control of the Admiralty and the new Ministry of Munitions, it was obvious that anti-war action here was more dangerous than in any other part of the country.

This was an explosive situation in a city which had probably the highest proportion of industrial workers in the world, a highly-developed trade union movement, and well-organised bodies like the ILP, BSP and SLP, which had been conducting intensive socialist propaganda for years. Glasgow, with its large immigrant Celtic population huddled together in slums round the factories and shipyards, with no great love for the Sassenachs or the imperialism which had uprooted them, was never completely submerged in the patriotic fever which swept the rest of the country. "Jingoism", wrote James D. MacDougall, "was at a discount in Glasgow from the very beginning of the war; it was the sole place in the British empire where there was perfect freedom of speech for international socialists and opponents of the war".[6] At first the anti-war men were looked on with hostility and scorn, but not subjected to the violence customary elsewhere. Then, as war-weariness and hunger crept in, the Glaswegians began to listen and then to act. Something of this is conveyed in the wartime section of this book, and a very brief and low-key description of his own experience is given by MacLean himself in his October 1922 election address.

His fight against the war made MacLean a world figure for the first time. Trotsky, writing in the Russian journal **Nashe slovo** about the Easter Rising, reported that "the Scottish soldiers smashed the Dublin barricades, but in Scotland itself coalminers are rallying round the red banner raised by John MacLean and his comrades."

In 1917 Lenin, now in Russia, wrote often about him, always linking his name with that of Karl Liebknecht. His most important assessment was made just before the October revolution:

"There can be no doubt that the end of the month of September marked the beginning of a new period in the history of the Russian revolution: and, very probably, of the world revolution.

The world working-class revolution was first begun with engagements by isolated combatants representing with unequalled courage all the honest elements of official 'socialism' — a socialism rotten to the core, which is in reality nothing but social chauvinism. Liebknecht in Germany, Adler in Austria, MacLean in England; such are the best known of these isolated heroes who assumed the heavy task of precursors of the revolution."[7]

Lenin went on to point out that the trickle of opposition to the war initiated by these men had grown into a flood, and this was the signal for the Bolsheviks to go ahead. That is why, after the revolution, the three men were selected, along with the Russians Lenin, Trotsky, and Spiridonova, as honorary presidents of the first All-Russian Congress of Soviets. And that is why MacLean proudly boasted at his trial in 1918 that the Red Clyde had helped to win the Russian revolution.

Lenin believed that they were on the eve of world revolution, and believed, as all marxists did at that time, that socialism could not be achieved except on a world basis because of the interconnectedness of capitalist economy. We find this again and again in MacLean's writings, and not least in the passage from which the title of this book is taken. "The times we live in are so stirring and full of change," he announced to his audience at a Co-operative Society Conference at the end of 1911, "that it is not impossible to believe we are in the rapids of revolution." Here he was not referring to an isolated British revolution but to the world situation, when he said: "We have but to think of all this to catch but the faintest outline of a world change that is so truly indicative of the triumph of knowledge and its application over the chaos of the past, and of the ultimate ascendance of the organised masses over the forces and resources of the world."

Since his release from prison at the end of June 1917, MacLean had been straining every nerve to bring about a revolutionary situation in Scotland. At the beginning of 1918 he was appointed Bolshevik Consul, partly because of his efforts to obtain the release of Peter Petroff and Chicherin (later to be the Bolshevik Foreign Minister) from London prisons. It was while carrying out his duties as Consul, and at the same time continuing his fight to spread in

15

Britain the flame lit by the Bolshevik revolution, that he was arrested again for sedition, and tried at Edinburgh High Court on 9 May 1918. The indictment essentially charged him with inciting the workers to turn the war into revolution, to strike the first blow on May Day, and to turn the House of Commons into a soviet. His speech from the dock was an attack rather than a defence: "I am not here, then, as the accused; I am here as the accuser of capitalism dripping with blood from head to foot", and ended with the classic marxist call for world revolution.

He was sentenced to five years' penal servitude, but released at the end of 1918 after a big public campaign. Such was his popularity by this time that when he was released from Peterhead Convict Prison, he was met at Buchanan Street Station in Glasgow by many thousands of people and was carried, waving a huge red flag, through the main streets on a horse carriage. It was this event which was the subject of Hamish Henderson's song "The John MacLean March" and Matt McGinn's "The Ballad of John MacLean".

Probably the nearest Britain has been to social revolution was during the first few months of 1919. In a secret memorandum Lloyd George described the situation:

"The whole of Europe is filled with the spirit of revolution. There is a deep sense not only of discontent, but of anger and revolt amongst the workmen against pre-war conditions. The whole existing order in its political, social and economic aspects, is questioned by the masses of the population from one end of Europe to another."

During these months, when the future of capitalism in Europe seemed in the balance, MacLean led another tremendous campaign for a general strike "round the mines as a nucleus", which was intended to paralyse British capitalism, prevent it attacking Russia, and possibly lead on to revolution. This was to a certain extent nipped in the bud by the fiasco of the premature Forty Hours' Strike in Glasgow (undertaken at that particular time against MacLean's advice), because it alerted the government to the nature of the attack being prepared. How the government warded off the threat and eventually out-manoeuvred the miners is described by MacLean in the articles at the beginning of the post-war section.

The murder of Rosa Luxemburg and Karl Liebknecht in January, and with this the defeat of the Spartacist revolution in Germany, was the bitterest disappointment of all. However, the subsequent rise of powerful anti-imperialist resistance movements in Ireland, Egypt and India provided a new lever for attack. It should be remembered that at this time British imperialism was the great power in the world. American imperialism was only beginning to develop and challenge British hegemony.

In Scotland, too, national feeling was stronger than ever before, and all three wings of the Labour movement had been demanding a Scottish Parliament since 1916. During the December 1918

16

election, at which MacLean had been the official Labour candidate for Gorbals, the Highland Land League and the Labour Party issued a joint appeal to the Scottish people to vote for candidates "pledged to the re-establishment of a Scottish Home Rule Parliament, and the ownership and control of the land of Scotland by the Scottish state".[8] It should be noted that the manifesto also stated that the English people showed "a marked disposition to conservatism while the Scottish people on the other hand are undoubtedly progressive in political thought and action". John MacLean had nothing to do with drawing up this manifesto, as he was in prison until the eve of the election, but it is obvious from later statements that he would have agreed.

This national feeling grew stronger in 1919, and was so strong in the labour movement by 1920 that the Scottish miners, the largest section of the organised workers, affiliated to the Scottish Home Rule Association. By this time MacLean was quite convinced that the Scottish workers were more advanced than the English, and would need to take the lead. In November 1920 he wrote in **Vanguard:**

"I hold that the British empire is the greatest menace to the human race. . . . The best interests of humanity can therefore be served by the break-up of the British empire. The Irish, the Indians and others are playing their part. Why ought not the Scottish? . . .

We on the Clyde have a mighty mission to fulfil. We can make Glasgow a Petrograd, a revolutionary storm-centre second to none. A Scottish breakaway at this juncture would bring the empire crashing to the ground and free the waiting workers of the world."

Again in April 1923 he wrote to James Clunie:[9]

"I'm certain London will never lead the Clyde or Scotland, so we must lead ourselves. A separate republic is justifiable as a step to keep Scotland out of future wars involving England; and breaking up the empire that most of all retards communism."

In the meantime in 1920 he became one of the founders of the Scots National League, the main object of which body was "the resumption of Scottish National Independence".

For this policy it was essential to have an autonomous Scottish communist party, but although he fought very hard for this during 1920, he was not successful. Many people believe that if he had gone to Russia like so many others did at that time, he would have been able to convince Lenin on this point. However, he made an issue of going openly and legally, as many others were allowed to do. But all his applications for a passport, both direct and indirect, were refused, and he did not go. This may have been one of the greatest mistakes of his life. The Bolsheviks, moulded as they had been by conditions of tsarist dictatorship and terrorism, were steeped in illegal and conspiratorial activity, and unable to

17

understand a deeply-rooted aversion to any kind of clandestine action. This could be regarded as an undesirable hangover from his Calvinist upbringing, but at the same time his kind of blazing honesty and integrity was part of the charismatic personality that drew the masses round him wherever he went. But his absence undoubtedly lent colour to the explanation given by Gallacher and others that he was a mentally sick man. His reactions to the official founding of the CPGB at the beginning of 1921 are recorded in his "Open Letter to Lenin".

I myself do not believe that the formation of a separate Scottish communist party affiliated to the Comintern would have made any significant difference to the course of events. Circumstances had forced on the Bolsheviks a party system of centralised military discipline. Before the revolution they had to operate in illegal conditions, and afterwards found themselves in the maelstrom of civil war and foreign intervention. In spite of the failure of the revolutions in the west, they still saw the Comintern as the body that was to lead the world revolution, and were convinced that it must have the same system of military discipline as the Bolshevik Party. This eventually meant Russian domination, with the national units having little say even in the formulation of tactics — a situation that was humorously expressed at a later date by a parody of an old music-hall song, "When Stalin says turn, we all turn!" Thus the Comintern soon became a supranational rather than an international organisation. Already in 1920 MacLean realised what was happening, and wrote in the December Vanguard ("A Scottish Communist Party"):

"We stand for the marxian method applied to British conditions. The less Russians interfere in the internal affairs of other countries at this juncture the better for the cause of revolution in those countries."

The accusation that in advocating Scottish independence MacLean was simply imitating Ireland and that the objective differences between the two countries made his position untenable has been made from time to time, the most recent occasion being in an article by Dr James Hunter in The Scottish Historical Review of October 1975. This is a grave reflection on MacLean's ability as a marxist to analyse events in a scientific and detached manner, and must be refuted.

While it is true that he had a great admiration for James Connolly, and was influenced by his ideas and by events in Ireland, it was the presence in Scotland of large numbers of Irish people that helped to determine his Scottish policy. The "black and tan" terrorism in Ireland in 1920 had a tremendous impact on these Irish people; it led to a growing hatred of "British" imperialism, which increasingly became identified as "English" imperialism. In August 1920 MacLean, along with the members of a propagandist group he had formed called the Tramp Trust Unlimited,[10] issued a leaflet

18

"All Hail! The Scottish Communist Republic!" which ended with an appeal to the Irish residents:

> "Many Irishmen live in Scotland, and, as they are Celts like the Scots, and are out for Irish independence, and as wage-earners have been champion fighters for working-class rights, we expect them to ally themselves with us, and help us to attain our Scottish Communist Republic, as long as they live in Scotland."

There were also large numbers of Irishmen in the armed forces, and when in 1920 the Connaught Rangers refused to fire on rebellious Indians, he saw this as the "greatest deed in British history". **The Manchester Guardian,** however, saw it as the most **dangerous** deed in British history, and warned that in the event of civil war every regiment would be "rent in twain", that there would be mutiny in every vessel of the navy, and that there would be an Irish outburst all over the empire. It seemed, alas, that many so-called revolutionaries were too busy arguing about the superior merits of political or industrial action or "whether Lenin can wink as well with the right eye as the left eye", as MacLean put it. "Unfortunately," he wrote, "lads who fancy themselves the only revolutionaries are to stupid or too obsessed with some little crochet to see with sufficient clarity the tight corner the Irish are placing Britain in".

Already at the beginning of 1919, MacLean had realised that unemployment was going to be one of the big problems of post-war society, and had declared in **The Call:** "Socialists everywhere, when unemployed, ought to organise, lecture and drill the unemployed, and so create a mighty menace to capitalism". He himself was one of the unemployed, having been dismissed as a teacher because of his first imprisonment in 1915. In spite of the fact that he had received the "King's pardon" after his release at the end of 1918, he was still banned from his profession and unable to get another job. So in the autumn of 1920, when unemployment was beginning to reach distressing proportions, he proceeded to carry out his own advice.

He was so successful that in his "Open Letter to Lenin" he was able to state:

> "It is by no accident that Dr Shadwell, after a recent tour over Britain, wrote in a series of articles to the London **Times** that the Clyde was the most revolutionary centre in Britain. . . . Three thousand five hundred unemployed meet twice a week in the City Hall, so that we may discuss principles and tactics applied to the present situation from a marxian point of view.
>
> As more and more are thrown idle and begin to starve — for the government means them to starve — you can realise that, sooner or later, a mass movement, vaster and bolder than ever before, is bound to show itself."

Before his plans for a new party could materialise, MacLean had to endure two more periods of imprisonment, because of his fight for the unemployed and his support for the locked-out miners. In May 1921 he was sentenced to three months, and in October to one year. Immediately after his release in October 1922 he plunged into a General Election, and again stood as a candidate in the Gorbals, not as the official Labour candidate this time but, proudly, "I stand in the Gorbals and before the world as a Bolshevik, alias a Communist, alias a Revolutionist, alias a Marxian. My symbol is the Red Flag, and it I shall always keep floating on high."

Several months later the SWRP was formed, but unfortunately the only record of its programmes and policies I have been able to find so far is contained in the various election addresses he put out, as the new party tried to establish itself by fighting as many by-elections as possible. But after only seven months of hectic activity, MacLean was dead, from an attack of double pneumonia incurred in the midst of fighting again in Gorbals in the 1923 General Election. He wrote his election address just one week before he died. It is a historic document. In essence his message was:

"The social revolution is possible sooner in Scotland than in England. . . . Scottish separation is part of the process of England's imperial disintegration and is a help towards the ultimate triumph of the workers of the world."

His sudden death at the age of forty-four shocked and dismayed thousands of Scottish people, most of whom were very well aware that he had been killed by government persecution, not by pneumonia — that he was, as Guy Aldred put it, "a martyr of the class struggle". His funeral was the most spectacular to have been held in Glasgow within living memory. Five thousand people marched the four miles from Eglinton Toll to Eastwood Cemetery in silence and with heads uncovered. Ten thousand followed the funeral procession, which was led by the Clyde Workers' Band.

Many years later, in 1937, a memorial article in **The Weekly Herald**, a Glasgow paper, ended with a moving description of the funeral:

"Although he was the dour Scots type, and a grim fighter, he was a man with a tremendous sense of humour, and quite the kindliest man I have ever met. In the winter of 1923, one of the worst I can remember, he was campaigning in the open in fog and sleet. Still living in dire poverty, his main food was dates and pease brose. The result was that, despite the tremendous vitality that made him a man apart, he caught pneumonia and died.

That was on Saturday, 30th November, 1923. There was a greater crowd at his funeral than had ever been seen in Glasgow before, and all the leaders of the working class were at the graveside. But not the leaders only: the rank and file were there in thousands, and there were many people wept that day who had never wept in public before.

20

And many lay stretched across his grave as they wept, having to be pulled away from it by force.

Only to a very great man are such tributes paid."

This article was called "Labour MPs Forget", but he was not forgotten by the rank and file. Every year until 1947 a "Silent March" was held again from Eglinton Toll to Eastwood Cemetery on the first Sunday in December, and in the evening a Remembrance Service was held in the city and a film of the funeral shown. At first large numbers took part, but through the years, as the SWRP dwindled until it was no more than a small sect, the numbers grew less until at the end only about fifty people took part.

William Gallacher's autobiography was published about this time. He paid generous tribute to MacLean for his work before and during the war, but brushed aside the even more important contribution made in the last years of MacLean's life, from 1919 onwards, as the work of a man unbalanced by a persecution complex. But there was one famous communist who did not turn a blind eye to John MacLean's real place in Scottish history, and that was the marxist writer and poet Hugh MacDiarmid. In a hard-hitting article in The Scots Socialist (November-December 1940), he castigated the labour movement for its neglect:

"It is indeed a scandal that a biography of this magnificent working-class leader — indubitably the greatest of modern Scotsmen — who had a far greater popular following than any other Scotsmen in the course of our history, should not have been written yet, seventeen years after his tragic death at the early age of 44. The consolidation of his great work called for the speedy and effective execution of this pious duty, so that, although dead, he might yet speak, and continue to be a great incitement and inspiration to the workers in Scotland, and to the workers of the world at large."

This challenge was accepted by the Scottish Committee of the CPGB, and in 1944 a short biography written by Tom Bell was published. This was obviously the result of careful research (most of it done by Harry McShane)[11] and was filled with interesting information. If it had been written by somebody who genuinely sympathised with and understood the totality of MacLean's marxist outlook, it could have been an electrifying book. But Bell had never worked with MacLean in any close fashion. He had been a member of the SLP, and the first president of the CPGB. Although a great revolutionary fighter in his youth, by this time he had obviously become just a party hack, determined to denigrate MacLean at every opportunity for his refusal to join the CPGB. This was done in such a subtle way that only those with a wide knowledge of MacLean's work could understand what was being attempted. For instance, he wrote in his assessment of MacLean's educational work:

"His weakness lay in the isolated character of his efforts (particularly in the last years of the war). How much more exten-

21

sive and permanent might have been the result had he laboured, not merely as an ardent individual, but as a member of a party consecrated to the same tasks!"

When it is remembered that MacLean was in prison for a great part of "the last years of the war", and that during his period of freedom he worked as one of the leaders of a party, the BSP, which was solidly behind him in his educational work, Bell's remarks seem very strange indeed.

Although the annual marches ceased in 1947, the legend did not die away. The upsurge of Scottish national feeling was even stronger after the second world war than it had been in 1919-20, and in 1948 the Scottish-USSR Society organised a mass meeting in St Andrew's Hall in Glasgow to mark the twenty-fifth anniversary of his death. A unique feature of this event was the presence on the platform of some of Scotland's foremost poets and literary figures, including Hugh MacDiarmid and Sidney Goodsir Smith, who recited poems of their own composition in honour of MacLean. Thus as a result of the Scottish literary renaissance which he himself had helped to inspire, the legend took on a new and immortal form.

During the revolutionary doldrums of the fifties and early sixties, it did actually begin to look as if the legend had died away and that MacLean had been forgotten, except in the pages of Mac-Diarmid's books and articles. Nevertheless, in 1956 James D. Young (then a student at Ruskin College) could write with assurance in **Forward:**

"A great army of orthodox historians have done their level best to cover John MacLean in obscurity. Most of the historians of the Labour movement have not done any better, for they have almost completely ignored his immeasurable contribution to British socialism. He was even ignored by G. D. H. Cole in his monumental book **A Short History of the British Working Class Movement. . . .**

In Scotland the man's name is a legend; indeed his incredible stature, his wonderful simplicity and unselfish devotion to a great cause have become part of our Scottish folklore. All the debunking in the world and all the attempts to surround his life and deeds in darkness cannot conceal his essential greatness."

This has been borne out by the level of the support gathered by the John MacLean Society since its formation in 1968. On the occasion of the fiftieth commemoration of his death two new biographies were published, but in my opinion the very heart of the legend is contained in **Homage to John MacLean,** a collection of songs, poems and verse (and some doggerel) written about Mac-Lean from 1918 until the present time. This unusual book was edited by T. S. Law and Thurso Berwick,[12] and in the preface they issue this challenge:

"Why should there be such a selective assessment of John MacLean as is given in the poems here? What is his significance? It has been said of him that 'he united the national sense and the international sense of the Scottish people', but there is a paradoxical situation of the betrayal of his ideas by the Scottish people after his death.

Our main consideration, however, is that Scotland also produced Hugh MacDiarmid, who countermanded the betrayal of MacLean. In so doing, MacDiarmid stands foursquare with MacLean for the honour of Scotland and the international proletariat.

By following the example of MacDiarmid, the poets contribute to the re-establishment of MacLean as a figure of epic significance. In the matter of whom do we remember and how do we remember him, the poets always have the last word, something which politicians among others should always remember."

So I shall let Hugh MacDiarmid have the last word. The following is a tribute paid to MacLean in 1976 on the occasion of a meeting called to commemorate the 97th anniversary of his birth. MacDiarmid was unable to attend, but sent this written statement:

"A few years ago the Edinburgh lecturer Hamish Henderson wrote a stirring song with the refrain 'Great John MacLean has come hame tae the Clyde'. There were few signs of that at the time, but things are very different today. Now that the predominance of the Labour Party is falling to pieces like a wet paper bag, it is noteworthy that no continuing influence attaches to the names of the Glasgow Reds of whom we used to hear so much. What do the names of Jimmy Maxton, Campbell Stevens, Neil McLean, and all the rest of them matter today?

Even more significant than the escalation of the Scottish National Party with its threat to what have been long considered safe Labour seats, is the research that has been going on in the last few years into all departments of our national life. And that research, among other things, has consigned to utter insignificance many names of men once considered important, and rescued from oblivion several men whose work has been unfairly neglected but is now seen to have been, and still to be, vastly more important than the alleged services of so many who occupied high positions in their own day — but are entirely without relevance to the problems of working people in Scotland now.

The name of John MacLean was largely forgotten. Young people had never even heard of him. Suddenly all that has been changed. No fewer than three books about MacLean were published simultaneously a few years ago, a monument was erected to his memory in Pollokshaws, plays have been written about him, and a John MacLean Society was founded and is now going ahead with the publication of MacLean's writings. In addition an effort is being made to revive and continue his great work in the establishment of a Scottish Labour College. Great is truth and it will prevail.

Why have so many men once considered great fallen into disrepute now? Why has the Labour Party shown such hypocrisy and lack of true political understanding in the miserable farce of its dealings with the question of devolution? For the simple reason that all their work and political policies were characterised by emotion without intellect. They would all have benefited enormously by attending John MacLean's lectures. He was the greatest working-class educator we have had.

Scottish politicians like Ramsay MacDonald, Campbell Bannerman, Bonar Law, and all the rest of them, mean nothing today in the light of Keir Hardie's declaration that Scottish MPs would be better advised to stay in Scotland and recreate an independent Scottish Parliament.

The vast revenues from North Sea Oil are to be devoted to paying England's Balance of Trade deficits — a purely English problem, since Scotland has no such problem. But to the British Labour Party and backlashing English Labour MPs it was, of course, unthinkable that Scotland, always regarded as a poor country and dependent on English charity, should suddenly become one of the richest countries in the world. That would never do for the English and their Scottish stooges, only concerned to keep their Westminster jobs and ignorant of, or indifferent to, the realities of Scottish affairs.

John MacLean wasn't. He was not a straw man blown hither and thither by the wind of party politics. He had the supreme disqualification of thinking for himself on the basis of a thorough grasp of marxist philosophy. The most advanced elements of the working class in Scotland owe him an enormous debt. Whether they like it or not they are going to have to discharge that debt now — or suffer the consequences. There is no other way. John MacLean was far in advance of his time. But he died over fifty years ago — and only now is an important section of socialist thought in Scotland beginning to catch up with him. It is not too late.

The message for which he gave his life is vital to us today — and he was alone in effectively expressing that message. It is indeed high time John MacLean came back to the Clyde. Unless he does there will soon be nothing worth coming back to in the great Strathclyde region. He is practically the only Scottish politician in the 84 years of my life worth a damn. Let us come to our senses at long last and renew and carry forward MacLean's great work. It is the only alternative to Scottish national suicide."

Notes
1. Many years later Johnston became the best Secretary of State Scotland has ever had.
2. "I for one will not follow a policy dictated by Lenin until Lenin

knows the situation more clearly than he possibly can know it from an enemy to marxian economic classes as Gallacher privately declared himself to me to be" (excerpt from "The Irish Tragedy" in **Vanguard,** November 1920.)
In various articles MacLean writes of Gallacher breaking up classes in Fife and Shotts. The latter's hostility is borne out in a negative way by the fact that his name cannot be found in any records as supporting marxist classes or the Scottish Labour College.

3. See introduction to Section 1, page 28.

4. This follows the end of MacLean's speech as reported in "The War: Its Cause and Cure", **The Scottish Co-operator,** 4 December 1914.

5. From Steve Vahrman's Introduction to a reprint by Socialist Reproduction of **The War after the War** (London, 1973).

6. See introduction to Section 2, page 71.

7. "On the Road to Insurrection".

8. From "The Gaelic Connection: The Highlands, Ireland and nationalism, 1873-1922", article by James Hunter in **The Scottish Historical Review,** October 1975.

9. Clunie, a friend of MacLean's, was a colleague of his in the Scottish Labour College, a member of SLP, and years later Labour MP for Dunfermline; he published letters from MacLean in a book of memoirs, **The Voice of Labour.**

10. Harry McShane, Peter Marshall, James D. MacDougall and Sandy Ross.

11. McShane was a foundation member of the BSP and a close personal friend of MacLean's. A member of Tramp Trust Unlimited and one of the leaders of Unemployed Committee formed by MacLean, he belonged to the CPGB from 1922 until 1953, and is now president of the John MacLean Society.

12. A pseudonym for Morris Blythman, now chairman of the John MacLean Society.

I

Pre-War Social Democracy

All MacLean's work, his writings as well as his speeches, were weapons forged in the heat of battle. He did not deal with theory abstractly unless it was vitally necessary, as in his economics classes. As he explained to Tom Johnston during the controversy in **Forward** mentioned in the Introduction:

"The historical and concrete method adopted by me may not appeal to Mr Johnston, but it is certainly the marxian mode of procedure no matter how clumsy may be my handling of that method. So far as I am concerned, I refuse to separate the Labour Party from its origin, its evolution, its deeds, its leaders, and the attitude of the rank and file. To discuss it from the abstract point of view alone, to me seems barren."

It is almost impossible, therefore, to arrange his work in any way other than chronologically.

The need to gather together his most important work in one volume necessarily limits the selection; this is particularly the case in connection with this first section. However, often a modern sketch consisting of a few essential lines conveys reality better than an old-fashioned drawing blurred with unessential details, and I hope the items chosen convey the essentials.

During this social democratic period, the theory that the struggle for reforms within the framework of capitalism was the only means available to achieve the final aim of social revolution lent itself very easily to the kind of opportunistic practice which regarded the reforms as ends in themselves — in fact, "revisionism". This was reinforced by the tendency of the leading European marxists, especially "Pope" Karl Kautsky, to regard socialism as "inevitable" in a rather mechanical way and as independent of the will of socialists fighting for it. This gave excellent cover for the growing schism between revolutionary theory and reformist practice.

At this time the Germans, possessors of the largest and most successful Social Democratic Party in the world, dominated world marxist theory. Much of German socialist activity had been concerned with wringing liberal democratic rights from a semi-feudal Kaiser, and it was natural that the leading German marxists should be concerned more with the political and cultural superstructure of capitalism than with the economic basis. This tendency led to a reaction in other countries which took the form of an over-emphasis on industrial action, for example in syndicalism. This can be seen to a certain extent in MacLean's work, although he was not a syn-

27

dicalist. This was partly because he himself was an economics expert, having been a brilliant student of orthodox economics at Glasgow University. Later, when running marxist classes, he concentrated on economics, leaving other subjects to James MacDougall and other colleagues.

British marxists of this period are generally regarded as being necessarily limited in outlook, because not all the works of Marx had been translated into English. However, the list of those available contained in Walter Kendall's book **The Revolutionary Movement in Britain 1900-21** seems to me not inadequate. MacLean did not appear to find the lack of even the third volume of **Capital** a great obstacle, as certain of his earlier writings on marxist economics demonstrate. In any case, he would not have approved of its being thought an obstacle, any more than he approved of the attitude of "Rob Roy" (a pseudonym for the right-wing Dr Robertson of Clydebank) when he tried to justify in **Forward** the conduct of the Labour Party by quotations from Marx. "Marxians do not fall back upon what Marx said here or there", MacLean wrote, "but apply his principles to each set of circumstances as it arises. 'Thus spake Marx' is not the marxian but the anti-marxian method."

The excerpts about municipal housing in this selection have been included mainly for their remarks about "municipal capitalism", since the remarks could also apply to the modern method of state ownership within the framework of capitalism and the capitalist state, which is "state capitalism" (although reformists call it "socialism").

It was customary at this period to deride marxists as "inhuman" (because of their efforts to view human events in a scientific, objective manner) and to accuse them of being concerned about "each for all" rather than "all for each". This was the opposite of the truth. For instance, MacLean from the beginning to the end of his political life was engaged in fighting cases of personal injustice and helping individuals, just as if he were the local MP or the parish minister. The excerpts from **The Greenock Jungle** have been chosen to show him engaged in fighting for justice for his comrades as well as fighting for social justice.

It was during the Singer's strike (see pp. 56-8) that the new tendency towards syndicalism and direct action first found concrete expression in Scotland. The "Industrial Workers of Great Britain" mentioned in the articles was a section of the Industrial Workers of the World (the "Wobblies"), which had been founded in America in 1905. Its principles were:

"1. There can be no peace so long as hunger and want are found among millions of working people, and the few who make up the employing class have all the good things of life.
2. The working class and the employing class have nothing in common.
3. Between these two classes a struggle must go on until all the toilers come together on the political as well as on the

28

industrial field and take and hold that which they produce by their labour through an economic organisation of the working class without affiliation with any political party."

The combination of industrial militancy and revolutionary socialist ideas was a dynamic one, and the IWW had a great influence in many parts of the world. In his articles MacLean gives the classical marxist reply to the anarcho-syndicalist position, although he obviously had great sympathy with their efforts. It should be noted that although the strike at Singer's was defeated and its leaders sacked, this did not in the end lead to any lessening of their influence on future events. Most of them found work in other factories or workshops up or down the Clyde, and when the industrial upheavals of wartime took place, these men occupied strategic positions throughout the whole Clyde area.

The extract from "Scottish Notes" on the foundation of the British Socialist Party is interesting because of the advocacy of a Scottish **National** Council, as opposed to the Scottish **District** Council of the old Social Democratic Party. Up to this time MacLean had not demonstrated any tendency towards nationalism, as far as we know, but this seems to indicate that even before the war he was very conscious of the fact that Scotland was a nation, and not merely a district of Britain.

1

Marxism, marxist economics and the Labour Party

Wage slavery
(Letter to *The Pollokshaws News*, 5 September 1902)
... "R" says the present form of society has been called commercialism. Not so. We call it capitalism. If he had the slightest knowledge of political economy and of logic he would not have tried the foolish sophistry of going to the dictionary for the meaning of scientific terms, whose precise meanings can only be obtained from the socialist school of economists. He denies wage slavery and the class stuggle without proof to substantiate his assertions. It would be as silly to merely deny the rotundity of the earth, its rotation, its revolution:

> "The wage-worker does not produce for himself; he cannot. All the things which are today indispensable for production — land and capital — are the private property of a comparatively small number of people. The worker, the person who has none of these, must either starve or sell the thing left to him, his labour-power, to the person who will buy it. That person is the *capitalist*. When the capitalist buys the labour-power of the worker, he does so only because he will produce more than he is paid for. If he produced only as much or less than he is paid for the capitalist would have no use for him, would not buy his labour-power, would not have him for a wage-worker. The wage-worker employed by the capitalist is the wealth producer. Out of the heap of wealth brought into life by the wage-worker himself, the capitalist takes a part, not more than one quarter, and returns that to the wage-worker in payment for his labour-power, as his 'wages'. The rest of the wealth, the three-quarters, is the surplus — i.e. the wealth produced by the worker over and above what was necessary to enable him to restore the force he expended in production. That surplus the capitalist keeps and calls 'profit'; it constitutes his income. Industrial capital, therefore, hatches profits by exploiting the propertyless wage-workers."

This plain extract shows the helpless condition of the wage-earner, shows that he is robbed week in and week out, and hence shows the justice of the term wage slave. Here is an extract from *The Clarion* of 1 August to show the precarious position of the slave and the safe position of the master:

"An explosion took place at Edge Green Pit, near Wigan, last April, in which the lives of nine men were lost. Mr Wm. A. Smethurst, colliery manager, was thereupon summoned at Wigan for two offences against the first and seventh rules of the Coal Mines Act. He pleaded guilty, and was fined by — what do you think — a fine of £10 and costs in each case, making £20 in all, or a little over £3 per head for the lives lost."

What about the slaves' lives when the masters' profits must be made!

To make wealth rapidly, capitalists have wrought men, women, and children long hours at high speed and for wages that just keep them alive. Here the class struggle begins with the desire to steal the maximum from the workers. The workers feel the necessity for united effort, so that they may resist the attacks of the enemy, the capitalists. Trade unions are formed, and the strike is used to get as much of the wealth produced as possible. . . . Hunger brings them to their knees, and so most strikes have resulted in loss to the men. Whatever gain is made is soon lost at times of depression, when masters need only threaten the lock-out to reduce wages.

Instances of strikes: the Belgian workers recognised that politics is closely related to economics, and so they struck work to force the capitalists to give them the political right of universal suffrage. Lord Penrhyn, trying to exercise feudal tyranny over his Welsh quarrymen, forced them to strike. The struggle has lasted two years, and is not settled yet. . . .

Just now the coalheavers and other workers in Gibraltar have been locked out by the Masters' Federation, because the workers dare to have a union. Governor White, the Ladysmith hero, assists the masters by using soldiers and sailors to scab on the workers. . . . Socialists have always shown that capitalists use Parliament to command the army, navy, and police force to subdue the workers, as well as to extend markets. . . .

That the class struggle is bitter, we need only reckon the annual death roll of the workers, the maimed, the poisoned, the physically wrecked by overwork, the mentally wrecked by worry, and those forced to suicide through desperation. It is a more bloody and more disastrous warfare than that to which the soldier is used. Living in slums, breathing poisonous and carbon-loaded air, wearing shoddy clothes, eating adulterated and life-extinguishing food, the workers have greater cause for a forcible revolution than had the French capitalists in 1789.

But the workers need not that method. Their hope lies in carrying the class struggle into the political field, and there they will meet and

31

defeat the capitalists, when all the workers see the need for solidarity and for loyalty to their class. The efforts of the masters to end the use of the strike through the Taff Vale decision has caused the miners to save their funds for labour representation. Next election we shall see a complete change in politics. The inevitable outcome will be the formation of two new parties with opposite interests, the parasites including capitalists, landlords, etc. on the one side, and the workers gathered round the trade unions and co-operative movement, on the other, the haves versus the have-nots. Socialists have pointed out this line of action and the masters have compelled its adoption.

When in Parliament, the new Labour Party will find its true mission to be not the shortening of hours, increasing of wages, and bettering of conditions, but the overthrow of the capitalist class and the landlord class, so that land and capital can be used to produce for consumption and not for profit. Remember the capitalist does not benefit the worker by giving him work; the worker benefits the capitalist by making him rich.

Time-saving and Karl Marx
(*Justice*, 14 December 1907)

By instinct the other evening I strolled up Sauchiehall Street towards the Fine Art Galleries, where at present are being exhibited all the latest devices and mechanisms that go to make up the modern office. Drawn thither by the spirit of enquiry that characterises the mind regenerated by socialist convictions, I enjoyed a mental feast, varied and palatable. I watched in operation machines for adding; machines for calculating the prices, wages, weights, etc.; machines for duplicating letters and drawings; in fact, machines for all kinds of work within the sacred precincts of business premises. I observed the latest methods of constructing and printing business books, the best systems of filing letters, the latest types of business furniture — all designed to create order and facilitate operations and calculations. . . . What underlies all these *facts*? What principle determines the whole exhibition? What is the philosophy of the whole affair?

Obviously, *time-saving*. The avowed advantage appealed to invariably by all exhibitors is — *the saving of time*. Clocks of various types and adapted to every purpose are there to lure the wary purchaser who knows that the struggle for existence in business is waged round the time-temple, and who knows that he who has the shortest cuts in the end will survive. "The race is to the swift", "time is money", "save time — save money."

This great truth inflames the imagination of the utopian socialist, who sees in all these things the means whereby the burden of humanity may be lightened in the new society.

To the marxist, the entire exhibition but reveals another aspect of the million activities of life, which all confirm the accuracy of his theory of value. But yesterday I heard of a clergyman giving a lecture on socialism, in which he reiterated the old bogey, that Marx had long since been discarded. Probably the wish was father to the thought; or, perhaps, parrot-like, it was simply repeating what socialists, who have not read or, having read, do not comprehend Marx, take a stupid delight in asserting. Many who are better caricaturists than thinkers or observers, delight in seizing hold of the technical language created by Marx the more easily to state his case and abridge later discussions of an intricate character, and by the skilful jugglery of the word-conjurer show the absurdities of marxian jargon. Others, less able, seize upon the awkward use of marxism made by zealous novices, and make that the base of an attack on Marx.

But all alike fail to present a serious refutation of Marx (even those who may have scanned the writings of Böhm-Bawerk), and to support any alternative theory other than those propounded by the orthodox economists, the capitalist hacks, whose whole business is to *justify the existence*, not *explain the origin* of profit.

These would have ignorant socialists believe that we marxists are narrow bigots, blinded by the prejudice resulting from an over-assiduous application of our minds to *Capital* and the other works of Marx.

This is absolutely false. Whilst the laws of capitalist production discovered by Marx form the foundations of our beliefs and actions, yet they have only become deep convictions as a consequence of using our own eyes and brains. Every new invention that saves time to the capitalist, and therefore is adopted by him, is simply further proof of marxian principles. Thus the significance of the business exhibition. It proves beyond dispute, *by facts*, that marxism is as true today as when discovered by Marx.

No other theory, and we marxians know these theories as well as our own, can find support from the display at the Fine Art Galleries.

It therefore becomes a duty for every socialist to comprehend marxian principles, because only by scientific knowledge can we know our social surroundings, can we explain social evolution and, therefore, efficiently and speedily accomplish the social transformation (i.e. the social revolution) necessary to the establishment of socialism.

See how successfully the Americans have applied science to industry, theory to practice; see how rapidly Britain is constructing technical colleges to follow suit; and see how the whole of Asia, with one fell swoop, is being lifted from barbarism and early civilisation to the highest form of capitalism by the wholesale absorption of Western science and arts.

If the capitalists can show us the importance of theory, and the certainty and celerity with which it can advance the political and economic structure, surely we socialists whose boast it is that we are ahead of the conservative capitalists, cannot afford to grope along in the dark in the good old(?) "rule of thumb" way, as did our fathers.

Capitalism is forging ahead at a terrific rate, and at an increasing rate; society is evolving at an unprecedented pace. Surely, then, we socialists cannot afford to grope; we must lead not follow capitalism. To that end we must have special scientific knowledge in our own lines of business; we must have half-an-hour's experiments every day in school for our children, instead of trying to follow Paul on his propaganda tours, or trying to parrot answers and inappropriate proofs to silly questions; and we must study Marx to know how best to lift society on to the higher plane of social evolution we are pleased to call socialism.

Böhm-Bawerk's theory of interest
(*Justice*, 6 February 1909)
I would like to say something on Böhm-Bawerk's theory of interest, now that the point has been raised in *Forward*. . . .

Thousands of years ago men began to lend money to others for usury, and were called usurers. "Shylock" typifies this class hated amongst men.

With the growth of world commerce and factories, these usurers evolved into bankers, and became "honourable" men. They lent money to manufacturers and governments for "interest". They also discounted bills of exchange. . . .

A bill, mature today, and worth £100, will exchange today for one hundred sovereigns; one due a year hence will exchange today for ninety-five. The difference between the price of the present bill and the price of the future bill is thus five sovereigns. The difference results from the usual interest transactions; and yet Böhm-Bawerk wishes to *explain* interest from this difference! He drags in mental operations to explain the difference; but as Marx has clearly shown the buyer's mind drives him in one direction and the seller's in the opposite with cancelling force. . . . This theory of Böhm-Bawerk's is almost the opposite of the "abstinence" theory.

Surely no sane worker believes that the luxuries of the rich are the result of this mental wire-balancing! We see that the workers are able

34

to make ten times more than they get in real wages, the surplus going to the owners of land and capital as interest, profit, rent, etc. If this is not true, then the claims of socialists are foolish and immoral. If rent and interest are not due to class robbery, then we must seek elsewhere the sources of the wrongs done the workers. The socialist theory is then false, and we must give up and seek the true one. If Böhm-Bawerk's theory is true then the ownership of capital by the few is not the ultimate source of interest and profit — in fact, interest is quite natural and just. If that be so, we have no reason to believe that the workers will be any better off in the future society than they are today. . . .

Karl Marx and the Labour Party
(Letter in *Forward*, 12 February 1909)
It shows a frightful chaos when professed socialists defend Böhm-Bawerk against Marx. This parallel can only be found when professed socialists appeal to Marx to justify the conduct of the Labour MPs who, whilst claiming political independence, silently listen to a wearisome discussion of the Licensing Bill during a period of almost unparalleled unemployment and starvation for the workers, and who strut about on liberal temperance platforms, exhorting the starving to end their drunken habits.

These phenomena result from the fear some men have of fully studying the marxian theory of value in economics and the marxian theory of the class struggle in politics, and accepting them as the basis of thought and action.

Marx could never brook sycophancy, and mercilessly flayed economic and political charlatans. The Labour MPs have fawned upon Asquith and his crew whilst at the same time using the vilest language against Grayson, Blatchford, Hyndman and others. They have created and aggravated schisms by trying to prevent the SDP putting up parliamentary candidates, and to that end have even gone against payment of members; or, where SDP candidates have been put up, have done all they could to prevent the workers supporting them. Whatever is proposed by the SDP is misrepresented, caricatured or opposed; but whatever comes from the Liberals receives adulation. It is a scandal to quote Marx as one who would support such a line of conduct. . . .

The probability is that "Rob Roy" in his attempt to justify the Labour Party by quoting Marx wishes to nullify the criticisms of those who are said to swear by Marx.

Unfortunately for him, marxians do not fall back upon what Marx said here or there, but apply his principles to each set of circumstances as it arises. "Thus spake Marx" is not the marxian but the anti-marxian method. No marxian, therefore, attaches any importance to the clever method of "Rob Roy".

The method of Marx, in testing the Labour Party and its leaders, is to examine whether they are constantly fighting in the interest of the wage-earning class. We marxists are in favour of the Labour Party because it is working-class; but we oppose the conduct of the MPs because it is reactionary and tends to lead the masses to Liberal petty patchwork rather than to the class struggle ending in the revolution of property-ownership which must inaugurate socialism.

Why a Labour Party? Come out!
(*Forward*, 30 July 1910)
Mr Thomas Johnston in his article "Why a Labour Party?" says the present British Labour Party "is the heir of the marxian tradition, for it is the wage-earners' party, paid for by the wage-earners, controlled by the wage-earners, expressing the political and economic sentiments of the wage-earners."

To this I beg leave to take exception. The Labour Party is a miserable caricature of marxism. Before January 1906, it stood, or its exponents said it stood, for political independence, but not for socialism, nor for socialist palliatives. Marxism, in the eyes of the world's professed marxists, stands for the revolutionary transformation of society. In fact, socialism established implies surely the overthrow of capitalism, and that is revolution. . . .

The Labour Party in Parliament does not seem to be controlled by the wage-earners. It brings in a miserable Women's Franchise Bill, whereas the trade unions are alone in favour of the vote for all women. Its representative men are anxious to flatter Liberal ministers, Liberal measures, and Liberal policy, and to keep the Liberals in power.

In doing so, it proves that it is controlled by the Liberals, and, if controlled by them, it is really fighting against — not on behalf of — the interests of the working class. . . .

The remedy now lies in the amalgamation of the SDP and the ILP. The energy of the two bodies today is more or less frittered away, and the progress that we should naturally expect is not visible. The rank-and-file hold the same ideas and the same principles as the rank-and-file of the SDP, and are only kept separate from their comrades by the grossest misrepresentation of the theoretical principles enunciated by the SDP.

We are said to be dogmatic. We are dogmatic in so far as we hold ideas that make us strive to end capitalism. We are dogmatic because we talk about surplus value, another expression for rent, interest, dividend, etc. We are dogmatic because we preach the class war, another way of asking the workers to cut adrift from the capitalist parties and form one for themselves in opposition to them. But surely that is the very dogmatism of the ILP too. If not, what does the ILP really exist for?

It is said that the SDP is too extreme. We fight for nothing short of socialism, because we believe that nothing short of that will save the workers. That, I understand, is the position of the ILP as well. If so, then it is apparent that the ILP are as extreme as we.

And, after all, extremity is a virtue. The international trustification of today is capitalism carried to an extreme. We, as socialists, hail that extreme development. Why? Because we know that it hastens the approach of socialism. Mild men are obstacles to progress because they are unscientific.

It is said that the SDP are unpractical. Dear me! He must be an ignoramus, indeed, who does not know the practical and economic programme of the SDP and of the marxist movement the world over. . . .

Examine whatever lie against the SDP you may, and after candid analysis you will find that it has been propagated for the purpose of keeping the two bodies separate. . . .

A United Socialist Party is the only way out of the political quagmire we have been led into by the supremely sagacious Labour MPs.

My objections
(*Forward*, 6 August 1910)
In my previous article I tried to show that the Labour Party is not "the heir of the marxian tradition", although Mr Johnston says I have not really faced the position he laid down. He further describes the Labour Party as "the proletarians on the move for economic change through political avenues" and as "the workers as workers, organised for the capture of economic power".

This I cannot accept. Richard Bell, to safeguard his Union and himself after the Taff Vale decision, gave the lead to the formation of the Labour Representation Committee, which undoubtedly came into being to protect trade unions, their funds and the salaries of paid officials. But all socialists saw in it the start of the workers on the political plane leading up to socialism, and hence did their best to give it a good send-off. Though "capture of economic power" did not inspire it at its inception, socialists believed that once in existence as a political party it would be compelled to make for our goal.

Perhaps prematurely the SDF (now SDP) tried to get the LRC to adopt socialism as its political aim, and, when defeated, wrongly (in my opinion) left. Just as wrongly did the ILP oppose the socialist resolution by amendment, speech, and vote, as this could safely have been left to Bell and Co. And here, might I add, that had it not been for the NAC of the ILP the socialist forces would have been fused prior to the birth of the LRC, and the present political chaos of the workers undoubtedly avoided.

I joined the SDP two or three years after its withdrawal, and I did so because I saw the need for only one Socialist Party. It was the oldest, and I felt that it alone was required. If the trade unions were anxious to enter the political arena as socialists, then I thought it was their duty to support the already existing Socialist Party. . . . I thought it my duty to join the SDF, and do my best to bring all bodies together should the occasion present itself.

The 1906 election saw the marvellous success of Labour candidates. It did not matter to me how some had won. A new party now existed to champion the cause of Labour. . . . Things looked rosier, and to finish up, at the 1907 Labour Party Conference a sort of socialist resolution was carried.

This gave some of us the chance we desired. Hyndman and some others of us advocated affiliation of the SDF in *Justice*, and supported a resolution to that effect at our 1907 Annual Conference, at Manchester. We were defeated.

Since then the Labour Party, instead of fighting for the working class and maintaining a sturdy independence, has acted as apologist for Liberal ministers, measures, and policy, and has, in consequence, proved the most efficient touting agency for that party. . . . The result was a partial collapse at the last election, with a resultant slump in socialism. . . .

The origin of the Labour Party, the repudiation of the SDF socialist resolution, the reactionary drift of the Labour MPs, and the lack of revolt on the part of the rank-and-file of the trade unions suffice to prove that the workers are not "organised for the capture of economic power" and not even political power, as the Osborne decision should have afforded that very chance we need to fight — fight mind you — for the payment of election expenses and MPs. . . .

Appeal to Marx will not do, especially by those who repudiate the economic principles of marxism, the basis of working-class politics. I believe, however, that Marx would have approved of the unity of socialist forces at this juncture, especially when we see the dissatisfaction and rebellion inside the ILP itself. . . .

Why a Labour Party

(*Forward*, 13 August 1910)

Again Mr Johnston maintains that I have not faced the issue. He wishes to settle whether we should have a Labour Party or not. For that matter the workers can have a thousand Labour Parties if they like. That was not the point which induced me to write. The question for me was and is — is the Labour Party a marxist one?

The SDP, since its inception almost, adopted what is sometimes called marxian socialism, the which has been usually sneered at by all outside the party. It was natural, then, that as a member of that party I should attempt to present the general attitude of that party towards the Labour Party to show that the claim made for it, that it was marxian, could hardly be upheld.

I endeavoured to give a general sketch of the Labour Party from its inception, the part played by the ILP in it, and the varying attitudes of certain SDPers towards it, to show that it would be inaccurate to describe it as marxian. The historical and concrete method adopted by me may not appeal to Mr Johnston, but it is certainly the marxian mode of procedure no matter how clumsy may be my handling of that method.

So far as I am concerned, I refuse to separate the Labour Party from its origin, its evolution, its deeds, its leaders, and the attitude of the rank and file. To discuss it from the abstract point of view alone, to me seems barren. I remember a journalist reading a paper on "War", in the midst of the Boer War, without even referring to it. When his hearers wished to get to grips with him on that war he absolutely refused to discuss it, as he maintained that such was irrelevant. Mr Johnston's attitude appears to me to be like that of this particular journalist. . . .

Mr Johnston holds that as the Labour Party is composed of workers, is maintained by workers, and fights for workers, it is all right, and is marxian. The old and the new internationalists used to let communist anarchists attend their congresses. Marx bitterly opposed them, although they were out for social ownership, because they refused to fight through political channels and had confused ideas. . . . At last these anarchists were excluded from international socialist congresses. Today the syndicalist trade unions of France and Italy, although they believe in social ownership, are opposed by the socialist parties of these countries because they repudiate politics. . . .

Here we see trade unions making for socialism, and yet opposed by the socialist parties. I fancy they have more right to maintain they are "the heir of the marxian tradition" than the Labour Party, in that they have their faces turned towards socialism, but are making through a bog;

the Labourists are on the solid road, but are marching to liberalism, i.e. in the direction opposite to socialism. All we Social Democrats wish them to do is to get them to right-about-turn.

And, bear in mind, that as trade unionists we are trying our best to get the workers into their proper unions, to get the unions fused or brought closer together, and to get the existing unionists converted to socialism. Furthermore, we try to get them to co-operate with us, and we co-operate with them, on all possible occasions. So far as my experience goes we get on well enough side by side; and in local elections in the West of Scotland Social Democrats have polled as well as Labour men who have fought a clean fight against capital, and we have done that, too, with the help of trade-union and co-operative organisations.

It is a significant fact, also, that the larger portion of our votes comes from those as yet unorganised, showing, no doubt, a strange phenomenon that men unprepared to unite economically or politically are still prepared to vote socialists into power. It does not follow, then, that socialism would wane away were the ILP to withdraw from the Labour Party and join with the SDP. . . .

Mr Johnston may say I have given away my case when I point out that the Labour Party is on the path, and that all we need do is to educate the rank-and-file to make them move in the right direction.

My point is, that because the Labour Party is marching into the capitalist camp, it needs must meet with the opposition of marxians, according to precedent. . . .

A workers' party necessary, but Labour Party useless
(*Forward*, 3 September 1910)
. . . Both Mr Johnston and myself, no matter what our differences may be, agree that a workers' party is necessary. The divergence arises as to whether the present Labour Party is the one. The workers' party that is of any use in my estimate is one that recognises that the workers are robbed by the capitalists, and understands how that robbery takes place; and is one that is organised to prosecute the class struggle politically until socialism is attained. Such would be a Socialist Party based on marxian principles. All other parties, no matter how named, and of whom composed, are useless.

The Labour Party of today, not being socialist, is useless. Yet admittedly we might postulate the possibility of it becoming the Socialist Party, the Marxian Party, when its usefulness would begin. Facts show that the Labour Party opposes socialism, and socialist candidates, and supports liberalism and Liberal candidates.

Many Labour men have been returned by Liberal votes, and openly proclaim themselves Liberals. . . .

The socialists inside the Labour Party are unable to stem this march to liberalism, and are through loyalty compelled to apologise for the party when they might be better engaged inculcating the principles of democracy and socialism. As a result, widespread discontent manifests itself inside the ILP, and will spread as the Labour Party moves along, the servant of liberalism. . . .

I would advise Mr Johnston to get past elementary and rise to advanced logic. Every path has two directions. It is possible for us to be on the right path but moving in the wrong direction. It is the function of marxists, who see just as great potentialities in the Labour Party as the non-marxists or anti-marxists, to oppose every motion of the Labour Party in the wrong direction. To do that more effectively the marxists, i.e. the SDP, withdrew from the LRC. And, like most marxists today, I think it advisable for the ILP to withdraw from the Labour Party and fuse with us for the specific object of advancing socialism, belief in which the rank-and-file of the Labour Party must have ere things will be done. . . .

The SDP is as entitled as any other to be considered the British Labour Party and it is more thoroughly democratic than the so-called Labour Party — because its members have but one vote, whereas ILPers who are at the same time members of a trade union have two votes for other members' one. Such is not democracy. This arises entirely out of the hotchpotch nature of the Labour Party.

Had there been but one Socialist Party prior to 1900, then certainly the true function of the trade unions would have been to urge their members to join the Socialist Party, and thus there would have been one man one vote. At the same time, political liberty would have been assured to all members of trade unions. Today conservative and liberal trade unionists are compelled to pay for a political party they oppose. . . .

Finale
(*Forward*, 24 September 1910)

. . . I am now firmly convinced that the prosecution of this discussion with Mr Johnston is useless meantime, as it has never really afforded the opportunity to thrash out the point I disputed — the marxian nature of the Labour Party. I fail to see that it is marxian. Mr Johnston clearly sees that it is. My conclusion is that we should agree to differ; but Mr Johnston will pardon a parting suggestion, and that is this. If he is still convinced that the Labour Party is a marxian one, and if he approves of it being so — as I am led to think by his articles — I should point out that it is his bounden duty to make the members of the Labour Party conversant with the writings of Marx, should encourage them to read the shorter and simpler ones, and should attempt to popularise the basic principles that are concentrated in the word marxism. Then there will be hope that soon the Labour Party will openly avow itself a marxist party. . . .

I ask Mr Johnston to create in the readers of *Forward* a thirst for the study of marxian economic and industrial history, and I am prepared in my classes to do my best to satisfy their thirst. Meantime, preparation for these classes compels me to apply the closure. . . .

The Labour Party muddle
(*Justice*, 29 October 1910)

It is with the deepest interest we Social Democrats must watch the campaign over the Osborne decision. For the first time since the formation of the Labour group in the House of Commons, the Labourists now have begun to realise the genuine importance of a national campaign. From now on till the autumn session begins, they are going to stump the country to create a public opinion that will cause the Liberals (their dear friends who love their presence in the House!) to reverse the "awful" decision that will deprive them of their wages.

Why did they not do that on behalf of the unemployed millions two years ago? Why did they not get thrown out with Grayson, and do as he did afterwards? Why did they not fight for the Tyneside engineers or the Belfast dockers? Their only excuse was that such was not statesmanlike, or not practical. Yet all the time they could stand on Liberal platforms and write in Liberal "rags" for free trade, temperance, and a change of the human heart through a Christianity they use but do not believe.

What did not become them to perform on behalf of the class that put them into Parliament and kept them there seems plainly to suit them now that their personal interests are affected. . . .

Shortly after the return of the Labour men in 1906, Hardie and other so-called "democrats" repudiated payment of members and election expenses, as their claim on trade unions gave them financial advantage over the Social Democratic Party. Their very attitude on this radical, chartist and real working-class economic reform certainly gave the clue that has directly led up to the Osborne decision. The capitalists' early dodges to kill the Labour Party completely failed, and in the end they had to resort to the risky expedient put into operation by Osborne. For, as we Social Democrats know full well, Osborne certainly did not initiate the action he took on his own account, but on account of the plunderers. Hardie's advantage has now gone, and he, with his invertebrate colleagues, are frantic. . . .

The practical question for us, however, is not merely the exposure of political incapacity of the Labour Party, but the carrying on of the class war under the circumstances, and thus giving the lead the workers really want. It is our business, as our executive is trying to do, to rally the support of the trade unions at present attacked by the masters, and to show the meaning of the simultaneous attack by lock-outs and Osborne decisions. Ours is also to point out the insincerity of the capitalists in their offer of payment of members and election expenses, but at the same time accept the offer by pressing for its realisation during the coming autumn session. . . . To this we must add the cry for a reversal of the Osborne decision, for such a hampering of the trade unions obviously tends to cripple them. The Taff Vale decision enabled the capitalists to steal, to confiscate the funds of the union did they dare to strike. This judge-made law was the final argument that forced politics on the unions. Obviously, then, to clear them out of political activity is the first step towards their ultimate annihilation. This is too much an insult to our class in this twentieth century of Christian civilisation under the benign régime of a paternal Liberal government. . . .

Inflation

(Letter in *Justice*, 12 November 1910)
. . . Hobart, in refuting G. B. Shaw's argument that an increase of wages would in the end stop destitution, falls back on the fallacy that wages determine prices — a fallacy long since exposed by Marx in his "Value, Price and Profit".

So long as surplus value is wrung out of the workers by the operations of the perfectly natural laws of capitalist production, just so long will the equally natural social consequences of unemployment and destitution continue to appear. . . .

But no matter how high wages may be, surplus value — as rent, interest and dividends — must still pour into the coffers of the plundering few, and therefore chronic unemployment, periodically accentuated by crises, must persist. This is a marxist reply to Shaw.

On the assumptions of Hobart, the real wages of the workers never for any considerable time vary, because the prices are regulated by wages. If wages rise, prices rise, and vice-versa.

During the last fourteen or fifteen years, prices have almost steadily risen, whereas wages, though fluctuating, have rather on the whole tended downwards. And had we the absence of trade unions, wages would markedly fall without at all affecting the upward movement of prices. The reverse of this we see in the increasing wages of German comrades organised into unions, unaccompanied by price increases greater than obtaining in other fully evolved capitalist countries.

Wages simply being the specific name for the price of labour-power, it must be theoretically apparent that a price cannot regulate prices in general. The above illustrations bear witness. The recent revolt against trust prices in America, and the dramatic strike of the railway workers for increased wages, to balance the increased cost of living, demonstrate that the masses had become conscious that their real wages — the mass of goods that money wages can purchase — had gone down.

I am one of those who believe that we ought to have a law of minimum wages, but ever increasing with every increase in prices, though never decreasing with price diminution, and a law of maximum for hours, ever falling with increased productivity. Tom Mann does right to insist on this as work for the organised workers, after they have organised industrially for fusion of unions already existing, and the absorption of those as yet unorganised. But the supplementary effort of parliamentary representatives I hold to be necessary, and here it is that a real Labour Party could fight the class war effectively in the "temple of time-servers".

So far as a maximum for prices is concerned, I imagine the proposal is utopian. Prices are, under perfect free competition and uniform composition of capital, determined by the exchange of gold for other articles in proportion to the time necessary to produce them socially. Thus ten hours of gold will normally exchange for ten hours of any other product. This gold, converted into coin, constitutes the price of all products finished in the same time.

If gold can be found abundantly in rich, easily accessible seams, or if by the application of improved mechanical and chemical agencies, it can be more easily produced, then its value declines, and prices generally rise. This is quite natural, and is operating today; and laws to limit prices would be just as silly as laws to end trusts. An agitation for the limitation of prices would imply that we favour the point of view opposed to marxism, that profits are the result of fleecing the consumer. No doubt profits are increased by the sale of adulterated goods, but normally profits are not made out of the consumer. Such a fight would blur over the class issue entirely, and would thus be tactically as bad as it would be economically.

It might be suggested that if a law of maximum in price is bad, so also is it bad in relation to hours, so also is the law of minimum in relation to wages. But an increase of wages and a shortening of hours all

44

round would in no way violate the operation of the natural laws of capital-ism, although it might result in the reduction of surplus value temporarily, and thus give an impetus to better methods of production and trustifi-cation. An agitation for this purpose would bring to the surface the fact that the producer creates profit, and would thus enable us to raise to eminence the fight of the workers against the capitalists.

As prices are rising in our country whilst the capitalists are using every cunning agency such as profit-sharing to speed up the workers as well as every form of cruel "sabotage" to cow and quell them, it surely is time our organisation made a concerted and well-planned attempt to get trade unions to fuse and fight with social-democratic arguments and, through the unions, to force the poor Labour Party to do something, just for once, on behalf of the men who pay them, for a reduction of hours and the establishment of a minimum wage. Efforts are being made, I know, but systematic effort is the only road to success.

The rise in prices
(*Forward*, 7 January 1911)
Nothing is of greater importance than to find facts and arguments that support the socialist case in books issued under capitalist auspices. And every fresh yearbook provides these requisites in ample abundance.

Here is the *Daily News* yearbook, for instance, giving us as substan-tial proof of the accuracy of marxian economics as the most ardent could wish for. On page 80 appears a brief article on "Gold", supplying us with facts anent the world's output of that "root of all evil". In 1890 the total production amounted to £29.2 million, and by 1909 this had risen to £92.1 million; that is to say, an increase of fully 200 per cent.

This tremendous increase has been essentially due to the develop-ment of the Rand and the cheapened cost of production — or, in marxian phraseology, the reduction in the time socially necessary for production.

In this article we are told that in 1904 the average revenue in gold derived from every ton of ore amounted to 30s 8d, the cost per ton for extracting, handling, etc., amounted to 21s, and the profit 9s 8d per ton; whilst in 1908 (the date of the latest statistic) the revenue was 31s 4d; the cost 17s 10d, and the profit 13s 6d.

What lessons do these facts teach us? First of all we see that in four years the cost of production has dropped about 40 per cent; second, this has led to an increased output of about 40 per cent (from £65.9 million to £92.1 million); third, it has been found possible to work poorer ores — in fact, ores 20 per cent poorer; fourth, so great has been the reduction in cost that even taking in the poorer ores, the profits have gone up fully 36 per cent.

Theoretically an increased supply has followed a reduced cost of production, and not an increased demand, as followers of Marshall might try to explain, from a psychological point of view; and next, in contradiction to the law of diminishing returns, the opening up of poorer mines has not been due to increasing demand at a higher price, but the reduction of the time socially necessary at a lower "price" for gold — to use the loose term of business men. . . .

Those unacquainted with economics will necessarily find it difficult to understand how "cheap" gold gives rise to high prices generally. But if they reflect they will see how it logically follows that the less valuable gold is, relatively the more valuable all other articles become when expressed in gold; in other words, their prices rise. . . . Whether the theory can be grasped or not, there we have it all the same — a general rise in prices essentially due to the facilitated output of gold. I say "essentially due" advisedly, because I am aware that corners, rings, and trusts all strive to raise prices above the level that would obtain were competition, with the great "law of supply and demand", prevalent.

As the output of gold yearly tends to grow larger, experts tell us that there is no end in view to the rise in prices. Now this is going to be serious, very serious, for the working class. Fabians and revisionists generally in this country have skilfully attempted to prove the falsity of marxism by a spurious use of Marx's prediction of the tendency of capitalism to make the lot of the workers worse and worse. They have triumphantly pointed to the reduction in prices shown by reference to Sauerback's index numbers from the early seventies, the time, by the way, when prices were highest since the end of the Napoleonic wars; by reference to the rapid extension of co-operation; and by reference to the marvellous expansion of municipal enterprise.

Superficially, it really did look as if the position of the people was rapidly improving, and that collective effort was expanding so rapidly that all we had to do was to go gently, and quite unconsciously to the mass of mankind, we would evolve into socialism without waging that hated "class war", etc., etc.

Unfortunately for such superficial scientists, the twentieth century is rapidly bringing these illusions to a sad end. Prices, since the century has begun, have risen at least 10 per cent, whilst the wages of the organised workers have risen only 1 per cent, and those of the unorganised have remained stationary. This proves that the workers are getting rapidly poorer, and that the trade unions, as constituted today, are sadly out-of-date, so far as holding their own against the solid forces of the masters.

46

The really tragic thing is that the revisionists in the trade unions are those who seem contented with things as they are, and that the revolutionary socialists are those really responsible for the move towards fusion of the scattered forces of the day. Trade unions will now have to learn that there is a class war, and that their lack of knowledge of this "compass" fact has led them off the track of that sound class organisation requisite at this juncture in the evolution of capitalism to even hold their own with the plunderers.

The growth of multiple shops and the rise of prices are very soon going to bring the happy forward career of co-operation to an end. Once the few remaining private traders are frozen out the class war in distribution and production will commence; that is to say, a bitter competitive conflict between the trusts with the government and the law courts behind them, and the co-operative movement, will begin, with all its sad awakening of utopists and revisionists who imagined that here at least was a path along which we might travel to avoid the class war.

In Glasgow we are likewise beginning to learn that Arthur Kaye and his Citizens' Union are just about as alert to the possibilities of municipal expansion as ever were the revisionists; and the consequence has been the rallying of the reactionary forces, the cessation of municipal expansion in new industries, the stopping of milk depots, and the attempt to throttle in an insidious manner real tramway progress by side-tracking the surplus profits for the benefit of the middle class. This, of course, is another manifestation of the class war.

These lessons should well suffice to rouse the workers to a consciousness of their true position in society, and the real practical work that lies before them, if they are to see salvation.

They must wage the class war; but the only way they can do this is by studying the principles of economics as formulated by Marx and by using these, not the fustian of capitalist-supporting economists, in waging that war. Now then, my revisionist friends.

(*Forward*, 28 January 1911)
. . . The whole tendency of my previous article was to show that the improvement in the lot of the workers from the early seventies on till near the end of the century, upon which revisionists dwelt in order to undermine marxism, has now given place to a decline due to the unconscious operation of economic law, and the conscious activity of the masters. A spurious use of the now famous chapter in Marx's *Capital* entitled "Historical Tendency of Capitalist Accumulation" enabled them to point out that Marx declared that the workers would become poorer and poorer,

and that, as a consequence, revolution would come, a forceful one, and sweep us on to socialism. Against this, they pointed to the reduction in prices, rise in wages, saving of profits through co-operation, and extension of local and national government enterprise as proof of the increasing wealth of the workers.

It was the purpose of Marx to show that the tendency of evolution was towards a centralisation of capital in the hands of the few, and the reduction to wage slavery of the many. We see this very tendency in operation at present in the East Coast herring industry. The many who owned or partly-owned their own sailer are now wage-earners on board "drifters" possessed by companies. He also pointed out that simultaneously the workers would organise and revolt. Such revolt has everywhere taken place, and has naturally lifted the workers' economic position above the level it would reach if they remained unorganised. But within capitalism there are limits to improvement in wages, etc., and there may be reactionary tendencies as well. The reaction has set in again within this century.

It naturally follows that opposition to revisionism makes those of us who are not ashamed to publicly proclaim our indebtedness to Marx and our support of the principles discovered or developed by him lay special stress on this worsening of the lot of the workers.

That does not, however, commit us any more than Marx to the theory of the intensified impoverishment of the wage-earners. The transition to capitalism and the development of capitalism imply the expropriation of larger and larger masses and the extension of the degradation to the position of wage-earner. That is entirely different from the distortion of the position imposed upon marxists by revisionists. It now lies with the erring critics of Marx to explain away their position.

Every marxist, as should be well-known, is in favour of any proposal that will temporarily improve the position of the workers. In fact, no proposal is before us today but has been promulgated for thirty years by Social Democrats. . . .

To us the fight for real democratic reforms, political and economical, are the life and soul of the working-class movement, and help to bring to the surface the fundamental antagonism of the classes. Only by struggling do we improve our organisation, and do we elevate the ideals of the masses above the immediate concessions to the heights of socialism. But we know full well that any advantages we may gain on the one hand may be liable to be negatived on the other by such contingencies as price increases or a widespread and severe trade depression, such as we experienced in 1908, and, therefore, act rightly in calling the workers to lay stress on the immediate and more on the approaching time, rapidly approaching as all indications show, when the workers will be able to control production and distribution by socially owning the great agents of production. What the workers have to learn is that the revolutionary social democrats are in the end the only practical men, because the only real practical work for the people is the transformation of capitalism into socialism.

2

Aspects of social democratic activity

Municipal housing
(From letters in *The Pollokshaws News*, 25 March and 8 April 1904)
. . . The point before us is houses. We should remind Mr C. that we write as social democrats, and our effort is directed towards public ownership of houses by this community, not personal ownership as he says in his letter. It is impossible for the working class to own, each and every one, a house for himself. The worker must follow his job, and so the arrangement would be inconvenient. . . .

He says we wish "to cripple the energies of the private owners and builders", and so bring about certain baneful effects. Mr C. is again wrong. We wish to abolish private enterprise, or more correctly *class* enterprise. Capitalist builders exist not to build houses (that may seem rather queer to some), but to make a profit. Profit is the hub of the capitalist world. We wish to abolish profit, and so find we must abolish the class which makes it. The community, if it builds, can afford to give better conditions to workers than have yet been obtained under precious private enterprise. Today we find people living in hovels, while masons, etc., are out of work and starving. This is proof of the "efficiency" of private enterprise. The thing must seem absurd to every thinking man. The people can solve all these problems, if they will so to do. . . .

. . . Mr Croall talks of municipal socialism; what he really means is municipal capitalism, a mere step in advance of individual and company capitalism. We socialists support municipal capitalism because it is the line of least resistance to socialist society. Next, *re* pauperism. Mr Croall uses this trick word knowing its effects on the people. He maintains that if Pollokshaws builds, a tax will be thrown on the shoulders of the people to support those who will live in the municipal houses. Then private speculators and house owners must be paupers. Every new park, every new street improvement, every demolition of slums, and every new tramline opened up enhances the value of their property. Therefore all municipal effort increases their profit, makes them paupers. Two-edged swords are difficult to wield, Mr Croall. Now, we ignorant socialists wish to stop this pauperism by advocating municipal houses. . . .

Socialism and the land question
(Letter to *Justice*, 1 September 1906)

Let me return to a proposal I made some time ago because I consider it important in the light of supplying work for the unemployed, of fostering the theoretical and practical side of scientific agriculture, and of taking the first step towards the national organisation of earth-culture. In each county with a good industrial population, there is or ought to be an agricultural college. To each college ought to be connected a large farm or colony, where scientific agriculture could be carried out in real life and where students could get that practical knowledge and dexterity without which theoretical knowledge is more or less valueless. On such farms unemployed labourers could find profitable and health-restoring outlets for their restrained energy under the direction of managers who, in the culture department, would be directly guided by the college authorities. Year by year these colonies could be extended until each county would be absorbed, until the whole country would be absorbed, when finally agriculture would be established upon a purely scientific basis under the control of local and national administrative bodies.

To urge such a scheme does not necessarily make us deviate from the paths of recent agitation and application since, obviously, it is surely a supplementary one in the realm of agriculture. In pursuance of the class struggle we ought to bring pressure to bear at as many points as possible, if it can be shown that such tactics will prove the most effective at the special time and under the peculiar circumstances. . . .

The above scheme is unique in that it permits of our tapping the Education Department, the Agriculture Department, and the Local Government Board, for the money necessary to carry it out. I do not suppose the money will at once be forthcoming, but that will merely give us data to work upon in developing the educated class consciousness of the workers — a consummation even more valuable than the execution of our palliative suggestions. . . .

A farm colony for Renfrewshire
(*Forward*, 2 September 1910)

Many of your readers may remember that I had the good fortune to read a paper on the above subject to the December meeting of the Renfrewshire Co-operative Conference. So favourable was the reception afforded the idea that Comrade David W. Hendry, secretary of the Renfrewshire District Council of the SDP, wrote to about two hundred and fifty working-class bodies within the area requesting delegates to be sent to a conference in Paisley for the further discussion of the subject. Although less than a week elapsed between the issue of the invitations and the date of the meeting, more than 80 delegates arrived upon the scene. . . .

To the socialist, the importance of experiments in agriculture, the application of mechanics, and the organisation of labour under competent management need not be elaborated. These things are rendered possible only on farm colonies under local and national authority.

The work of distress committees having failed, a National Conference was called last autumn in Manchester. The Unemployed Act (1905) was condemned, and the government was called upon to undertake the organisation of the unemployed itself. At that conference farm colonies were approved of. To those unacquainted with the minority report, it is well-known that such colonies are also approved of, but, again, under the aegis of the state.

So far as I am concerned, I see no reason why the state should not delegate the practical executive work to the respective county councils, contenting itself with the higher co-ordination of production and ultimate distribution of products.

All socialists believe in the ultimate organisation on social lines of agriculture, as well as factory production, and hence must support such a scheme as that of a farm colony that certainly has within it the potentiality of expansion into the full-fledged system of agriculture that will prevail under the coming co-operative commonwealth. . . .

Public health

(From *The Greenock Jungle*, pamphlet 1907)
The following history has been written to give the people of Greenock and other towns in Britain an accurate though brief statement of the recent scandalously lax and unscrupulous method of supervising the slaughterhouse of Greenock; the events that led up to the final exposure; the treatment meted out to Mr James Houston; and the duty that yet devolves upon the citizens of finding work for this genuine man who by his efforts has done so much to rid the community of a most pernicious traffic in unwholesome flesh.

As the whole narrative circles round the person of Mr Houston, it is but appropriate to give the reader one or two facts in connection with him, so that a clear comprehension of the events as they arise may be possible.

In the employment of R. Ramsay & Co. Ltd, Hide and Skin Brokers, Glasgow, for thirty-one years, Mr Houston spent the last eighteen at the Greenock slaughterhouse. Whilst there from day to day he witnessed the violation of the law by the cow-butchers, who were regularly engaged in *selling diseased meat and vile sausages* for large profits, although they well knew that the poor who had to purchase these articles were liable to the deadliest of working-class maladies — consumption.

This slaughterhouse is owned by the town council, and is managed by a committee which, prior to April 1907, employed a Mr Ballantine to inspect, amongst other duties, all carcases taken out of the premises. Every carcase showing traces of disease ought to have been detained by him until thoroughly examined by a competent veterinary surgeon, Mr Pottie. . . .

On frequent occasions Mr Houston noticed that Inspector Ballantine let out diseased cows without calling in the services of the veterinary surgeon. . . . So lax became the inspection of carcases at the slaughterhouse that for years Greenock became the dumping ground for old dead and dying cows within a radius of twenty miles. If a cow turned sick and showed signs of dying then off to Greenock was it sent, there to be killed and sold as wholesome food! . . .

Convinced that the continued sale of putrid flesh was bound to undermine the constitutions of those upon whom it was being imposed, Houston nevertheless carried out in a successful manner *an experiment* which conclusively proved the relationship that exists between bovine tuberculosis and human consumption. He took two young healthy cats into his office and with the utmost care fed and tended them until they grew sleek and fat! He thereupon began to feed one of them solely on tuberculosis flesh similar to that sold for food. Very soon it began to look sickly, become thin, and cast its hair. At last it could scarcely stand on its legs, so weak and puny did it become. At this stage Mr Ballantine consented to kill it, and make a post-mortem examination of its remains; and just as expected, it was found that the lungs were completely rotten, and its digestive organs had almost gone. Tuberculosis had been doing its deadly work. Mr Houston hinted that he intended to show the carcase to the veterinary surgeon as an object lesson, and for that purpose he covered it up, and left it in his office till the vet's arrival. When he did arrive, the body was gone. . . .

Haunted more than ever now by the thought that the poor were not only being mercilessly cheated and defrauded, but also were threatened by consumption, Houston cautiously dropped hints here and there, where he thought they would be effective and lead to an inquiry or a stricter supervision of the slaughterhouse. By this process rumours did actually circulate about town, and more than once the Health Committee made investigations, but failed to find specific information. Houston at this time thought it inadvisable to make a statement of what he saw going

53

on, lest he might lose his job. That, of course, is the position of the wage-slave who has a wife and family to maintain.

At length appeared Upton Sinclair's *Jungle*, containing a graphic account of the tinned beef factories of Chicago. Fired now with an intensi-fied desire to expose the still grosser evils of the beef trade of Greenock, he *determined to speak* out against the next irregularity.... On 31 August and on 4 September 1906, two carcases, bad with tuberculosis, were let out. He at once informed Ballantine that he was going to report to the Sanitary Inspector. . . .

[The result was that a completely ineffective committee of inquiry was set up by the town council, and a report was made that Houston's charges had not been substantiated. Some councillors, however, insisted that the Local Government Board should itself institute an inquiry. This was done, and in a very short time made an extensive report which con-cluded that "the inspection of carcases at Greenock slaughterhouse has been extremely lax during the last ten years" — N.M.]

The doctor, in his concluding remarks, suggests that a fully-qualified inspector of meat, aided by an assistant, should be engaged to supervise the slaughterhouse. From April, since the appointment of the new inspec-tor, the number of condemnations has risen very rapidly. But how long will this last, seeing that Houston has been driven out of his job and that Mr Banks, the cow-flesher, though defeated in the fourth ward at the Novem-ber election last (1907), was appointed by the town council to fill a vacancy in the fifth over the head of the defeated candidate for that ward?

So long as profit can be made out of the sale of diseased carcases, just so long shall these be sold. This is just as true as the statement so persistently uttered by those of us who are Social Democrats, that so long as the present class ownership of the factories, ships, mines, land, etc., lasts, just as long shall the working class be robbed of at least two-thirds of the wealth they produce.

As Social Democracy is the only organisation of industry able to stop this robbery, so municipal supply of beef, provisions, and milk will alone lead to the ending of this capitalist infamy of adulterations. . . . If the people of Greenock are wise, they will bestir themselves and never rest till the beef and other foodstuffs are sold for the benefit of the con-sumers and not for the enrichment of a few privileged merchants. If a municipal slaughterhouse, why not municipal cattle and municipal flesher-shops? . . .

We cannot close without further reference to the hero of this tra-gedy, Mr Houston, who has had to suffer for his action in this affair.

He has now been out of employment eight months, compelled to resign after thirty-one years' service under the same employer. *As a socialist,* Houston clearly comprehended the danger his action would lead him into, and therefore for years he smothered his indignation, until at last his family had grown up. Once his duty towards them was fulfilled, he risked his all to save the health of many of his class from disease and death. How can we refrain from admiration of the courage of one who so nobly plunged into the ranks of the enemy single-handed to rescue his dying comrades? . . . *The purpose of this pamphlet* will not have been completely accomplished until such times as the citizens of Greenock recognise in a more tangible form the respect they owe to one who so unselfishly sacrificed himself in the best interests of his fellow-beings. Without delay the Corporation of Greenock ought to provide him with a comfortable and well-remunerated position. If the government can and do reward the outstanding generals, admirals, and statesmen, for their supposed great services to the nation, surely Greenock is not so base and mean as to let suffer one who has nobly done his duty to the community at large. . . .

Democracy and the coming coronation

(*Justice*, 13 May 1911)

At the recent half-yearly Conference of the Scottish Branches the following appropriate resolution was passed: "That this Conference of Scottish Social Democrats, repudiating monarchy as contrary to the principle of democracy, deprecates the needless waste of public time and money on the coming coronation, and demands that time and money be granted to carrying into effect the following political measures of justice to the working class: payment of members and election expenses, male and female adult suffrage, proportional representation and devolution."

I should imagine that it is useless to waste time in proving that all Social Democrats are in favour of such a resolution. . . . But some inside, as well as many outside, may desire to know why our protest against the mockery of the coming monarchical mummery should take the form of a demand for more political freedom for the masses instead of a direct demand for the establishment of a republic. . . .

The well-known fact that the position of the king in the British empire is merely nominal, and that the monarchs for two hundred years have practically contented themselves with "sitting tight", and doing nothing except with the consent of the aristocracy or the plutocracy, has been largely instrumental in inducing the people to tolerate a position as obsolete as the wooden warships of Old England. We Social Democrats, republicans though we may be, have been essentially responsible for teaching the people that the real political enemy of our class is not the king, but the propertied class that, out of the plunder taken from us, is prepared to spend the sum needed to maintain the royal family.

The capitalists cheerfully pay out this sum, as the maintenance of royalty at this critical juncture in the country's history seems to them necessary as an agency that helps to cover over with superstitious ornament the class war between the capitalists and the workers, and which thus helps to stave off those demands for political equality that would naturally ensue upon the establishment of a republic.

The capitalists cannot afford, then, to dethrone the monarch in this country, especially on account of their supreme control of the political machinery of the land and on account of their fear of the people's desire for participation in the gentle art of law-making and administration. And on account of their propaganda, the people are conscious that the social inequalities in the land are in no way due to the crowned head; and, naturally, they cannot be expected to take but a languidly philosophic interest, meantime, in the deposition of a harmless nonentity like Geordie the Fifth.

But the workers are ripe, and over-ripe, for the passing into law of a new political People's Charter. . . . Our action must take the form of a demand, and that demand must be for the People's Charter. And such a demand is timely, whilst the measures demanded are long overdue. It surely must be admitted that a Parliament that can suspend operations to carry out a silly old mediaeval custom can with good will settle down for three or four days, or, rather, a few minutes on each of three or four days, for the passing of a one-page Bill granting the vote to all men and women; granting the money needed to pay the expenses of parliamentary elections and the salaries of members of Parliament; granting proportional representation, the initiative, referendum and recall; and granting a few other details needful to put all classes on the same political level of opportunity. Time and money can be spent on royalty. Our demand must be that time and money must be spent on the commonality.

The strike at Singer's
(*Juctice*, 1 April 1911)

Last summer, owing to a reduction made in piecework rates by the managers at the Neilston factory of the English Cotton Thread Trust, the cop-winding girls affected came out on strike and shortly afterwards, the whole mill of almost 2,000 employees came out in sympathy. At once, we East Renfrewshire Social Democrats arrived on the scene, just in time to help the organiser of the Women's Federation to get them into that union. So loyal and plucky were the girls that we were encouraged to hold meetings and collect on their behalf all round Renfrewshire. Others carried the work over the West of Scotland, and after the strike got all the Neilston workers to join the Women's Federation, and since that time I understand that, as a consequence of women striking here and there over the West, thousands of other women have poured into the Federation.

But perhaps the most significant in this plucky revolt of women workers against the driving that has become excessive these last few years back, is the strike of a few women polishers in Singer's Sewing Machine Factory at Kilbowie, Clydebank, down the Clyde and a few miles from Glasgow. Clydebank has grown with mushroom-like rapidity as an outcome of the rapid growth of Singer's and the establishment and the extension of such famous shipbuilding yards as John Brown's and Beardmore's. . . .

Here you have, then, a new town after the heart of the hustling Americans. And the American Singer's concern is Yankee from stem to stem. It is a trust that, as far as I know, monopolises the output of sewing machines in Britain (with but one exception). It has plant in America, Germany and in Russia. It has agencies all over the world. At Clydebank it employs over 12,000 hands, of whom about 3,000 are women. There are 41 departments, and the various processes have been so divided and subdivided that I believe few outside the office staff will know exactly how many processes the wood, the iron and the steel have to go through before the machine is completed. Within recent years the sub-division of labour has been rapidly developed to an extreme, and new automatic machinery in many departments has displaced labour, or, at least, enabled the management to enormously increase the output without a very great absorption of fresh workers. All, except a few moulders, engineers and joiners, are tied down to work no longer skilled. All are practically on the same level, and all the departments are interdependent. Apart from the mechanics alluded to, no organisation of workers has existed, and no union, so far as I know, has attempted to absorb these workers.

Here was a chance for the Industrial Workers of Great Britain, a few of whom slave for the Singer Company. They set about holding midday meetings, and concentrated the attention of huge crowds daily.

A few weeks ago a small strike took place, but at once the difficulty was smoothed over. Last Tuesday, however, the girl polishers came out against more work being imposed without extra pay. The propaganda of years, nursing the class solidarity of the workers, showed itself in a striking manner by the immediate stopping of work by all women, and then by all the men not in trade unions. Soon it became apparent to a number of the engineers, amongst them some Social Democrats, that to remain at work was blacklegging on the strikers, and they naturally dropped tools in sympathy. Most of the unionists have clung to their toil pending decision of the EC of the ASE. It is certainly to be hoped that the august body will adjust itself to the new circumstances, and thus avoid unnecessary friction in Clydebank during this rather romantic effort.

The whole circumstances are uniquely appropriate for the immediate application of industrial organisation of the up-to-date type. A monopoly centred in one workshop; minute division of labour; unskilled labour; absence of trade unions; a sudden and spontaneous strike of unprecedented dimensions in this industry of making sewing machines.

The result will largely depend on the course and the conduct of the strike. The strikers have no means behind them, except what may yet be collected from a sympathetic public. If the ranks are held in hand unbroken, if discipline is maintained in a loyal manner, and if the large committees are firm in attitude and unanimous in spirit and objective in tactics, then in the state of present trade, the trust will have, for the time being at least, to yield to the strikers. Should success be attained by the workers, then nothing will stand in the way of an immediate organisation embracing the workers in every part of the factory.

It is my earnest desire that all this should happen and that all should end well, as it certainly will act as an incentive to comrades in old unions to proceed with the utmost rapidity in the agitation for the fusion of all unions engaged in the same and closely allied industries. Trustification of industries, through fusion, must obviously bring in its train trustification of already existing unions and the closing of their ranks internationally. . . .

The end of the Singer's strike
(*Justice*, 15 April 1911)
The end of the strike at Singer's has come. Readers will perhaps remember that in my former article I pointed out that Clydebank had grown with American rapidity; that Singer's factory was a typical American concern; and that the workers in defence had adopted the projected American form of economic organisation — industrial unionism. It but remains to state that the company has now outflanked the strike committee by American capitalist application of the plebiscite or referendum. . . .

What will eventually transpire time in its progress will unfold. Meantime we must learn the lesson of this dramatic strike. The referendum as above applied, and applied so successfully, will undoubtedly appeal to capitalist federations. We must, in consequence, expect its application in nearly every strike that will take place in Britain if necessity demands, until something superior supplants it. That being so, it is our duty to discover wherein its efficiency lies, as that more readily may enable us to devise some method of destroying its effectiveness. I think this referendum is clever, because it appeals to the individual in the quiet of his own home, and because it enables the firm to deal with each unit separately. If all workers were class-conscious socialists, this method would fail, but as they are not it tends to succeed. And perhaps even tried socialists would yield for a time or two.

What, then, should be done? Certainly not blame incipient industrial unionism as useless. All Social Democrats are industrial unionists. We differ from others in that we insist real industrial organisation must arise out of the fusion and federation of already existing trade unions and the extension of the scope of the forces to rope in workers and industries hitherto unorganised. And, furthermore, we rightly insist that economic organisation is subject to political organisation, in that the workers, here having the completest basis of unity, are better able at once to form a party representative of the interests of the workers as a whole, and affording an outlet for the energies of many capitalists and intellectuals who cannot very well come within the scope of a purely economic instrument.

Again as politicians we rightly hold that the socialisation of industry cannot be accomplished by the direct seizure of the factories and the land by the unions. This latter method denies (tacitly, of course) the naturalness of the state and politics, the which we as scientists cannot uphold. The state is the natural outgrowth of a growing economic structure of expanding society, and upon it, in rapidly increasing numbers, devolve duties formerly undertaken in a voluntary manner. It is only consistent with impartial scientific survey to carry forward this growth of the duties of the state until the social revolution has been accomplished. And this course is the only true one for the party that claims to be marxist and believes in the class war.

We must blame the lack of feeling of, and confidence in, class solidarity. It is our duty, then, to foster this by further inculcating the principles of unionism, co-operation, and socialism. Essentially we must get the masses to test their confidence in one another by giving them ample opportunity of voting "class" at every election when candidates are available. The man who votes for a representative of capitalism can hardly be trusted to hold against the strike referendum. Hence the continued necessity for political action as the best agency for fostering nascent class solidarity, in that no risks are run from the very secrecy of the vote. . . .

The Scottish Co-operative Conference
(*Forward*, 13 May 1911)

Up till the present, comparatively little public attention has been concentrated on the annual gathering or parliament of Scottish co-operators. But the momentous developments that co-operation will participate in within a very few years necessitate our ruminating on the significance of the role that the co-operative movement must play in the unfolding of capitalism and the help it will be in the transition to a fully established social democracy.

From a Scottish point of view, the most important gathering is perhaps the annual conference, where views are expressed on the general tendencies within the movement, the possible immediate developments and the dangers looming ahead — dangers that naturally must be encountered and surmounted by every growing organism. Readers may therefore pardon me if I crave their indulgence for a few moments whilst I give the reflections of a Social Democrat on the proceedings of the conference held at Perth last Saturday, 29 April. . . .

The forenoon was largely given over to a general discussion of overlapping. The very growth of the separate societies has brought neighbouring ones right up against one another, and frequently energetic societies have been guilty of poaching on the preserves of others. Success obviously must come to the one which dangles the largest dividend before the glittering eyes of anxious housewives. Hence bitter quarrels and competitions between rival societies!

As a consequence, amalgamation among societies has been suggested as a first step towards one great organisation all over the British Isles. Curiously, this is exactly the course many of us are suggesting to the trade unions; or at least amalgamation of such trades and workers as are directly engaged in one branch of industry. Unfortunately, it will take some considerable time before socialists (who believe in peace and the unity of mankind!) will think of fusing all their rival organisations in this country.

In the afternoon a paper was read by Mr Huggin, Scottish Wholesale Society, on "The Rise of the Multiple Shop: its Methods of Doing Business, its Effects upon Retail and Wholesale Co-operation". It was an admirable paper, but it simply dealt with the surface facts in the history of the multiple shops and their methods of doing business, and only dealt with immediate suggestions that have been thrown out from time to time to make the movement more efficient and economical.

Most of the men who go to co-operative conferences of one kind or another are generally very much older than those attending trade-union or socialist ones. . . . These, therefore, are mostly Liberal in their outlook and method; that is to say, they look a very short distance in front of them, are prepared to see only detail difficulties, and are consequently only prepared to consider, as a rule, such detail suggestions as may appear to them competent to solve these difficulties. This to them is the essence of practicability. We cannot condemn them. We can only hope that the younger men will fall into line with us, and having the socialist objective in view — as had the pioneers — take that larger view of the evolution of society and the coming conflict with the trusts in their manifold forms. . . .

The older co-operators do not know that society from its origin in the mists of hundreds of thousands of years ago has passed from primitive communism to slavery, from slavery to feudalism, from feudalism to capitalism, and now it is in the process of preparation for the transition from capitalism to socialism. These older men fail to perceive that their form of joint effort is but a necessary outcome of the conditions of capitalism, and is but one petty manifestation of the universal tendency towards conscious unity of effort for definite, specific purposes. The multitudinous functions of the state and the various local governments are other signs of this drift towards mutual aid. And the formation of joint stock companies that inevitably give rise to trusts and monopolies in all branches of industry and in all capitalist countries likewise illustrates the general merging of identical interests.

Some at first might conclude that if the law of cohesion of men and forces be universal then there is no need for fears, there is but room for jubilation; for all will blend into one consistent whole, the Co-operative Commonwealth.

Unfortunately, that will not come without conflict, without fear and trembling. Capitalism, like its two preceding forms of society, is characterised by opposing classes, and opposing class interests. In the workshops are the working men, trade unionists, opposed to the capitalist owners. In politics the working men, socialists, are opposed by representatives of the various parties that stand up for capitalist property. And here now is the working men's co-operation in sight of a desperate struggle with capitalist trusts.

We socialists who know how our class is mercilessly robbed of hundreds of millions of pounds annually by a tiny fraction of the community are aware of the tremendously rapid spread of capital to all ends of the earth. . . . It is but natural to expect that very soon huge masses of capital will flood into the distributive trade and there begin an internal conflict that will end in higher trustification. But it is obvious that when the ultimate struggle between the huge trusts and co-operation takes place, an ultimate amalgamation along capitalist lines cannot take place, because it will be a fight between capital and labour. . . .

We socialists cannot afford to let the trusts win. It therefore is up to us (as our Yankee comrades say) to settle down to the education of our fellow co-operators as to the real meaning of the mutiple shops, trusts and combines, and show them that the only way ultimately is the political way by which we can seize hold from above of stores and trusts alike, and unite them on a local, national or international basis as circumstances demand, and thus establish the highest and completest form of co-operation, in other words — social democracy.

Co-operation and the rise in prices

(Speech to the Renfrewshire Co-operative Conference, 25 November 1911) The times we live in are so stirring and full of change that it is not impossible to believe we are in the rapids of revolution. Truly, the development in every branch of industrial, commercial, political, social, and intellectual activity is so apparently quick that even the dullest must admit that the old order of society is passing away, to give place to one that with our aid will eradicate for ever the inequalities, the injustices, and the oppression that characterises the present. We have but to think of the increasing thousands of inventions and discoveries that facilitate production; of the swift spread of the most perfect modes of transit and communication; of the amazing expansion of capitalism through the export of capital from developed to underdeveloped countries; of the unprecedented grabbing of occupied lands for the extension of trade and of empires; of the sudden arrival of mammoth trusts controlling colossal masses of capital and slaves; of the tremendous uprise of the masses in the co-operative, the trade union, and the socialist movements, to find a growing expression in productive and distributive activity, economic revolt, and political agitation; of the modern political upheavals, starting six years ago in Russia, and passing in rapid succession through Turkey, Persia, Portugal, and Mexico, to find a momentary culmination in China, in what may ripen into the most magnificent and dramatic transformation ever witnessed by man — I say, we have but to think of all this to catch but the faintest outline of a world change that is so truly indicative of the triumph of knowledge and its application over the chaos of the past, and of the ultimate ascendancy of the organised masses over the forces and resources of the world. These are but a few of the outward and visible signs of the evolution of capitalism — an evolution so fraught with impending dangers to the co-operative movement that it is our imperative duty to investigate from all possible standpoints the nature and the extent of these dangers, and thus prepare to adopt such new methods and agencies as will enable us to survive under the new commercial conditions so rapidly rising above the economic horizon.

The better to understand the present and the tendencies towards the future, let us glance backwards for a moment. The industrial revolution towards the close of the eighteenth century, when machinery sprang into use, saw the birth of the factory and the rise of the capitalist class enriched by the wholesale spoliation of the new poverty-stricken wage-slave class. One of the capitalist class was Robert Owen who, taking pity on his workers at New Lanark, established a store that led to his future attempts at productive and distributive co-operation. Failures though these may be considered by many, yet they led up to the Rochdale system that holds the field today. The successful start and development of this Rochdale system is explicable in the petty nature of the businesses carried on forty or fifty years ago by shopkeepers, who had in consequence to levy large profits to make a living. Charging the same prices and obtaining the same profits, the early co-operators were encouraged to go on themselves and pull others into partnership. The timidity and the poverty of the workers, however, for a long time made the competition hardly felt by the old-fashioned traders, who largely profited by the rapid increase of the town population and the slight increase of their purchasing power, due mainly to advancing wages and dropping prices. The fall of prices from 1876 to 1896 certainly had an effect on the people who, under such favourable conditions, were less inclined to leave retailers for whom they had a personal liking. Certain it is that the rivals both flourished during that period, if the number of shops be any index of development, for between 1875 and 1897 the number of shops rose from 295,000 to 408,840 — an increase of almost 39 per cent in 22 years. Under the circumstances, it was impossible for private traders to build up such an efficient organisation as could crush out the co-operative stripling. When they did get alarmed it was too late; co-operation had struck its roots too deep and spread its branches too wide. Their onslaught but fostered our growth. Today they are sinking to their doom, whilst co-operation is flourishing like the green bay tree.

But the opposition has not ceased with their demise; it cannot, this side of the establishment of the full co-operative commonwealth, social democracy. Whilst the private traders were waging their war against us there appeared in their midst far-seeing men who learned from us the lesson of owning many shops. These saw that if one shop could only afford a tenth of a living, then they must own at least ten. Hence, by adaptation to a new environment, they developed the multiple-shop system. Through lack of capital and experience, the application of this system was practically local at first; today, its extent we know. In 1896, whilst this new departure was in its infancy, a change had also manifested itself in the price of commodities. From the seventies till the nineties prices had steadily fallen, as already indicated, but by 1896 the tide turned, and from that date till this prices have steadily risen, till at present they are from 15 to 20 per cent higher. . . . At first the rise was not felt by the working class, because from 1895 till 1900, a period of expanding trade, wages rose. But since 1900 prices have gone up 10 per cent whilst wages have dropped over £92,000 per week and unemployment has become more prevalent. This means that the workers' purchasing power within the first decade of this century has considerably declined, a situation accentuated by a rise in rents and rates of 40 per cent in many cases. And, as we know, this year of grace (1911) is experiencing exorbitant prices for sugar, eggs, butter, cheese and other commodities, with little or no relaxation in those of the remainder.

Whilst I admit the drought of this summer explains, or is used to explain, the present year's rises, yet, apart from this operation of the law of supply and demand, there still remains the steady upward tendency of prices. Many are the explanations of this. One thing is certain, the rise is world-wide. It follows that a universally applying cause must be sought. The trusts, say some. Personally, I think many trusts have actually been forced into existence by the rise in raw materials, aided by growing competition. There, then, but remains the rapidly growing output of gold, especially from the Rand. . . .

I hold that one result of the intensified poverty of the people, due mainly to rising prices, has been the crushing of the private trades, whose customers have either come to our societies or gone to the multiple shops. . . . The keener struggle to make ends meet has submerged the old sentiment binding the housewife to the retailer. As we have seen, with the sentiment is going the retailer too.

As hinted above, many have been attracted to our movement but certainly not by prices lower than those obtaining amongst private retailers, for our prices have risen with the rest. Of that I have ample proof. . . . There only remains the dividend as an explanation of the influx of members, aided, no doubt, by the superiority of our products. Whatever the explanation, the movement has rapidly grown between 1900 and 1908. . . . Our members and our sales have increased, but the growth of the multiple system has been more rapid. . . . It is noteworthy that multiple companies often do their own manufacturing and wholesale work, and that manufacturers also tend to open shops to dispose of their specialities. Alongside the multiple shops spring up into pre-eminence the universal providers, with many departments concentrated under one roof, and supplying wide areas by train and motor. . . .

Whilst we were yet young and growing the private traders also grew, but the turning-point came as we well know today. To leave well alone in face of a rapidly growing menace, assisted by rising prices, is nothing short of suicide. What the upholders of this slothful policy fail to grasp is that the multiple shops are spreading more rapidly than ours. . . . Instead of giving way to fear or despondency, let us more rigorously analyse the situation and plan out what may be attempted to attain yet grander and grander successes. I, for one, feel triumphantly hopeful as I recognise that the coming conflict between the capitalist trusts and co-operation will be but another aspect of the great class war that inevitably must lead to the victory of the workers by the overthrow of capitalist predominance. That co-operation is going to play a great historical part in the ultimate transformation of society I am convinced, or it would have little of my time.

The growth of the great American trusts throws light on the methods of those determined to freeze out or squeeze out dangerous rivals. Capture the raw materials, get rebates from sellers and railway firms, cut prices below cost on the basis of a large reserve fund. Such are a few of the ways adopted by capitalist against capitalist. Do you imagine similar tactics will not be used against us by the growing distributive-productive capitalists? If so, you have not grasped the import of the boycott and of the exclusion from sections of the Glasgow Meat Market.

The fleecing of the Canadian farmers by the railways and the owners of elevators has urged them to demand the national ownership of these parts of capital. It would be easy to manipulate the railway and ships against us in the interest of our opponents. Hence it is that we should fight for the national ownership of the means of transit by land and sea. Carnegie was forced into the Steel Corporation of America because it owned the raw material requisite for his works at Pittsburgh. Others have been treated similarly by those holding the sources of supply. It follows that we ought to take warning, and demand the national ownership of land and all its mineral wealth.

As grain, corn, and other products have on occasion fallen into the hands of manipulators to the detriment of farmers and public alike all the world over, it should be our duty to get started everywhere co-operative associations of farmers pledged to trade directly with us. Such independent sources of supply would enable us to escape agencies that might naturally ruin us by exorbitant demands. All the suggestions hinted at are broad and general, but are necessary if we wish to secure raw material at favourable prices.

Next, we must extend our production by hook or by crook. As I have said, manufacturers are beginning to retail their own products, and large retailers are tending to produce their principal articles of sale. That being so, we must see to it that we are not cut off from manufactured articles, for that would be just as fatal as a drying up of the sources of raw material. . . . As the movement contains many highly skilled men in every branch of industry carried on within our isles, and as such men would be only too willing to render first aid to the directors and officials of the Wholesale in any venture, it now lies with the directors to take speedy though safe steps in the extension of production. Grow or go under is the alternative. We must grow.

Suppose that we succeed in getting our raw materials to our factories there to be prepared for sale, we shall still have to face the enemy in the retail market as before alluded to. Here the fight is one of prices. We have seen that both the multiple firms and our societies have benefited by the rise in prices at the expense of the single shopmen. The bait of the mutiple shop has been the cutting of prices in certain articles and the sale of inferior qualities of articles at reduced rates. . . . So sharp is the struggle that some managers have been enticed to pass the Wholesale for cheaper articles bought elsewhere. . . . Some of these opponents cut prices not only in leading articles but in others as well, for profit can be assured by faking and adulteration, one of the characteristic fine arts of this free-trade capitalism of ours. . . . So extensive is adulteration that we need spend no more time on it, except to emphasise its importance in baiting people who find it increasingly difficult to make ends meet. . . .

What should we do to meet all possible types of opposition? So far as adulteration is concerned we should help on any movement compelling government to intervene on behalf of innocent purchasers and of the health of the community. Suffice for that.

Next, I strongly hold that the depreciation of plant and property should be increased at the expense of a reduced dividend. Some of us years ago howled at the Wholesale on the trust question, and the outcome was increased depreciation. Since then managers and Society directors have demanded a reduction of this rate of depreciation so as to get a bigger dividend from the Wholesale. . . . The Scottish Wholesale gives 8d per £ dividend whereas the English Wholesale only gives 4d. I would advise the Scottish directors to gradually reduce theirs to 4d as well, and use the difference to hasten depreciation. They should also clear out sur-

66

plus capital by reducing their various rates of interest and thus set the example to retail societies. . . . Over and above that the reserve funds should be more speedily inflated so that ultimately interest-bearing capital may be dispensed with. The ideal is thus property absolutely free of charges and a further capital free of interest, able to be used at any moment for extension purposes or making good any losses incurred by selling under cost price.

And yet all this could not save separate societies when facing a national trust, as the latter is a higher form of co-operation than ours. We must, in consequence, also evolve such a higher form by the ultimate establishment of a National Co-operative Society. None comprehend the dangers to democracy in such a proposal more clearly than I do, but I am confident that the suggested co-operation of co-operative organisations could ultimately be founded on a democratic basis. An attempt has been made in Glasgow to weld the respective societies. The sooner this is done the better, and the sooner the Glasgow Society evolves into a West of Scotland one the better still.

The ultimate abolition of dividend I hold to be the natural consequence of our evolution. City societies have to put up with smaller dividends than country societies, in some cases only half. It follows then that dividends could easily be lowered still further. . . . The argument that the dividend is excellently suited for paying rent I trust will soon receive its quietus by the passing of the House Letting Bill. When the Bill becomes law, weekly rents will take the place of quarterly ones, and under such new circumstances I should imagine that the abolition of dividend would enable housewives better to pay the weekly rent.

I am out, then, for the abolition of interest and dividend, with free capital and a national Society, as the basic condition in the struggle. I am out for high wages and short hours to all workers as long as capitalism lasts, and, therefore, if we are going to do justice to our servants we must have a fusion of the two trade unions and the growth of a Workers' Federation. By such means will we prevent the enemy beating us through sweated labour. Lastly, we will have to bring our methods up-to-date. A national society could do this better than individual ones, and hence I am confident that when we reach this stage of our development we will not be defeated by the enemy carrying on trade at a less expense.

Sufficient for the day. Let me conclude by hoping that I have induced no trace of fear into the minds of my hearers. Potential dangers lie ahead. My purpose has been to indicate these. Call me alarmist if you will, I have quietened my conscience, and therefore am satisfied. Bear in mind I have no fear of the future. The working class is going to win by the establishment of socialism even were co-operation to go under. But the working class cannot afford to let this great popular movement sink before the opposition of a class that, having performed its work in history, must inevitably yield supremacy to ours, the last class to attain freedom. In my eyes, just as trade unionism is playing its part, so also must co-operation in the great human impulse towards that time when, the world-wide Co-operative Commonwealth having been established, man for the first time shall rise dictator over the forces and resources of nature, and ensured through life of the material, mental and moral requisites of a grand and noble existence, shall also for the first time cease from robbery and cease from conflict.

The foundation of the British Socialist Party
(*Justice*, 9 December 1911)
I believe I express the sentiments (admitting that we canny "NB-ers" have sentiments) of all north of Berwick and many of our dominant race south thereof when I say that we are proud of the latest "combine", the combine of socialist forces. This amalgamation is not perfect yet — in fact, cannot be so long as avowed socialists remain apart from the British Socialist Party. The men of the ILP still hold that union with non-socialists is more advantageous to the cause of socialism than union with fellow socialists. That I cannot see.

A composite body can never attain socialism; that alone can be accomplished by determined and openly avowed socialists. Neither is socialist opinion more rapidly advanced by such an alliance if socialists are themselves apart from one another. Socialists who are more anxious to join with non-socialists and sometimes anti-socialists than with fellows of kindred opinions have a strangely distorted point of view. I should imagine that a completely united body of socialists would be better able to carry the working class with it than a disrupted one. The socialist movement, composed as it is largely of trade unionists, can just as effectively convert the membership of the unions whilst retaining its separate identity as when definitely allied. There is nothing that the ILP can do today inside the unions that the BSP cannot achieve.

Where socialists maintain separate organisations they naturally clash with one another, and frequently attempt to undermine one another. For example, at the beginning of this summer an organiser of the ILP in Scotland declared his intention of starting branches in every town where the SDP ruled supreme. Had the ILP had domination over all other parts of the country I could have understood this move. But we know that the ILP was languishing for lack of speakers in very many parts. Hence we were forced to the conclusion that sinister motives actuated that organiser, and that his specific object was more to weaken the SDP than to advance socialist principles. Unable to accomplish his ends openly and directly, this individual has for months been trying to do so through the old trade unions, through new ones, or through new branches of old ones.

What does all this prove? Surely that the policy of separateness leads to antagonism and active opposition and that means a brutal waste of socialist energy. This difficulty must be got over in Scotland once the British Socialist Party gets on to its feet. At least an effort must be made to get ILP branches to fall in line with us.

Whilst still having the larger outlook constantly in view, we must meantime set our house in order. Linking up all the new forces will present a few difficulties, but the sooner we commence business the better.

Scotland will need a national council. The basis of such already exists in the Scottish District Council. This body could easily be adapted to fulfil all the functions required of a national council. I think it would be wise, then, for the secretary of the SDC to get into touch with all new branches of the British Socialist Party, and arrange for an informal conference during the New Year at Glasgow. At this gathering preparations could be made for something more definite in the spring. Officials and a committee could be appointed to prepare a policy for Scotland and make arrangements for summer propaganda over the country. For this work three or four organisers will certainly be needed. The sooner we work out the matter the better.

District organisations will also have to be set up for local work. Areas might easily be mapped out at this conference, and so save friction and overlapping of work. The principal area will be Glasgow and district. This might at first include the whole West of Scotland from Dumfries right up with an inner committee for Glasgow proper. So far as this city is concerned it might be advisable to have a gathering of all members during the New Year week also — before or after the larger one, as thought fit.

All will admit that the New Year season is the one best fitted for new resolves and new impulses; it is a season when all factory workers are idle, and therefore able to foregather; it is far enough off to enable preparations to be made; and it will give the SDP branches a chance to wipe out all debts so as to be ready for a new start.

Meantime, I appeal to all old comrades to be up and doing. Those of you who have lapsed, return; those who have lost heart, cheer up; those who have heart, pull in the indifferent and stimulate dormant or defunct branches. Let us "ring in the new" with rejuvenated animation.

II

Wartime and Revolution

The selected items again give only a partial picture of the Scottish revolutionary movement in action against the war, because MacLean was in prison for almost two years of this period. In addition, for a full year he had no party organ in which he could write freely, having been banned from **Justice** after the letter of 17 August 1914 in which he challenged the chauvinism of the Hyndman clique which controlled it.

The situation regarding **Justice** must have been a bitter pill for MacLean to swallow, as he had been conducting for years a campaign for the transfer of the paper's control to the party's executive committee. But his resolution along these lines at the 1914 conference was defeated by a large majority. However, although the majority of the party was anti-war, the position taken by **Justice** made it appear as if the party as a whole was pro-war.

I have included "The War: Its Cause and Cure" because it was in effect his swan song in the co-operative movement, which became rapidly pro-war. It is unusually interesting because of the different views of the two men who were later to become notorious as the two most dangerous revolutionaries in Britain. The social democratic outlook of MacLean and the anarcho-syndicalist outlook of Gallacher (see Introduction, page 12) were to become transformed by the cataclysmic events of the war and the Russian revolution. It is instructive to compare this speech of MacLean's with his speech from the dock in 1918.

While the columns of the pacifist **Forward** were still open to MacLean in a general way (for example, the bitterly sarcastic article "Scottish Chivalry and Freedom in Pollokshaws"), it was not until September 1915 that he was again able to write freely, when the Glasgow District Council of the BSP produced the first issue of **The Vanguard**. Only four issues were published before it was suppressed (Lloyd George declaring in Parliament that it was the worst paper in the country), but these issues contain a mine of information about the struggles on the Clyde. The articles selected give an indication of the kind of activity that, in MacLean's words, "will ever make famous the class-conscious workers of the Clyde Valley". James MacDougall described the background to these events:

"The experience of wartime produced a revolution in the psychology of the Clyde workers. The gigantic expansion of the 'shops' for the provision of huge supplies of munitions attracted a multitude of industrial recruits into the Clyde area. The

71

pressure on the housing accommodation became very severe; the 'factors' then seized their opportunity and rapidly raised the rents to an extortionate figure; this was answered by the tenants through rent strikes, resistance to evictions, and finally a stoppage of the munition workers, which forced the government to institute the legal control of rents for the duration of the war. At the same time speculators in flour and shipping were coining in money hand over fist. The cost of living was rising rapidly, without any compensating increase in wages being granted. The trade union officials had entered into a patriotic truce with the employers and would do nothing for their members. The rank and file thereupon kicked over the traces and proceeded to build up a new representative system on the basis of workshop committees and shop stewards with which to fight for their wage claims.

Jingoism was at a discount in Glasgow from the very beginning of the war; it was the sole place in the British empire where there was perfect freedom of speech for international socialists and opponents of the war. The brave stand taken by John MacLean, for which he had to suffer the repeated imprisonments that killed him, inspired faith and courage in the revolutionary minority; and the classes in economics and history conducted by MacLean, with the assistance of others, every Sunday, became the rallying centre of the most militant of the shop stewards.

Out of the resistance to the Munitions Act there grew up the Clyde Workers' Committee, on which all the shops and yards soon had their delegates. In 1916, a vigorous agitation against conscription was conducted by the CWC, and this culminated in extensive political strikes, which the government countered by sending MacLean, Maxton and others to jail, while deporting Kirkwood and several prominent shop stewards. These events reverberated throughout the factories and made an indelible impression on many workers formerly indifferent to politics."*

The paucity of items by MacLean about the international movement was due to the fact that these were provided by other contributors, especially Peter Petroff who had a special knowledge of this subject. Petroff was a Russian refugee who had been wounded in the 1905 revolution, had escaped from Siberia and made his way to Scotland where he was succoured by MacLean. After MacLean had taught him to speak English, he departed to join the colony of Russian refugees in London, and there became an active member of the SDP and one of the leaders of the left-wing opposition to Hyndman. When events on the Clyde began to come to the boil, Petroff was invited to come to Glasgow (this is explained in Mac-

*"Clyde Labour: a Study in Political Change", in **Nineteenth Century,** 5 February 1927.

Lean's letter in **Justice** of 30 December 1915). Both Lenin and Trotsky were quite unknown in Britain at this period, but Petroff knew them and the other leaders of the Russian Social Democratic Labour Party, having been a member since 1901. He sent information to Trotsky who was at that time editing **Nashe slovo** in Paris, and this information was transmitted to Lenin in Switzerland. According to Harry McShane, MacLean was the first person he ever heard calling himself a leninist.

On 5 January 1916 a Conscription Bill was placed before the House of Commons, and that was the signal for a government attack on the Clyde. First came the arrest of Petroff, who was jailed in Edinburgh Castle as a prisoner-of-war. **The Vanguard, Forward** and **The Worker** (organ of the CWC) were suppressed, and then came the arrests of the main leaders, including MacLean, Mac-Dougall, Maxton and Gallacher. By May, when they were all safely in jail and the leading shop stewards deported, it seemed as if the anti-conscription campaign was completely squashed. But, of course, this was not the case; the fight against conscription began to take the form of individual conscientious objection and the Anti-Conscription League was formed. While revolutionaries did not believe that this kind of individual action could have any practical effect in halting conscription, many members of the BSP, in default of revolutionary mass action, did become conscientious objectors. Meanwhile, leading shop stewards exiled to different parts of the country encouraged the extension and unification of the shop stewards' movement.

The founding conference of the Scottish Labour College, held on 12 February 1916, had to take place without MacLean, who had been arrested on 6 February and held in Edinburgh Castle without bail. He had been due to deliver the inaugural address, but had not quite completed its preparation, so it was finished and delivered by James MacDougall to an enthusiastic audience of about five hundred delegates from all sections of the labour movement. This was a truly significant event to occur in the second city of the British empire in the midst of an imperialist war still regarded by the vast majority as a heroic and glorious affair (the battle of the Somme and other bloody disasters had still to come). The address, which is produced here in full, is clear and simple, but readers should note the first paragraph, signalling as it does big developments taking place in government: "The government will have to pay interest on the War Debt, and in consequence, will be compelled to interfere in the economic life of the nation more than ever before", and again, "political problems are going to be essentially economic problems".

MacLean received the heaviest sentence of all the Clyde leaders, and was the only one to become a convict. On 11 April he was sentenced at Edinburgh High Court to three years' penal servitude, and taken to Peterhead Convict Prison. A fortnight later came the Easter Rising in Dublin, which Lenin regarded as the first big blow against the mighty British empire. Whether or not Mac-Lean heard about it at the time I do not know, but later he was to state in his 1922 Election Address: "When Jim Connolly saw how things were going in Edinburgh he resolved on the Easter Rebellion in Dublin, the beginning of Ireland's new fight for freedom."

The Easter Conference of the BSP that year was a historic event, with the decisive defeat of the pro-war Hyndman section, which promptly left the party, taking **Justice** with it. For the first time MacLean was elected a member of the executive committee; a new paper **The Call** came into being, edited by E. C. Fairchild, a veteran of the anti-Hyndman struggle. **The Call** led the campaign for MacLean's release, which came eventually in July 1917, after the February revolution in Russia had galvanised the movement into militant action. He had served only fourteen months of his sentence.

The other leaders were back in circulation again and the Clyde Workers' Committee sprang into life, but the most militant action now came from the miners, who had also undergone a "revolution in psychology". In "Miners' Historic Protest against Profiteers" Mac-Lean acclaimed their one-day strike against rising prices (another political strike): "The organised miners have now raised themselves to the highest level; that is, as champions of the whole working class, and not merely of miners as miners."

It is a great loss to the working-class movement that none of MacLean's lectures on economics were ever recorded, but his pamphlet **The War after the War**, written in the winter of 1917-18 for his Glasgow class, helps to fill the gap, and we can see how all that was going on in the outside world was interpreted according to marxist doctrine. This was the first publication of the Scottish Labour College, which had begun to function in real earnest that autumn, with over 500 pupils enrolling in the Glasgow class and about 125 in the Greenock one, to mention only the two largest. The classes had scarcely begun before news of the Bolshevik revolution arrived. MacLean and the BSP gave full support, and when the news came through that the new Soviet government was calling for a peace without annexations or indemnities, the enthusiasm knew no bounds.

Another encouraging event was the mass meeting of Clyde shop stewards which took place on 28 January 1918, in St Andrew's Hall. It had been called by the government for the purpose of gaining support for the new Manpower Bill for the conscription of lads of eighteen. However, there was unanimous opposition, and the audience left the hall **en masse** to hold an anti-war meeting at George Square.

Two days later, on 30 January, the **Glasgow Herald** reported the message sent out by the Russian government's radio station: "The Department of the Occident of the Commission for Foreign Affairs announces that the Consul-General at New York, Usti-noff, is dismissed and John Reed is appointed in his place.

74

John Maclin is appointed Consul at Glasgow, Scotland."

There was certainly no prestige attached to this job, only toil and trouble; soon he was arrested again to face his most famous trial. He conducted his own case, refused to plead and, when the Lord Justice General intimated that he could object to any particular juryman, replied: "I would object to the whole of them." He was sentenced to five years' penal servitude, plus the remaining twenty-two months of his previous sentence, after delivering a seventy-five minute speech attacking capitalism and the war, with no holds barred. As he left the court, he turned and shouted to his friends in the gallery, "Keep it going, boys! Keep it going!"

Doubt has recently been cast by certain academics about the reality of the "Red Clyde", the suggestion being that it is all a myth manufactured by "politically motivated" leftists. While it is true that the part played by the Clyde Workers' Committee and some of the leaders, for example David Kirkwood, has been exaggerated, the fact that May Day in 1918 was held for the first time in Glasgow on 1 May, and that one hundred thousand workers took the day off to march in it, is proof positive. This great celebration finished up with a huge crowd marching to Duke Street Prison, where MacLean was awaiting trial. They shouted "John MacLean!" hoping that the man inside would hear. Such was the public interest in the trial that for the first time in the history of criminal trials at Edinburgh High Court the queue system of admission was introduced, and many, including some of those who had marched overnight from Glasgow, were turned away.

3

The anti-war struggle and the Russian revolution

War and robbery

(Letter in *Justice*, 17 September 1914)

In last week's *Justice* E. Belfort Bax exhorts us to "hate the present military and bureaucratic state system." Our first business is to hate the British capitalist system that, with "business as usual", means the continued robbery of the workers. After that I for one will transfer the larger portion of my hate to Russian soil against the devilish autocracy that prevents the peaceful development of the workers' organisations by organised murder, torture, and scientific cruelty, with a regularity and on a scale that would make the Kaiser with all his evils intensified a thousandfold blush with shame.

So far as I can see, it will be impossible to tell whether Russia or Germany is immediately responsible for the war. . . .

Even supposing Germany is to blame, the motive force is not the ambitions of the Kaiser, nor the brute philosophy of the Prussian militarists, but the profit of the plundering class of Germany. Colonial expansion was denied the Germans because the British, the Russians and the French had picked up most of the available ports of the world. What could the Germans do but build up an army and navy that would hold its own against all comers? This it has done steadily for the last generation. It is mere cant to talk of German militarism when Britain has led the world in the navy business. It is merely the "struggle for existence" on a capitalist, national scale. The inspiration of German militarism comes as much from Darwin and Huxley, and applied by British economists and sociologists against us socialists, as from Bernhardi or any other German apologist of organised murder. Capitalism has neither conscience nor morality when it is brought to bay.

Every interested person knew that Germany's easiest road of entry into France was by Belgium. Sir Edward Grey had only to wait till Belgium's neutrality had been broken to seize the "moral" excuse for Britain taking up arms. The real reason was, and is, that he and his class knew that war between Britain and German capitalism had to come sooner or later. Now was the day, and Britain struck. Plunderers versus plunderers, with the workers as pawns taking the murdering with right good will. The working class at home is beginning to be starved, and is being buoyed up with the assertion that this is the last great war.

Unless the social revolution bursts forth in Europe at the close of this present murder campaign, Russia will make a bold bid for Turkey, Asia Minor, Poland, and a bit of the Persian Gulf area, with Sweden added shortly after that. If its allies try to intervene, we may have another war.

Even should this not happen, we all know that the commercial rivalry of Japan and the US — similar to that between Britain and Germany — must lead to a war in the Pacific basin. Canada and Australia will side with the States so that Britain will be dragged in or lose those colonies. . . .

In view of eventualities like those indicated, it is our business as socialists to develop "class patriotism", refusing to murder one another for a sordid world capitalism. The absurdity of the present situation is surely apparent when we see British socialists going out to murder German socialists with the object of crushing Kaiserism and Prussian militarism. The only real enemy to Kaiserism and Prussian militarism, I assert against the world, was and is German social democracy. Let the propertied class, old and young alike, go out and defend their blessed property. When they have been disposed of, we of the working class will have something to defend, and we shall do it.

The war: its cause and cure

(Report of speech made at a Renfrewshire Co-operative Society conference, *The Scottish Co-operator*, 4 December 1914)

. . . The chairman then introduced Mr John MacLean, MA, who was to read a paper entitled "The War: Its Cause and Cure". The chairman intimated that whatever opinions might be expressed by Mr MacLean, the council was not to be held responsible for them.

Mr MacLean, in the course of his paper, said that the attitude of co-operators should be such horror of war as would compel them to take steps to eliminate all possibility of its recurrence. They must adapt their environment so as to give opportunity for the full fruition of an all-embracing co-operation. Hitherto the world waste on war or preparations for war had not met with that consideration or discussion in co-operative circles that every form of waste ought rightfully to receive. . . .

He was convinced that there was one fundamental cause of all modern wars. Bearing in mind international episodes during the past ten years, they could not but come to the conclusion that defence or theft of territory had much to do with all modern wars. But territory was not the sole object which nations had in view; coupled with it were the material advantages which today went hand in hand with the ownership of huge tracts of land. Monopoly of colonies for capital investment, for the sale of surplus produce, and for the settlement of surplus population, as well as the extremest exploitation of the native labour, was the steady and increasing force actuating the most civilised and so-called cultured races towards preparation for war and its regular recurrence. Men were not by nature friends — not even the despised Germans — but the struggle for material existence or for material supremacy made friends of most men. All the great nations of today had followed the lead of Britain in passing from an essentially agricultural economy to an industrial and commercial economy. Capitalism brought in its train machinery driven by vast forces of nature. Capitalist rivalry brought with it the ever-pressing need to revolutionise the methods of production, and it followed that more commodities per worker were turned out — that more wealth in the aggregate was being created.

Most of them were now convinced, however, that, whilst prices had risen everywhere, wages had not risen as rapidly. The workers were producing vastly more than formerly and yet were getting in return a diminished quantity of the wealth they formed and fashioned. It was obvious, therefore, that the stores at the command of the capitalist class must be on the increase at a terrific rate. This class was forced to market a growing portion elsewhere in the world, and this was true not only of Britain and Germany, but of every other capitalist country. Experience had shown that colonies gave market advantages to their owners; they also provided the safest park for investments of surplus capital. The surplus of goods produced could not, however, be got rid of as quickly as they were produced, and thus trade depression, unemployment, and industrial unrest arose, and became a political danger to the state, which could best be got rid of by emigration to the colonies. All colonies had been taken by force and must be kept by force. It was therefore by no accident that Britain had the supreme navy of the world, and it was no freak of Kaisers and politicians that other nations had imitated her in the building of ships of war. The economic necessity was the ever-pressing force. Those who tried to delude the people into believing that this was the last war were either fools or knaves, and he inclined to think there were more knaves than fools. Until capitalism with its growing robbery of the workers ceased, warfare and murder would ever recur.

If this explanation was the true one, it became comparatively easy to suggest the cure. They must get rid of capitalism. Mr MacLean said divergences of view existed as to how this could best be done. Everyone admitted that the various states were the supreme representatives of asso-

78

ciated mankind. If peace was to be established, these states must be captured by the workers. Once captured, the process of state ownership of the land and the means of production must be proceeded with at the utmost speed, until the creation and distribution of every product necessary for the existence of mankind was in the hands of each respective state. When industries were thus in the hands of the workers, rent and other forms of plunder would cease and capitalism would meet a well-merited death; national co-operation would logically develop, and national independence would force the respective states to justly exchange their surplus produce; and this would call into existence a world parliament, binding race to race and man to man in one universal co-operative brotherhood. In such a commonwealth it would become transparently clear that the making of munitions of war or the maintenance of a soldier class was sheer, absurd and barbarous economic waste. Consequently, armies and navies must vanish and war, the fiend, disappear. . . .

Scottish chivalry and freedom in Pollokshaws
(*Forward*, 15 May 1915)
When recruiting showed signs of flagging, our courageous and high-souled Scottish press turned on the tap of German frightfulness, especially towards women and children. The natural implication, of course, always was that *we* (the landlords and capitalists, I suppose, as the masses are always an afterthought) were the very acme of benevolence, generosity, courtesy, and gentleness towards the weaker of our race.

And were we not also sustained in our bold enterprise by the thought that we free Scotsmen were sacrificing all for the Kaiser-ridden people of Germany?

Had we "queer folk o' the 'Shaws' " innocently accepted such plausible suggestions, we would have been rudely awakened, as I was at 6 a.m. on Monday, 3 May, by the boisterous shouts of rebellious girls and women.

For me it was a red-letter morning, as is any other when I have to rise at such an unearthly hour. At last I shall have a chance of seeing a Zeppelin, thought I; but to my astonishment it was a procession of striking women, striking as much for their impoverished and work-worn appearance as against their kind and generous employers, Messrs Stevenson & McKellars, Bleachers and Dyers. When the Neilston strike was on some of us tried to get these very women to revolt; but Scottish pluck prevailed against us.

There appears to be a limit to the acceptance of generous-hearted philanthropy, strange to say, for the women bleachers have come out into the sun to avoid it. I presume they got worried over the red ruin facing their benefactors, if they accepted their bounties any longer. At any rate, whatever the explanation, out they have come.

I happened to meet Mr William Rushworth, organiser of the Amalgamated Society of Dyers etc., among the women, and tried to find from him why these workers should dare enjoy the sunshine when the men were in the trenches. I give you his explanation, although I fancy he has been enraptured by the large-heartedness of the aforesaid worthy gentlemen.

First of all, he gave me a list containing the names of 117 of the women and girls, the wages paid, and the wages that ought to be paid according to the rates prevalent in the West of Scotland. He assured me that some of the women had worked for over thirty years for this firm. I gathered that only 25 were under 18 years of age.

I see by the list that one female gets 6s, 5 get 6s 6d, 6 get 7s, 12 get 7s 6d, 19 get 8s, 22 get 8s 6d, 14 get 9s, 13 get 9s 6d, 7 get 10s, 3 get 10s 6d and 15 get 11s: an average of 8s 9d. Some are married women with families. Theirs must be exciting lives indeed, finding out ways and means of spending their princely incomes. It is really astonishing the government has not appointed a committee to solve the stupendous problem for them.

Friend Rushworth assures me the average ought to be 12s 2d, if the district rates were paid. A cynical, still, small voice whispers 52s 1¼d would be nearer the mark for 55 hours a week, in a steamed atmosphere, in some cases of 100 degrees Farenheit. Rushworth alleges that the women came out for 1s a week more, owing to rising prices.

One old woman assured me she was thankful to get dry bread at her mealtimes. I tried to set matters right by coaxing her to give less after this to the Prince of Wales Fund and the Belgian Relief Fund. I learned later that this extravagant person refused to adopt my wise suggestion.

I cannot see why these women ought not to be happy and contented, when I remember that the government pays a soldier's wife 12s 6d a week. If it takes 12s 6d to keep a soldier's wife at home, surely it ought not to take more than 8s to keep a woman 55 hours in a salubrious bleach-field.

The thirty odd men get an average of 19s 10d, and request 2s extra. I fear that these men might become as bad as the Clyde engineers if they got their own way — drunken and lazy.

The trade union is paying these wicked strikers money to keep them out in the sun. As the sums granted are 5s for women and boys, and 10s for men, collectors are going the round of the work-gates on pay days to get more to encourage them in the bad practice of sun worship. A very silly person suggested that I might urge *Forward* readers to do their best to back up the sun-worshippers. But, really, when I think of the great freedom to toil (55 hours) under such nice conditions (in some cases 100 degrees Farenheit), for such a munificent reward (8s 9d), I feel so proud of the 'Shaws, so proud of Scotland, and so proud of our great race and privileges, that I have not the heart to do so. I would rather die in the trenches!

We are the very acme of benevolence, generosity, courtesy and gentleness towards the weaker of our race, and we are justly entitled to sacrifice all for the Kaiser-ridden people of Germany!

Our freedom is going
(*The Vanguard*, October 1915)

Britain entered this war to safeguard freedom; so said our masters, pastors, pressmen, and politicians. We did not believe them a year ago; still less do we credit them today when we see the developments against the rights and privileges of the wage-earners. The workers are economic slaves; in other words, they live not for themselves, but for landlords and capitalists. Yet, they have had a certain right to organise in unions, and to strike against irksome impositions of the bosses, to move from workshop to workshop (unless when a master wished to victimise a hard-hitter inside the workers' ranks), to enter or keep out of the army and navy (unless when hunger compelled), to express their thoughts in press or in public, and to vote in local or national elections.

Without the workers' vote on the matter, this country was plunged into the war to fight for one gang of robbers and swindlers against the supporters of another such gang. To raise popular support, the hirelings of Parliament and our robber masters shouted that our freedom was in danger. Now, the tough task of laying out the Germans is driving our masters to put the grip of tyranny on the workers; for the assumption always is that the workers alone are bad, drunken, and lazy, and alone need the whip of compulsion to make them do their "duty to their country".

Economic pressure had to be brought to bear on many young men to force them into the fighting ranks. Bitterness was developed by hair-raising stories of German brutality — as if war could ever be carried on in kid-glove fashion. . . . Yet this has not seemingly sufficed to raise the forces requisite for the crushing of Germany. So compulsion is going to be resorted to unless we hit out hard against it. . . .

The Munitions Act, better known as the Industrial Slavery Act, since it was meant to tighten the chains of economic slavery on the workers, was the outcome of the suggestions of Mr William Weir, of Cathcart, whose usual arrogance forced his men to stop work and precipitate the Clyde Engineers' Strike, the first great workers' revolt after the Great Slaughter Match commenced. He demanded that the government ought to prevent the workers' unions from being used to force up wages or improve conditions during the war. The government has not only practically adopted his ideas, but it has appointed him supreme controller of munition supplies in Scotland. The men, and even the women, inside his big workshop are bubbling over with discontent, as are those employed from end to end of the Clyde smelting, engineering, and shipbuilding areas. . . .

The root of the unrest is that the plundering class, at home and abroad, has added almost three hundred million pounds to the workers' cost of living since the war started. . . . Prices are still rising, and pounds are being put on to rents. The limit is not in sight. When the workers ask more to meet the increased difficulty to live, they are insulted as traitors who ought to be shot. These insults and threats come from the very men who ask us to throw away our lives for freedom! If the workers strike to get more money they are denounced as drunkards and shirkers, and are held responsible for a war failure absolutely due to the incompetence of the men who blackguardise them. They are fined or imprisoned if few in numbers. They are called nice fellows if they are determined Welsh miners who defy and nullify the Munitions Act.

Lloyd George . . . and his capitalist friends would have the workers doing twelve hours a day for seven days in the week, and for fifty-two weeks in the year — with perhaps five days off in the summer — and for the old rate of wages no matter the rise in prices.

If he and his friends imagine the workers are going to stand that, without striking and fighting, they are woefully mistaken. . . . It is a capitalist war, so let the masters die for their precious property, and pay the war expense. If these capitalists imagine we are going to be forced to fight their battle and pay the piper as well, then they must be taught a lesson. The partial freedom, radical and chartist, trade-union and co-operative, working men worked and fought for — often at terrible cost — we are not going to allow our Junkers to seize from us. No, we intend to press on incessantly towards that social ownership of the very earth itself, when all shall be workers and all shall be masters, when robbery shall have vanished, when national hatred and antagonism shall have faded away, and when armies and navies shall have disappeared amidst the concord of a united mankind. . . . To prove our sincerity, let us see to it that military compulsion is not introduced, that industrial compulsion through the Munitions Act is swept away, and that either the workers get a wage

82

commensurate with the increased cost of living, or a reduction of prices to pre-war level.

If the masters are anxious to win, we challenge them to hand over their land and capital to the people, and to let the workers organise all industries, including those necessary for the conduct of the war, and control the products of labour, and we can assure them that all will go well at the front. In other words, let them adopt socialism and victory is assured. We know they would rather accept defeat than adopt socialism. . . .

The fight for freedom in Glasgow
(*The Vanguard*, October 1915)

The rushing of anti-socialists, brought to a socialist meeting place by the police to break the socialist gathering during a war, is a tremendously significant fact. If the authorities do not comprehend its full import, we do. If men are dying for a country which is not theirs, then we are prepared to suffer any penalty for a country we mean to make the people's. It is the duty of every man of the slave class to rally round us in this bitter fight to retain the freedom won by our fathers from the fathers of the Junkers who, today, ask us to die for them. Let them die for themselves, and we will look after ourselves against German and all other Junkers who crash up against us.

The "Punch-like" notions of our Junkers seem to infer that because we are not anxious to throw away our lives for them, we are anxious to have the German Junkers as our masters! No, we are not anxious to swap masters; we are out to get rid of all masters. No man has the right to be any other man's master. It is because we object to the slavery implied in mastery, the mastery over the land and the capital of the world, that we are socialists, and nothing but socialists. It is in our estimation a base myth to think that we shall gain our freedom more easily from British than from German capitalists.

The war has brought out the fact that Germans own, and will own after the war, property in this country, and we are convinced that if we attempted to take our land and means of production, we should have to face not only the "loyal" section of the British army, but a contingent sent over by our "beloved" enemy, the Kaiser. Remember how the Germans released French soldiers to shoot down thirty thousand men, women and children in the streets of Paris, simply because the workers dared to establish a Commune in 1871 at the close of the Franco-Prussian War. . . .

The Clyde unrest

(*The Vanguard*, November 1915)

The situation in the Clyde area is just as interesting as it was recently in South Wales, and as it is presently in Dublin where the transport workers have paralysed work at the docks. Unrest and dissatisfaction manifest themselves in many directions, but principally in opposition to the Munitions Act, the raising of rents, and the threat of conscription. We think it necessary to deal with these in the order mentioned.

Since the introduction of the infamous Munitions Act, in the output of which the leaders of the trade unions have played their treacherous part, the workers of the Clyde have found themselves bullied and ordered about by foremen and managers as never before. Men, seeking to leave one factory for another, have found themselves detained to suit the interests of the employers. Others, wishing to stay, have been dismissed without a clearance card and have thus been kept six weeks out of work to satisfy the desire for revenge of some vicious foremen or managers. . . .

In such circumstances, the men stop work and, of course, in due course become victims under the vile Slavery Act. Penalty after penalty, always against the workers, has convinced the workers on the Clyde that the purport of the Munitions Act was not increased supplies to the soldiers, but the crushing of trade unionism. In that we think the workers right. . . .

The capitalist class seized on the Marshall case to demonstrate that the men were doing their utmost to hold back production, and the presiding Sheriff gave a savage sentence to frighten others who might be thought guilty of the ca' canny policy, although Marshall was simply charged with an ordinary assault.

Things did not turn out as the silly old Sheriff and his class expected. The Beardmore workers, aroused by this vile spleen, rallied round Marshall and his family. At the same time they prepared to strike if he was not liberated. He was liberated.

This Marshall case revived the unofficial committee of shop-stewards in the engineering works, and as luck would have it the Fairfield Shipwrights' case arose as the Marshall one faded away.

The unofficial committee decided to widen its borders so as to include unofficial representatives from all allied trades in the engineering and shipbuilding shops. Now railwaymen and miners are admitted — and even a teacher [i.e. MacLean himself—*N.M.*] — to show the solidarity of brawn and brain workers.

This wise provision entitled and enabled the committee to consider the Fairfield case and decide upon action, if need be. . . .

A move began among the Fairfield and other Govan workers to prepare a strike for the release of the three brave and good men.

The unofficial committee also roused itself to the occasion, and resolved that if the shipwrights and other workers in Fairfield struck the whole Clyde area would be paralysed. . . .

It is no surprise, then, to learn that the three men were released on Wednesday, 27 October, after three weeks in prison, the fine having been paid. We know the imprisoned men did not pay the fine and did not consent to its payment. Either the official gang or the government did it to save their dirt-stained faces. . . .

Grey is a fossil who has bungled his department; Asquith can only "wait and see" while the Germans spread themselves around; Lloyd George is a good jumping-jack, and most of his other colleagues would do very well in a Berlin Museum. It is men of this kidney who would make criminals of our class.

It is up to the unofficial committee now to forge ahead, refusing to recognise officials who have betrayed the workers (as Highland chiefs and Indian princes have betrayed their peoples in the past to the English), and are equally ready to again do the trick. The withdrawal of the charge against our comrade Bridges, of Weir's, by the Minister of Munitions, shows that fear of a strike is the only thing recognised by the Russo-Prussians who rule this country. The very fact that Bridges was summoned because, as shop steward, he approached a man to join the union is further proof that the attempt is to crush the unions and to continue the stupid methods of irritation started under the protection of the Munitions Act.

Unless the Clyde men act quickly, determinedly, and with a clear object in view they are going to be tied up in a knot. We know that the Glasgow press was threatened with the Defence of the Realm Act should it make mention of strike had one broken out. We know that the military authorities had engineers and allied workers in the army at home ready to draft into the Clyde works in the event of a strike. We know also that, despite the clamour for munitions, young men are being dismissed from all the Clyde works in order to force them into the army. When the occasion arises they will be reinstated in their old jobs, but now as military slaves — worse even than munition slaves. Quick and firm action is needed if slavery is going to be abolished and conscription defeated. We must now fight boldly for the common ownership of all industries in Britain.

Rent victories

(*The Vanguard*, December 1915)

Through the tireless energy of Mr McBride, secretary of the Labour Party's Housing Committee, and ardent support of the Women's Housing

Committee, an agitation was started in the early summer against rent increases in the munition areas of Glasgow and district. Evening and midday work-gate meetings soon stimulated the active workers in all the large shipyards and the engineering shops.

Emboldened, the organisers by demonstration and deputation tried to commit the Town Council to action against increases. As it acts as the executive committee of the propertied class, the Council shirked the responsibility of curbing the greed and rapacity of the factors and house-owners.

Enraged, the workers agitated more and more until the government intervened by the appointment of a commission of inquiry — Dr Hunter and Professor Scott. This was the signal for all the factors in the city to give notices of increase in rent. They anticipated that this united front would influence the commissioners (as it did), and that the government would compromise the situation by allowing half the demands to be made legal.

They all calculated without consideration of the awakened anger of the whole working class. People in the previously unaffected areas saw no objection to munition workers paying more, but when they themselves became liable to increased rent they adopted the aggressive. Encouraged by the universal working-class support, and irritated by the operation of the infamous Munitions Act, the Clyde workers were ready to strike. This several yards did when eighteen of their comrades appeared before Sheriff Lee. Beardmore's workers at Dalmuir sent a big deputation to tell the Sheriff that if he gave an adverse decision they would at once down tools. We have been favoured with a report of the proceedings in the Sheriff's room from the principal spokesman. It is intensely interesting as described by one of the spokesmen. In the circumstances the Sheriff wisely decided against the factors' demand for an increase. We state the cause of triumph in these terms advisedly, for it really was due to joint action and not to the justice of the case (and there could be no juster) that success came to our side.

The strike having taken place, the workers were bent on letting the government know that out they would come again unless it restored rents to their pre-war level. It now transpires that a Rent Bill will be passed, forcing all factors of houses, rented at £21 and under (£30 in London), to reduce the rents to the levels prevailing immediately prior to the outbreak of the Great Slaughter Competition. . . .

It should be noted that the rent strike on the Clyde is the first step towards the political strike, so frequently resorted to on the Continent in times past. We rest assured that our comrades in the various works will

86

incessantly urge this aspect on their workmates, and so prepare the ground for the next great countermove of our class in the raging class warfare — raging more than even during the Great Unrest period of three or four years ago.

Bear in mind that, although the government has yielded to enormous pressure, it must do something to balance the victory. Remember how Lloyd George came out with the Munitions Act as a reply to the victory of the striking Clyde engineers, and let that put us all on our guard. . . .

It is up to the workers to be ready, and resist with a might never exerted before. Whether the Clyde Workers' Committee as constituted to-day is able or willing to cope with the situation is doubtful; but it is just as well to give it a further chance with the added support of miners and railwaymen. However, just as this unofficial committee views with suspicion the official committees of the various unions, and attempts to act as a driving force, we warn our comrades that they ought to adopt the same attitude towards the unofficial committee and see that it pushes ahead. If it still clings on to academic discussions and futile proposals, it is their business to take the initiative into their own hands as they did in the case of the recent rent strike. Remember that the only way to fight the class war is by accepting every challenge of the master class and throwing down more challenges ourselves. Every determined fight binds the workers together more and more, clears the heads of our class to their robbed and enslaved conditions, and so prepares them for the acceptance of our full gospel of socialism, and the full development of the class war to the end of establishing socialism.

A victory at football, draughts, or chess, is the result of many moves and countermoves. We do not lie down and cry when our side loses a goal. No; we buckle up our sleeves and spit on our hands, determined to get two goals in return, or more. So is the game of life. It advances from move to move, ever on grander and grander scale. Prepare, then, for the enemy's counterstroke to our victory on the rent question!

The conscription menace
(*The Vanguard*, December 1915)

This war was declared to be a war of freedom. We socialists considered that a deliberate lie, because the promoters of the statement know quite well that the workers of the world are their slaves, and will continue to be their slaves no matter the issue of the war. It certainly is a war of freedom for one national section or other of the robbing propertied class to corner for itself the whole, or the greater part, of the surplus wrung from the wage-slave class. Obviously, that is no concern of the

87

workers one way or the other.

We have repeatedly expressed our perfect willingness to let those who benefit by capitalism enter the war, and slaughter one another to their heart's content. That is their affair, not ours. Their mutual extermination might, in fact, smooth the path leading to socialism, so that even many socialists might be excused if they departed from the policy of indifference and became active recruiting agents amongst the propertied class, urging them with fiery eloquence to defend *their* king and *their* country.

We have furthermore refrained from the attempt to prevent workers enlisting if they sincerely believed that Britain was entitled to enter the war. In fact, we usually insisted on them enlisting as the only logical outcome of their beliefs.

It is an entirely different matter when an attempt to force conscription on us is threatened. We socialists, who believe that the only war worth fighting is the class war against robbery and slavery for the workers, do not mean to lay down our lives for British or any other capitalism. If we die, we shall die here defending the few rights our forefathers died for. To us it is nobler to die for our own class than for the class which has robbed, ruled, despised, and imprisoned us.

They dare not murder us, for that would lift the veil of cant they have blinded the eyes of neutrals with. . . . They also had better not enlist us, for we will prove more dangerous with arms than without them. A reign of terror would certainly ensue. History backs us up in that assertion, for the mass of the men who refuse now to enlist do so on principle and not through fear. . . .

So far as mere trade unionists are concerned, we warn them that conscription means the bringing of all young men under the control of the military authorities, whether they be in the field of battle or in the factory and workshop. Every controlled factory comes directly under military discipline as well, and thus the old as well as the young will be bound hand and foot to Mr William Weir and his capitalist friends. Military conscription implies industrial conscription, the most abject form of slavery the world has ever known. . . .

To the old, as to the young, we appeal for stern opposition to conscription. . . .

The only way to retain our freedom — the small shred of it we now possess — is by solid combination as a class. The only weapon we can use today is the strike. We urge our comrades to be ready to use that weapon to prevent the coming of absolute chattel slavery.

Do not be paralysed by academic quack socialists, who insist that the only occasion justifying the strike is for the establishment of socialism. These men admit that the masses are still far from socialism. That means we must defer the strike to the remote future. See how absurd the position is, and act accordingly.

German industrial development
(*The Vanguard*, November 1915)

To those who have unthinkingly accepted the popular press statement that this war is due to the caprice or pushful designs of the Kaiser, aided by his Tory landlord class (the Junkers), it must come as a shock to hear us state that it is the unavoidable outcome of capitalist development in Germany, inside a world already very largely staked out and claimed by the powers arrayed against her.

We intend to give a few facts to show the marvellous development of Germany and the urgent economic necessity imposed on them of expanding or bursting. Even the most stupid or laziest now admit that economic competition inevitably leads on to trusts. The small firms are absolutely crushed out. There is no morality on this side of business. Crush your opponents lest they crush you! What we wish the most stupid and laziest now to grasp and admit is that the modern political machinery of any state acts as a uniting agency of the strongest industrial and money kings of that country, and that this political machinery must be used to form "political trusts", or "empires", for the further enrichment of these powerful capitalists. Armies and navies in this case do the crushing of less powerful rivals, and absolutely no heed is paid to the "rights" of tiny nations like Belgium, Turkey, Greece, Persia, Morocco, or Egypt. The only difference between price-cutting warfare and the present enthusiastic worship at the shrines of Thor and Mars is the slaughter and maiming of millions of men. The object is the same — the control of men and wealth.

Marx, in his "Revolution and Counter-Revolution", let us know that even as late as 1848 the thirty-six states now called Germany were practically in the feudal condition, the condition from which England freed itself during the time of the early Tudors. There were few capitalists, and these were so scattered as to be politically powerless. Remember that this was at the end of "hungry forties", when the English capitalist class had not only formed the Liberal Party, but had used that party against the landlords to obtain what they have called "free trade". Most of the Germans were small traders, shopkeepers, artisans, or peasants.

Since 1851, the date of the first Exhibition in England, springs up capitalism in Germany. Because of Germany's economic backwardness, we have few figures prior to 1871 that can be considered reliable or of real value. It was in 1871 that the empire was formed by the uniting for political as well as economic purposes of the mass of small states round Prussia.

In 1871 the population was 41,058,792; in 1910 it was 64,925,993, an increase of 24 millions in thirty-nine years. Latterly, German population has been increasing at about a million a year. This swelling of population is one of the features of the growth of capitalism in every country, and forces on statesmen the finding of new lands on which to dump the overflow, and yet retain their economic and political services for the state's, and therefore the property-holders' benefit. . . .

The use of coal and iron is a means of measuring a country's industrial advance. Let us quote a fact or two. Between 1900 and 1911 Germany's output of coal rose from 109 to 161 million metric tons. Over a half is used directly in industry. . . . Surely this shows the predominance of industrial undertakings.

Between 1880 and 1890 Germany produced between 3 and $4\frac{1}{2}$ million tons of pig iron a year, just about half Britain's output. In 1903 Germany beat Britain, and thus alarmed Joseph Chamberlain and his Birmingham iron and steel friends. That explains the "tariff fever". In 1911 Britain's output was 10 millions and Germany's $15\frac{1}{2}$ millions. This marvellous superiority of German iron output gives full explanation of her gun, shot, and shell superiority in this war. Germany has shown most initiative and scientific ability so far in attack, and likewise she was first to see the need of converting her huge iron and steel producing power to purposes of war.

We draw the attention of our readers to this to prove that it has been the past inferiority of Britain's capitalists in the iron industry and their present inability to adapt their plant and material to war purposes that have given the Germans their advantage up till the moment of writing, and has led to the needless death of thousands of the physically finest of our people. . . .

Germany shows the same company and trust development as here and in America, and the same mighty growth of concentrated capital. Their capital, however, rose from £243,800,000 to £736,865,000 — an increase of 203 per cent. This shows that the average business needed more money to run it and was consequently growing in size.

This growth of size is markedly seen in 1909. . . . This shows a grand total of 229 companies. . . . Over and above these companies there are between 550 and 600 cartels and syndicates which exist to control markets, prices etc., and in time lead up to the absolute solidarity of capital inside a few immense trusts.

So far as shipping is concerned, here is what Sir Owen Philipps, of the Royal Mail Company, said in June 1914, on the eve of the war: "British trade is represented by some 300 individual and separate (shipping) lines, with no unity of action or purpose. German trade is centred in seven big lines. Behind them, using every power of persuasion and influence to secure harmonious working and co-action, is the greatest commercial director of the world — the Kaiser." The result he shows thus: "On every great trade route in the world, in every great commercial port, you will find German ships. They are the only formidable rivals British shipping has to face. . . ." German shipping was absolutely necessary to dispose of Germany's surplus of goods.

In the world market international antagonism becomes very sharp, and forces on the stealing of other people's land as colonies.

This rush for colonies necessitates secret diplomacy (polite lying and cheating) and when the liars find one another out diplomacy gives place to warfare.

Germany being late in the development of capitalism was late in the search for colonies, and hence had to attack whilst Britain had to defend. Not any special virtues, then, but historical circumstances have placed Britain in the position of the injured one in the eyes of the blind. . . .

We are fully justified, then, in designating this war as another capitalist war that will bring no grist to the workers' mill. On that account we are forced into the position of demanding that this war cease, and that the respective countries return to the territory possessed before the war began. . . .

Zimmerwald

(*The Vanguard*, October 1915)

In spite of the British government's prevention of British socialists attending a gathering of representative socialists in Switzerland by the refusal of passports, a most successful conference took place, not at Berne as originally intended, but at another town.

The conference was attended by seven delegates from the anti-war section of the German Democratic Party, two from the French trade unions (the French Socialist Party being hopeless), three from the Italian Socialist Party, and others representing Bulgaria and the other Balkan States, Norway, Switzerland, and Russia. "Socialist patriots" were excluded.

The proceedings lasted three days. The German delegates asserted that the majority of the members of their party are opposed to their Executive and to the Reichstag group who voted for the war credits, but the opposition had so far lacked cohesion and therefore effectiveness. The

French pointed out that the opposition to the war and the "socialist patriots" is growing. At a recent conference of French trade unionists a resolution against the war was rejected, but about a third favoured the resolution. Although no Belgians were present, it was asserted a large number of Belgian social democrats treat Vandervelde with the perfect contempt we think he merits.

Both sections of the Russian social democrats at the conference are internationalists and are fighting the Russian government with all their might. The "majority" section declares that the defeat of the Tsar's army would be the lesser evil for the Russian and European democracy. They urge civil war for the establishment of a democratic republic in Russia, and international action to stop the war and defeat the bourgeoisie. The "minority" oppose the "lesser evil" idea, and declare against defeats or victories. (We learn that a gigantic political strike has already been declared in Petrograd and other important centres. We wish our comrades every success.)

The third and last day of the conference was devoted to the consideration of a manifesto against the war to be issued to the workers of the world.

From the *Avanti*, the central organ of our Italian party, we learn that efforts are being made to discredit the conference by allegations to the effect that it dissolved without coming to any agreement. Those responsible are ex-socialists attached to the European capitalist press. The editor of the *Avanti* asserts that about forty delegates participated in the proceedings, and at least twelve nations were represented. The manifesto above referred to is to be issued in German and French, and will be signed by two from each nation. Emphasis will be laid on the only war worth fighting — the class war for social democracy. This the editor considers will renew the workers' solidarity, which no militarism ever again will destroy. Even should those controlling the International Socialist Bureau continue the policy of keeping the respective parties apart, this conference clearly indicates that the International itself will go on. The traitors to the International will have to be treated later on.

We side with Morgari of Italy when he charges Vandervelde with doing everything to prevent the International coming together.

We draw attention to the fact that Hyndman's paper *Justice*, which boasts its international information, was totally innocent of the international conference. At least, it said so. "None so blind, etc." From what we have seen in Britain, we must put down the bell on those who are constantly whining, "trust your leaders". Faithful social democrats here have been led a sorry dance by the bourgeois members of the central branch of the BSP. Our business is to trust ourselves and our cause and line up with our world comrades as quickly as we can.

We assure our comrades that we in Glasgow are internationalists first, last, and all the time.

Speech from the dock, 1915 (excerpts)

Recently I have considered and lectured upon the economic causes and results of the present war. All the lectures which I have given have been directed from the workers' point of view, and the object has been to show that economically the workers have suffered and are suffering much as the result of the present conflict.

These lectures have been delivered in different towns, but principally in Glasgow.

The locus of the offence first charged in the complaint against me is a place well known for the holding of open-air meetings of all sorts. . . . I have no notes of what I said at this meeting. . . . I had been specially dealing with articles and certain economic statistics which were contained in the *Labour Gazette* issued about the end of August. . . . I finished my lecture and the meeting was thrown open for questions. Two or three questions were asked, and I then proceeded to close the meeting. I was making some general remarks, and asking members of the audience to become members of the BSP, when a man from the audience cried "away and 'list". I did not notice the observation till it was repeated by the same person, who had a loud and rough voice, two or three times. This observation had no connection whatever with anything that I had said, and was altogether irrelevant and impertinent. At last I said, "I have been enlisted for fifteen years in the socialist army. It is the only army worth fighting for; God damn all other armies."

The remark did not cause any comment or trouble. It passed altogether without notice. There were policemen there at the time, and they never spoke to me about it. In making the statement I knew that I was doing so in the presence of the police, but never felt that I was committing any breach of the law.

I did not use the expression referred to in the complaint against me, i.e. I never said, "God damn the other army". It was quite opposed to my own views and the views of my party to say this. I have friends and dear friends in the British army. But I am opposed to the present military system. It was regarding this that I said, "God damn all other armies." Rightly or wrongly I feel conscientiously that this is not the way to settle national disputes.

The second charge referred to a meeting which I addressed at Langside Avenue and Pollokshaws Road on 2 September. . . . I gave an address on economics. In the course of the address I referred to the war as "this murder business". There were two or three soldiers in the audience, some having a little drink. When I spoke of "this murder business" one of the soldiers in the audience said, "Do you call me a murderer?" and I replied, "No, I do not."

I never used the expression mentioned in the complaint. I never said that a soldier who killed another soldier was a murderer, or words to the same effect. . . .

Peter Petroff
(Letter to *Justice*, 30 December 1915)

On the fourth page of *Justice*, 23 December, you have a note entitled "Who and What is Peter Petroff?" You say: "He has been for some weeks on the Clyde. What he is doing there, and what may be his object, is best known to himself."

He was invited to Glasgow by the Glasgow District Council of the BSP to address a meeting in the Panopticon. He spoke on the Russian revolution to an audience of over a thousand. After arrangements for this meeting were made, I was summoned under the Defence of the Realm Act. Expecting six months, I wished to see that my "withdrawal" would involve no hitch in the conduct of our economic class, the issue of the *Vanguard*, and the other activities that are helping to make the Clyde Valley the danger spot to capitalism. I therefore suggested to the GDC that Petroff be kept in Glasgow as our second organiser. This was agreed to, and here he remains, with his wife, as a BSP organiser. . . .

To make Petroff safe, I took him to the Free Speech Committee, to the Clyde Workers' Committee, and to other bodies of Clyde Workers. He has no status on the Clyde Workers' Committee. Everybody knows that; but still, Petroff speaks at it.

His attack on Vandervelde was "plotted" in my house. We think Vandervelde a traitor to socialism, and hold him partly responsible for the breakdown of the International. The BSP tried to send delegates to the unofficial International Socialist Conference in Switzerland. We in this part stick by that conference. We object to money being sent to Vandervelde in the name of the International. The Austrian socialists are now lining up with the Swiss conference, as will many others very soon. Petroff is not alone in this, and Petroff does not do our thinking. We put Petroff in his proper place every time, and will continue to do so. . . .

Speech from the dock, 1916 (excerpts)

I am a socialist, and a member of the British Socialist Party. I am closely associated with the efforts being made for better housing of the workers, and am secretary of the Scottish National Labour Housing Association. . . . For a number of years I have been a close student of and lecturer on economic and social questions. Classes were conducted under the auspices of the Eastwood School Board of which I was lecturer. I have conducted classes in connection with the co-operative movement. I have organised and carried on large classes in Glasgow for the study of industrial history and economics.

I am an opponent of compulsory military service. I believe that the present war is a war of capitalist aggression and defence. If I were asked if, having been attacked by Germany, we were bound to defend ourselves, my answer would be that the matter of defence is the business of the capitalists whose interests are more immediately concerned. If we had conscription of property and capital I would instantly concede it to be the duty of the workers to defend. This has been my attitude all along. . . .

I have recently been engaged in the agitation against the Military Service Bill no. 2, now an Act of Parliament. I attended the various meetings referred to in the charges against me.

With regard to the charges generally I have to observe that I have not a recollection of what I precisely said at these meetings. I speak extemporaneously. I use notes of things said by statesmen and speakers. I quote largely from current well-known newspapers. . . .

I remember the meeting on 9 January in the Morris Hall, Govan. It was arranged by the Govan ILP Branch (Central). I had been invited to speak. . . . In my speech I dealt with conscription. . . . I never said at that meeting or at any other meeting that if the government were to enforce the Military Service and Munition Acts the workers should down tools but do it discreetly. I do not know what the word "discreetly" in this capacity would mean, and the words were certainly not used by me.

With reference to the statement that if the British soldiers in all parts would lay down their arms I was certain that the Germans and the soldiers of all other nations who are fighting would also lay down their arms as they were all tired of the war long ago. In dealing with peace in my address I referred to the incident that had taken place in Flanders where on Christmas Day 1914 the soldiers of Britain and Germany fraternised. I gave this as an illustration of my belief that it was not the soldiers that had caused the war, and that they were quite willing to agree together. . . .

I was present at Brunswick Street, Glasgow, on 16 January 1916. A meeting had been advertised to take place there at 7 o'clock to be addressed by myself. It was thereafter arranged that Miss [Sylvia] Pankhurst should speak. Miss Pankhurst was addressing a meeting at Clydebank that day, and she was late in arriving. I was chairman and kept the meeting going till she came.

At that time there was a controversy in the newspapers regarding the Clyde workers being bribed by German gold. I told them that I did not just need it yet as the three months' salary which the Govan School Board had given me* was not exhausted. I did say that if there was any gold of German origin among the workers it must have been given by Lloyd George to the shop stewards when he was up to see them on Christmas Day. Miss Pankhurst arrived and I told her that if she had come up from London in the expectation of getting German gold here, she was too late as it was all done. . . .

I was present at the meeting on Monday 17 January, at Weir's Gate, Cathcart. . . . The time was the breakfast hour which is between 8.55 and 9.40. . . . I dealt with the question of the newspaper controversy and proceeded very much on the same lines as I had done on the previous time. I pointed out as I had done before that if the workers had got German gold it must have been quite legitimately, say through the visit of Lloyd George to Glasgow . . . in connection with which each of the shop stewards got 6s. My point was that this and the wages paid to them for their work came out of the war loan and that the war loan was contributed to a considerable extent by German financiers like the Rothschilds and Schroders. . . . I pointed out that the money that these men were getting from Messrs Weir might be German gold in the sense already indicated. . . .

I was present on Thursday, 20 January 1916, at Nelson's Monument, Glasgow Green, at the meeting convened by a united committee. The purpose of the meeting was to protest against the Military Service Bill. . . . Mr Shinwell was chairman. . . . I was among the audience and listened to Mr Shinwell and a number of other speakers. . . . After the others had spoken Mr Shinwell called upon me. . . . I spoke very shortly on conscription. . . . I did not say that the Clyde workers should strike at once and that the men should not go back to work and that those of them that had guns should use them.

As a matter of fact I have always been against the use of arms for the purpose of securing redress. I have pointed out again and again that that type of thing might be good enough for men in Dublin, but that it was no good whatever for the Clyde workers who, even if they had the in-

---

*Upon his dismissal.

96

clination to use guns, have not got them. I certainly did not use the expression quoted against me.

With regard to the meeting on Sunday, 30 January, held at Nelson's Monument, I was present at it. . . . It was held under the auspices of the united committee before referred to. The Military Service Bill by this time had been passed, and the resolution was to agitate for the repeal of it. I moved the motion and in concluding my address referred to the German clocks. I do not remember the exact words, but I think it was almost as follows: "You men are all patriots and won't use any goods of German manufacture. I understand that you have all got German alarm clocks to waken you in the morning. As patriots you surely can't continue to use these. You should pawn them or sell them. Be sure to do it all at one time, and then you will all sleep in in the morning."

Miners' historic protest against profiteers
(*The Call*, 2 August 1917)
At last the miners of Lanarkshire have put a move on and not too soon either. During January 1916, I held several meetings at pitheads and in halls in Lanarkshire with the object of rousing the miners to resist conscription, on the ground that the capitalists would use this weapon after the war for the intensified robbery of the workers. That intensified robbery has already been put into practice throughout Britain through the gentle art of raising prices and keeping wages at the old level. . . .

Last Thursday, the whole of the miners of Lanarkshire, with the exception of Harthill, where a holiday was held on Friday, did not dig coal, but made a hefty dig at the paunch of the profiteers and their flunkey government. More than 50,000 were engaged in this most healthy exercise. After processing, they assembled at thirteen places of meeting to call on the government to reduce prices immediately. Smillie himself hinted to the whole working class that, if the government did not take the hint they ought to "take action".

This event is certainly the most important in the whole history of the working class in Scotland. It easily transcends the spontaneous strike on the Clyde that forced the government to give us the House Letting Act. At the time those of us who did our bit in getting that Act realised that for the first time the workers of Scotland (perhaps Britain) struck for a political object of a class nature. In this case the object is also political, but it is a larger object — the whole cost of living. More significant still is the fact that the strike has been organised by the EC of the Lanarkshire miners and loyally supported by the rank and file. . . . The greatness and grandeur of Bob Smillie (the mightiest fighter the workers of Scotland have ever had) is seen in his refusal to accept the food controller's job thrown at him by the government, and the powerful lead he's giving our class to force the government's hand on the food question. The organised miners have now raised themselves to the highest level; that is, as champions of the whole working class, and not merely of miners as miners. That is the beginning of the end of capitalism after other organised workers follow suit. I am confident, at any rate, that my comrades in the engineering and shipbuilding industries of the Clyde will fully appreciate the significance of Thursday's great event in Lanarkshire. . . .

Significance also attaches to the extra resolution passed in the Coalburn district, where the men threaten a "down-tools" policy against the further application of military and industrial conscription. This is the work of the South Lanark Miners' Reform Committee, a link-up of the socialist forces in South Lanarkshire. This area is the centre of revolutionary fervour in the country, and I think McDougall and myself can claim our share of credit in the work. Significantly enough, economic classes have been successful here, the last having been conducted by our comrade George Pollok. . . .

Comrades, let Thursday inspire us to beat the Russians in the revolutionary race.

Russian distress fund
(Letter in *The Call*, 21 February 1918)
Kerenski last summer committed himself to a Convention with the Allies empowering each country to send back eligible men to their respective countries or to enlist them in its own army. In consequence, many Russians in the autumn were transported to Russia, leaving behind them their families.

After delay the government provided money to be disbursed by the parish councils to those families. In the meantime the late Glasgow Consul, Mr Denham, started a Russian Relief Fund. The money gathered has been distributed through the agency of the Charity Organisation Society in a most unsatisfactory manner, as might be expected by those conversant with the methods of the COS.

The acute poverty now prevailing in the West of Scotland has compelled the Russian women to form the International Women's Protection League, and I have been asked by them to appeal to the working class to immediately come to their aid. I have consented to act as honorary treasurer.

My suggestion is that the matter be brought before the notice of the shop stewards' committee in all workshops by readers of this appeal, in order that a systematic subscription may be obtained. This does not preclude individuals from forwarding donations.

Comrade Litvinoff is at present pressing the government to give more generously to these Russian families or to grant facilities for their return to Russia. Meantime it is our duty as socialists and members of the working class to show our gratitude for the triumph of socialism in Russia by subscribing liberally at once to this fund.

Subscriptions to be sent to John MacLean, Russian Consulate, 12 South Portland Street, Glasgow.

Correspondence on the Russian Consulate

Russian Consulate,
12 South Portland Street,
Glasgow.
March, 1918.

The Postmaster,
Glasgow.
Dear Sir,

Allow me to indignantly protest against your policy of withholding communications to me when they contain the words on the address "Russian Consulate".

I understand that your duty is to officiate over the transmission of communications, and not to express political opinions.

Yours sincerely,
John MacLean.

12 South Portland Street,
Glasgow.
26 March, 1918.

Secretary,
Home Office,
Whitehall.
Sir,

My secretary, Mr Louis Shammes, was arrested in the above office on Friday, 22 March, at your instigation and now awaits deportation to Russia. He has a wife and child who must be kept alive.

I would be pleased to know what provision you intend to make for their maintenance, so long as they remain in this country.

Yours sincerely,
John MacLean.

4

"Unconstitutional action"

Speech from the dock, May 1918

It has been said that they cannot fathom my motive. For the full period of my active life I have been a teacher of economics to the working classes, and my contention has always been that capitalism is rotten to its foundations, and must give place to a new society. I had a lecture, the principal heading of which was "Thou shalt not steal; thou shalt not kill", and I pointed out that as a consequence of the robbery that goes on in all civilised countries today, our respective countries have had to keep armies, and that inevitably our armies must clash together. On that and on other grounds, I consider capitalism the most infamous, bloody and evil system that mankind has ever witnessed. My language is regarded as extravagant language, but the events of the past four years have proved my contention.

He (the Lord Advocate) accused me of my motives. My motives are clean. My motives are genuine. If my motives were not clean and genuine, would I have made my statements while these shorthand reporters were present? I am out for the benefit of society, not for any individual human being, but I realise this, that justice and freedom can only be obtained when society is placed on a sound economic basis. That sound economic basis is wanting today, and hence the bloodshed we are having. I have not tried to get young men particularly. The young men have come to my meetings as well as the old men. I know quite well that in the reconstruction of society, the class interests of those who are on top will resist the change, and the only factor in society that can make for a clean sweep in society is the working class. Hence the class war. The whole history of society has proved that society moves forward as a consequence of an under class overcoming the resistance of a class on top of them. So much for that.

I also wish to point out to you this, that when the late King Edward the Seventh died, I took as the subject of one of my lectures "Edward the Peacemaker". I pointed out at the time that his "entente cordiale" with France and his alliance with Russia were for the purpose of encircling Germany as a result of the coming friction between Germany and this country because of commercial rivalry. I then denounced that title "Edward the Peacemaker" and said that it should be "Edward the Warmaker". The events which have ensued prove my contention right up to the hilt. I am only proceeding along the lines upon which I have proceeded for many years. I have pointed out at my economic classes that, owing to the surplus created by the workers, it was necessary to create a market outside this country, because of the inability of the workers to purchase the wealth they create. You must have markets abroad, and in order to have these markets you must have empire. I have also pointed out that the capitalist development of Germany since the Franco-Prussian War has forced upon that country the necessity for empire as well as this country, and in its search for empire there must be a clash between these two countries. I have been teaching that and what I have taught is coming perfectly true.

I wish no harm to any human being, but I, as one man, am going to exercise my freedom of speech. No human being on the face of the earth, no government is going to take from me my right to speak, my right to protest against wrong, my right to do everything that is for the benefit of mankind. *I am not here, then, as the accused; I am here as the accuser of capitalism dripping with blood from head to foot.*

In connection with the "ca' canny" question at Parkhead Forge, I wish to take up some of the particular points first of all before I deal with the revolution. It is quite evident that it was in connection with a report in the *Forward* that reference was made to David Kirkwood. It was reported that Kirkwood had made a record output. Now David Kirkwood, representing the Parkhead Forge workers, at the end of 1915, when the dilution of labour began, put forward a printed statement for the benefit of Mr Lloyd George and his colleagues, the first sentence of which, in big type, was — "What you wish is greater output". He said that the Parkhead workers were then prepared to give a greater output and accept dilution if they, the workers, had some control over the conditions under which the greater output would accrue. That was his contention. Since he was got into position he seems to have boasted that he has got a record output. The question was put to me. Was this consistent with the position and with the attitude of the working class? I said it was not consistent with the attitude and the position of the working class, that his business was to get back right down to the normal, to "ca' canny" so far as the general output was concerned.

The country has been exploited by the capitalist in every sphere, to get the toilers to work harder to bring victory. I said at the commencement of the war that while this was being done, and while assurances were being given that at the end of the war the people would get back to normal, I said that circumstances would make such a return impossible. Now I have ample evidence to support that belief; I have used it at my meetings at Weir's of Cathcart — that they were asking the workers to toil harder, not only during the war, but after the war they wish them to work harder and harder, because there is going to be "the war after the war", the economic war which brought on this war. You see, therefore, the workers are brought into a position where they are speeded up, and they are never allowed to get back again. They are speeded up again and again. What is the position of the worker? This country is not a free country. The worker is deprived of land or access to the land; he is deprived of workshops or access to the materials and tools of production; the worker has only one thing to do in the market, and that is to sell his labour power. The capitalist purchased that labour power, and when he gets the worker inside the workshop, his business is to extract as much of that labour power out of him as possible. On the other hand, when it comes to wages, then the employer applies the principle of "ca' canny". "Ca' canny" is quite justifiable when it comes to the employer giving wages to the workers, and we have seen it since the commencement of the war. Prices rise right away from the commencement of the war while the workers' wages were kept at the old normal. Their wages were kept low. The purchasing power of the workers' wages was therefore diminished. They were therefore robbed to that extent. At the same time the workers were asked in the name of the country to work harder. "But," said the employers, "we will not give you any more money, although the money you are getting is purchasing less in the way of food, etc." That is the position.

The employers are changing their opinions now as a result of experience, but in the past they considered it in their economic interest to pay as low a wage as possible. On the other hand the position of the workers is to give as little of their energy as they possibly can and to demand the highest wage possible. If it is right for the employer to get the maximum of energy and pay the minimum of wage, then it is equally right for the worker to give the minimum of his energy and demand the maximum of wage.

What is right for the one is equally right for the other, although the interests of the two classes are diametrically opposed. That is the position, and in view of the fact that many of the workers have over-worked themselves and have had to lie off through overstrain, and considering the treatment they get when thrown on the scrapheap — kicked out like dogs when they are no longer useful — they are compelled to look after their own welfare. The worker has therefore in the past adopted the policy of "ca' canny", and I have in the interests of the working class advocated the policy of "ca' canny", not because I am against the war, but, knowing that after the war the worker will have the new conditions imposed upon him, I hold still to the principle of "ca' canny". I accede to that.

102

So far as Parkhead Forge is concerned I also pointed out that none of the great big guns had been made for some time prior to the great offensive. When the offensive came, Gough, the friend of Sir Edward Carson, the man who before the war was going to cut down the Irishmen, retreated and lost so many guns, and then the Glasgow workers had to give over their Easter holiday in order to make those guns. We have, therefore, Beardmore and others responsible for shortage of certain material, and we know from further disclosures that millions of shells have been useless, and perhaps that has been due to the fact of over-speeding, so that even over-speeding may do nothing for the advancement of the war. Furthermore, if big reserves of material are going to be built up, and the Germans are to be allowed to get them, that is going to be to the advantage of the Germans, and not to the advantage of the British.

With regard to the next point, "down tools", so far as Glasgow is concerned, I do not think I told the workers to "down tools". I am of the opinion that I said, "Now that you are determined to 'down tools' it is of no use standing idle; you must do something for yourselves." As a matter of fact my statement was based on a resolution that had been passed by the ASE in the Clyde area, the official Engineers' Committee. It met, and it determined to down tools against the introduction of the Man Power Bill.

At the same time that was supplemented by unofficial effort at Geddes's meeting in the City Hall. There a resolution was put up by the workers and carried virtually unanimously, that if the Man Power Bill was put into operation, the Clyde district workers would "down tools". It was unnecessary for me, therefore, in light of these official and unofficial statements, to urge the "down tools" policy.

As a matter of fact, we were told that the government had dismissed many munition girls just immediately prior to the great offensive, so that if the workers are guilty of stoppage of output of munitions, the government is likewise responsible in the dismissal of those thousands of girls.

Now then, food and farms. I pointed out to the workers that what was necessary if they stopped work was the getting of food. There had been a shortage; the government had held up the supplies, for several reasons probably — perhaps to get this rationing passed, in order to have a tight hold on food, and also lest the people get out of hand in reference to this Man Power Bill. I know that there was plenty of food in stores in Glasgow, and that the farmers had food stored up in their farms. The farmers have used the war in order to make huge profits for themselves, and then the government assisted them in connection with the potato regulations; and latterly, at the end of last year the Corn Production Act was passed, not in the interests of the farm labourers, but in the interests of the farmers.

When the demand for more food production was made, the farmers said they would do their best, and the government refused to give the farm labourers a minimum wage of 25s to 30s a week — 25s at that time being equivalent to 10s in normal times. The farmers were going to get extra as a consequence of the Corn Production Act. I therefore pointed out that if the workers went to the farmers and did not get the food stored up in the farms, they should burn the farms. We as socialists have no interest in destroying any property. We want property to be kept because we want that property to be used for housing accommodation or other reasons, but I specially emphasised about the farmers for the purpose of drawing attention to this particular point.

In the same way, when it came to a question of seizing the press, I suggested that when the *Daily Record* was seized, the plant should be broken up. I did not say that in connection with the *Glasgow Herald*. I said so in connection with the *Record* not that it is a good thing to break up printing plant, but in order to draw attention to the Harmsworth family and to the Rothermeres and so on, and their vile press which seems to be an index of the culture of Britain. I mention that particularly here, that I said the *Record* plant should be broken up, in order to emphasise the disgust of the organised workers with regard to that particular family of newspapers.

So far as Ireland and America are concerned, that was mentioned particularly for the purpose of getting food from the St Lawrence, food from the United States, and food from the Argentine. What was needed was food in order to hold our own, for, as the *Glasgow Herald* pointed out, when the Bolsheviks first came into power, Britain was withholding food from Russia, in the expectation that frost and famine would over-throw the Bolsheviks. That is to say, they were anxious to murder women and children inside Russia, as well as men. The suggestion I made was in order to draw attention of the workers to the need of having plenty of foodstuffs to keep them going.

So far as the government's responsibility for the murder of women and children is concerned, the reason for my statement is perfectly ob-vious. They have been accusing the Germans of killing women and child-ren in this country. Perfectly true. Of course bombs dropped in Germany have not killed women and children, marvellous to say! But that apart; we had the government getting hold of the food supplies immediately prior to and immediately after the New Year, and creating a shortage. The government was therefore responsible for the queues.

Women were standing in queues in the cold, and women had died of what they had contracted during their standing in the queues. The women had died therefore in consequence of the action of the government, and I threw the responsibility upon the government — and I do so still.

We know that women and children — human material — have been used up inside the factories, and the housing of the working class in this country has been so bad, and is so bad today, that the women and children of the working class die in greater proportion than the women and children of the better-to-do classes. I have always pointed out that the death rate among the working classes has always exceeded that in the better-to-do districts.

I also pointed out that the British government had sent Russian subjects back to Russia to fight, and had given their wives 12s 6d per week and 2s 6d for each child. Now, when I was functioning as Russian Consul, two deputations of Russian women came to me and they told me sorrowful tales of depression, disease and death in consequence of the fact that they had received 12s 6d per week and 2s 6d for each child. I wrote to the Secretary for Scotland in regard to that, and I received no reply. The children ought not to suffer because their fathers have been taken, but those children have suffered. There is not a Lithuanian family in the West of Scotland but has trouble today as a consequence of the starving of these people. These women and children of the Russian community have died as a consequence of the meagre supplies given to them by the British government, and I seize this opportunity for the purpose of making my statement public, in connection with these women, in the hope that the public in general will press the government to see that these women and children are attended to at least on the same scale as the wives and dependants of British soldiers.

With regard to the Yankees, I said, and I say today, that the Yankees are out for themselves. The British press — the British capitalist press — sneered and jeered at the Americans before the Americans came in, and pointed out how the Americans were making piles of profit out of the war, but were not participating in this fight for so-called freedom. Those insults were offered to America, and when Mr Woodrow Wilson said that America was too proud to fight, then that was used venomously. Therefore, if I erred, I erred on the same side as the capitalist class of this country. I made the statement on American authority, not off my own bat. My authority is Professor Roland G. Usher, Professor of History at Washington University. I think his statement in *Pan-Americanism* is one of the finest, showing the moves throughout the world leading up to this war, and Usher has his bias in favour of Britain.

What I wish to particularly refer to are his two books, *Pan-Germanism* and *The Challenge of the Future*. In *Pan-Germanism* he surveys North and South and Central America. He takes the Atlantic first, and explains what will be the consequence of the war as regards South and Central America whichever side wins, and then he takes the Pacific. He works it out from a material and economic point of view, his purpose being to get Central and South America to work in with the United States. In his later book he modifies that position — that is to say in *The Challenge of the Future*. He points out that America is still today economically dependent, that is to say she has got to pay interest to financiers in France, in Britain, and therefore America cannot afford to carry out the bold schemes referred to in his book *Pan-Americanism*.

I may now state that today the businessmen of this country know perfectly well that the Yankees are boasting of their independence. Therefore when you see references to American independence, that means that she no longer needs to pay interest to investors from outside and that her policy will be modified in consequence of that new phase. This gentleman points out that as a consequence of American dependence she must say which side she will take. This book was printed prior to America entering the war. Woodrow Wilson's policy works in admirably with the suggestions in that book of Professor Usher, *The Challenge of the Future*.

We know quite well, too, that the United States of America prevented Japan in 1915 getting economic and political control over North China. Twenty-one articles were imposed on China after the Japs had released their grip of the Germans there. America, alive to her own interests, getting to know of these twenty-one points, forced Japan to withdraw. America was there working in her own interests.

Japan has been, I think, incited to land at Vladivostok in consequence of the Russian revolution, and in order to crush the Bolsheviks. The allies on both sides are united to crush the Bolsheviks. America did not take that course. America early on began to back up the Bolsheviks because America was afraid that, if Japan got half Siberian Russia, that would give her a strategic control of Siberia, and it would mean a closed door to American contact across the Pacific with Russia proper. America therefore has been looking to her own interests, and for that reason I contend that the Yankees, who have been the worshippers of the mighty dollar, are looking after their own interests in the present war; and as to the great boast they have been making about what they are going to do, and their inadequate returns — that, I think, shows that America has not been over-anxious to plunge right away into this war and made all the sacrifices she has said. I know, of course, that America has had her own troubles at home,

106

racial troubles, and also troubles with the workers. Numerous strikes have taken place in America since the commencement of the war, not only in consequence of the war, but also in connection with the economic position.

Now then, I come to the doctors. The doctors I referred to were the prison doctors. When I was in Peterhead it was plain sailing until the middle of December, and then the trouble began. I was fevered up, and being able to combat that, I was chilled down. Two men came to see me at the end of December, a prominent lecturer in this country, and Mr Sutherland, MP, and to them I protested that my food was being drugged. I said that there was alcohol in the food lowering my temperature. I know that potassium bromide is given to people in order to lower their temperature. It may have been potassium bromide that was used in order to lower my temperature. I was aware of what was taking place in Peterhead from hints and statements by other prisoners there; that from January to March, the so-called winter period, the doctor is busy getting the people into the hospital, there breaking up their organs and their systems.

I call that period the eye-squinting period, because the treatment then given puts the eyes out of view. Through numerous expedients I was able to hold my own. I saw these men round about me in a horrible plight. I have stated in public since that I would rather be immediately put to death than condemned to a life sentence in Peterhead. Attacks were made upon the organs of these men and also upon their nervous systems, and we know from the conscientious objectors that the government have taken their percentage of these men — some have died, some have committed suicide, others have been knocked off their heads, and in this way got into asylums. The very same process has gone on here. Mrs Hobhouse has done a good service to mankind in registering the facts, but, unfortunately for Mrs Hobhouse, she does not know how the results have been obtained. I experienced part of the process, and I wish to emphasise the fact that this callous and cold system of destroying people is going on inside prisons now.

Whatever is done to me now, I give notice that I take no food inside your prisons, absolutely no food, because of the treatment that was meted out to me. If food is forced upon me, and if I am forcibly fed, then my friends have got to bear in mind that if any evil happens to me, I am not responsible for the consequences, but the British government. If anything had happened to me when I was last in prison, it would have been attributed to John MacLean, not to those who are working in the interests of the government. I have been able to lay down my principle and policy, not from mere internal and personal experience, but from objective experience. I studied the matter carefully, I combated the evils that were going to be perpetrated by the government by reducing my food to the minimum, and the present Secretary for Scotland knows that when I was in Perth I wrote to him asking for more food because of my reduced weight. I was about eight stones in weight at the time, and the doctor after weighing me had to grant me more food. The food, however, was of no use to me. I threw it into the pot. My position is, therefore, that I take no more government food, that I will not allow any food to be forced in upon me, and if any food is forced in upon me I am not responsible for it, but when the government can launch millions of men into the field of battle, then perhaps the mere disposal of one man is a mere bagatelle and a trifle.

So far as Russian freedom and British slavery are concerned, I wish to draw attention to the fact that an article appeared in *The Scotsman* the other day about Bolshevism, and I have a feeling that that article was written especially for this trial, to create a feeling against Bolshevism. The statements in that article are a travesty. Inside Russia, since Lenin and Trotsky and the Bolsheviks came into power, there have been fewer deaths than for the same period under any Tsar for three hundred years. Capitalists have been killed perhaps, officers have been killed perhaps, because they have not submitted to those who have come to the top — the majority of the people — in the name of Bolshevism. Some may have been put to death.

When there was a shortage and disorganisation of the food supplies before the Bolsheviks came into power, there may have been individuals who, in their scramble for food themselves, have gone to excess, but the crimes of individuals cannot be charged to governments. No person would hold the government responsible for the action of those individuals. The Bolshevik government has not given orders to kill men. They have to imprison men until a complete reconstruction of society has come about. It may be news to some of you that the co-operative movement in Russia has grown more rapidly than in any other part of the world, and since the Bolsheviks have come into power, co-operation has been growing more and more rapidly. The universities have been used during the day, and in the evenings, to train the working classes in order that they may manage the affairs of their country in an intelligent manner. The schools have also been used in the evenings, the music halls have been used, and the theatres, and the picture houses, all have been used, not for the trivial trash which is given to the people of this country — but all for the purpose of organising the production of food and the work inside the workshops and factories.

We saw that prior to our comrades in Russia signing their treaty, when the Germans made their advance into Estonia, Lithuania, and so on — the border countries between Germany and Russia — the capitalist class in the respective towns had lists of men who were members of the soviets, and those members of the soviets were taken and put against a wall, and shot at the instigation of the propertied class of Russia. They have been responsible for more deaths than the soviets. Our Finnish comrades, the Red Guards, have pointed out that the ordinary procedure of war has not been acceded to them, that as soon as the White Guards, the capitalist class, take any one of them prisoner, they immediately put them to death. It has been said that our comrades over there in Russia were working hand in hand with the Germans, and the proof of this was that the Germans allowed Lenin to pass through Austrian territory. Our comrades have stood up against Germany as best they could, and the capitalists — the so-called patriots of Russia — have been working hand in hand with Germany in order to crush the people of Russia. That has been done in the Ukraine. It has been done in the various states stolen by Germany from Russia.

The Lord Advocate pointed out here that I probably was a more dangerous enemy that you had got to face than in the Germans. *The working class, when they rise for their own, are more dangerous to capitalists than even the German enemies at your gates.* That has been repeatedly indicated in the press, and I have stated it as well. I am glad that you have made this statement at this, the most historic trial that has ever been held in Scotland, when the working class and the capitalist class meet face to face. The Bolsheviks got into power in October, and the people wished peace, and they were doing their best to get peace. The Bolsheviks wished peace throughout the world. They wished the war to cease in order that they might settle down to the real business of life, the economic reorganisations of the whole of Russia. They therefore got into negotiation with the Germans, and they and the Germans met at Brest Litovsk.

Towards the end of December there was a pause in the negotiations for ten days, in order to allow the British and their allies to go to Brest Litovsk. Ten days were given. The last day was 4 January of this year. Great Britain paid no attention to this opportunity, but on 5 January Lloyd George, in one of his insidious speeches, seemed to climb down as it were. He was followed by Mr Woodrow Wilson. But a speech by Mr Lloyd George on the 5th was of no use. It was mere talk. It was mere camouflage, or, a better word still, bluff, pure bluff. Why did the government not accept the opportunity and go to Brest Litovsk? If conditions absolutely favourable to Germany were proposed, then Britain would have stopped the negotiations and plunged once more into the war, and I am confident of this, if Germany had not toed the line and come up square so far as peace negotiations were concerned, that the Russian workers would have taken the side of Britain, and I am confident of this, that the socialists in all the allied countries would have backed up their governments in order to absolutely crush Germany, and we would at the same time have appealed to the socialists of Germany to overthrow their government.

Great Britain did not do so. On the other hand, they came on with their Man Power Bill, and also with their factor of short food. All these things must be considered in their ensemble, before you can understand the position taken up by myself. When this universal peace meeting was held at Brest Litovsk, then Trotsky played a very, very bold game. He knew the risks he ran. He and the Bolsheviks spread millions of leaflets amongst the workers of Germany in the trenches — the German soldiers — urging them to stop fighting and to overthrow the Kaiser, the junkers, and the capitalist classes of Germany. They made a bold bid by trying to get the German workers on to their side. Great Britain has been doing the very same thing since the commencement of the war. Great Britain has been trying to bring about, and hoping and urging for a revolution in Germany, in the hope that the working class would overthrow the autocratic class there and give us peace.

From a British point of view, revolution inside Germany is good; revolution inside Britain is bad. So says this learned gentleman. He can square it if he can. I cannot square it. The conditions of Germany economically are the conditions of Britain, and there is only a very slight difference between the political structure of Germany and that of this country at the best. And so far as we workers are concerned, we are not concerned with the political superstructure; we are concerned with the economic foundation of society, and that determines our point of view in politics and industrial action. Our Russian comrades, therefore, did the very same as the British have been doing; they appealed to the German soldiers and workers to overthrow their government.

Strikes broke forth in Italy. The strikes in January passed into Germany, more menacing strikes than have taken place inside the British Isles. An appeal was made from comrades to comrades. Many soldiers in Germany mutinied; many sailors of Germany mutinied, and these men are being shot down by their government. All hail to those working men of Germany who refused at the bidding of the capitalist to go on with this war. Their names will go down bright and shining where those of the capitalist of today and of the past will have been forgotten.

It would be a very bad thing for the workers of the world if a revolution were developed and carried through to success in Germany and no similar effort were made in this country. The German workers' enemy is the same as our enemy in this country — and if it was their business and their right and their duty to overthrow their autocratic government, then it will be a duty on us not to allow these men to overthrow their government, and then to allow France, Britain and Italy to march over them and make these German workers slaves at the dictates of the capitalists of the other parts of the world. There was the situation from their point of view and from our point of view too.

It has been pointed out that if we developed a revolution the Germans would come over and, instead of having liberty, we would be under the iron heel of the Kaiser. If I grant that that is true, it is equally true in the other case that the allies would do in Germany what the German Kaiser with the capitalist class of Germany would do in this country. There can only be a revolution when the workers of all the countries stand united and capitalism is crushed, and until then the war must go on incessantly and incessantly. It is not because I am against my own people. My own people are the workers here, and the workers in Germany and elsewhere.

It was not the workers who instigated the war. The workers have no economic interest to serve as a consequence of the war, and because of that, it is my appeal to my class that makes me a patriot so far as my class is concerned, and when I stand true to my class, the working class, in which I was born, it is because my people were swept out of the Highlands, and it was only because of my own ability that I remained. I have remained true to my class, the working class, and whatever I do I think I am doing in the interest of my class and my country. I am no traitor to my country. I stand loyal to my country because I stand loyal to the class which creates the wealth throughout the whole of the world.

We are out for life and all that life can give us. I therefore took what action I did in the light of what was transpiring inside Russia, inside Austria and inside Germany. You have got to bear that in mind when you wish to understand my remarks. I therefore urged the workers of this country that if they were going to strike, mere striking was useless, because they would be starved back into work again, and that if they were going to be against the Man Power Bill, it meant that they were out for peace. And as there was no sign on either side of coming to an amicable constitutional conclusion, then it was the business of the workers to take the whole matter in hand themselves.

War was declared! No matter the motive, no matter the cause, all constitution and order was thrown aside, and in the prosecution of the war the British government found it necessary to throw aside every law in this country and to bring in the Defence of the Realm Act, which means the negation of all law in the country. I have repeatedly pointed out that if the government wishes to get a grip of any individual, they do so under the Defence of the Realm Act. The government have power to do anything they desire. That may be right, or it may be wrong, but the position is this, that the bringing in of the Defence of the Realm Act has thrown aside all law and order as we know it during normal periods.

In the plunge into the war we have the abolition of constitutional methods, and therefore I contended, and I contend today, that if it is right and proper on the part of the government to throw aside law and order — constitutional methods — and to adopt methods that mankind has never seen before, then it is equally right that the members of the working class, if the war is not going to cease in a reasonable time, should bring about a reasonable settlement to the workers in no victory to either side.

If one side or the other wins, then the revenge will come, as France today is seeking revenge after the drubbing she got in 1871. Realising that we, as representatives of the workers of the world, do not wish one side or the other to be the victors, we wish the status quo prior to the war to be re-established. If the workers are going to do that, then it means that they have to adopt methods and tactics entirely different from the methods which would be adopted, or could be adopted under normal circumstances. Abnormal lines of action must be taken such as our comrades in Russia took. The very circumstances of the war forced in upon the Russian workers' committees and their national soviets the line of action which they adopted, and the only way we could do it would be to adopt methods peculiar to the working-class organisation in this country in the interests of the workers themselves.

The suggestions I made were intended only to develop revolutionary thought inside the minds of the workers. I pointed out at the meeting on the 20th that representatives of the police were present, and therefore if the workers were going to take action themselves, it would be absolutely foolish and stupid for them to adopt the suggestions I had given them. I only gave out these suggestions so that they might work out plans of their own if they thought fit to take action to bring about peace. I was convinced, and I am still convinced, that the working class, if they are going to take action, must not only go for peace but for revolution. I pointed out to the workers that, in order to solve all the problems of capitalism, they would have to get the land and the means of production.

I pointed out to them that if capitalism lasted after the war, with the growing size of the trusts, with the great aggregations that were taking place, with the improved machinery inside the works, with the improved methods of speeding up the workers, with the development of research and experiment, that we were going to have the workers turning out three, four and five times as much wealth as they had done in pre-war times, and a great problem would arise — a greater problem than ever before — in this country of disposing of its surplus goods on the markets of the world, not only of getting markets for these surplus goods, but of getting the raw materials. We see today in the committees appointed by the government that they are anxious to get control of the markets of the world in order to exclude the Germans.

Our government has already appointed a Land Organisation of the Board of Trade and of the Foreign Office whereby it is going to plant agents here and there throughout the world, so that in a scientific method British products may be thrown on to the markets of the world. This is scientific method applied to commerce internationally as well as nationally. These preparations are being made, it is being said, for the purpose of carrying on the war after the war. Nobody denies that there is going to be a war after the war, an economic war between the Germans and their friends, and the British and the Americans and their friends, and there is going to be a war between the nations and the respective governments will take care that, as far as they can, their capital will be planted in areas over which they have control.

You have, then, the rush for empire. We see that the Americans already have got one or two of the islands in the West Indies, and I understand that America has also got hold of Dutch Guiana. It has also been suggested that Mexico be brought into the American States. Britain herself is looking after her own interests. She has taken the German colonies, she is also in Mesopotamia and in Palestine, going there for strategic reasons, but when Britain gets hold of Mesopotamia, Palestine, and Arabia, she will use them for her own ends, and I do not blame Britain for that. Britain has got many troubles.

We see Japan also on the outlook. Japan has been trying repeatedly to get control of Northern China. She would also like to get a great big chunk of Siberia. Even today we see the tentacles being sent out, all anxious to grab more and more power. We know the secret treaties and disclosures made by our Bolshevik comrades. We know that these nations have been building up their plans so that when the Germans have been crushed they will get this territory or that territory. *They are all out for empire*. That was absolutely necessary for the commercial prosperity of the nations.

All the property destroyed during the war will be replaced. In the next five years there is going to be a great world trade depression and the respective governments, to stave off trouble, must turn more and more into the markets of the world to get rid of their produce, and in fifteen years' time from the close of this war — I have pointed this out at all my meetings

113

— we are into the next war if capitalism lasts; we cannot escape it.

Britain has the wealth. Britain did everything she could to hold back the war. That necessarily had to be the attitude of Great Britain, but in spite of all Great Britain's skill or cunning, there has been war. I have heard it said that the Western civilisations are destroying themselves as the Eastern civilisations destroyed themselves. In fifteen years' time we may have the first great war bursting out in the Pacific — America v. Japan, or even Japan and China v. America. We have then the possibilities of another war, far greater and far more serious in its consequences than the present war. I have pointed that out to my audiences.

In view of the fact that the great powers are not prepared to stop the war until the one side or the other is broken down, it is our business as members of the working class to see that this war ceases today, not only to save the lives of the young men of the present, but also to stave off the next great war. That has been my attitude and justifies my conduct in recent times. I am out for an absolute reconstruction of society, on a co-operative basis, throughout all the world; when we stop the need for armies and navies, we stop the need for wars.

I have taken up unconstitutional action at this time because of the abnormal circumstances and because precedent has been given by the British government. I am a socialist, and have been fighting and will fight for an absolute reconstruction of society for the benefit of all. I am proud of my conduct. I have squared my conduct with my intellect, and if everyone had done so this war would not have taken place. I act square and clean for my principles. I have nothing to retract. I have nothing to be ashamed of. Your class position is against my class position. There are two classes of morality. There is the working class morality and there is the capitalist class morality. There is this antagonism as there is the antagonism between Germany and Britain. A victory for Germany is a defeat for Britain; a victory for Britain is a defeat for Germany. And it is exactly the same so far as our classes are concerned. What is moral for the one class is absolutely immoral for the other, and vice-versa. No matter what your accusations against me may be, no matter what reservations you keep at the back of your head, my appeal is to the working class. I appeal exclusively to them because they and they only can bring about the time when the whole world will be in one brotherhood, on a sound economic foundation. That, and that alone, can be the means of bringing about a re-organisation of society. That can only be obtained when the people of the world get the world, and retain the world.

Letter from John MacLean's wife to E. C. Fairchild, editor of *The Call*
(23 October 1918)

I was up seeing John at Peterhead yesterday. I have repeatedly asked for a visit and have always been refused, so in desperation I asked for the visit due to me in November, and it was granted.

Well, John has been on hunger strike since July. He resisted the forcible feeding for a good while, but submitted to the inevitable. Now he is being fed by a stomach tube twice daily. He has aged very much and has the look of a man who is going through torture. The doctor all along has told me he is in good health, also the Prison Commissioners, and I knew nothing about the forcible feeding until John told me in the presence of the doctor and two warders. Now, Ex-Inspector John Syme told me at the beginning of John's imprisonment that I need not worry about the fear of his going on hunger strike, as they dare not start forcible feeding without letting the relatives know.

Seemingly anything is law in regard to John. I hope you will make the atrocity public. We must get him out of their clutches. It is nothing else but slow murder. I feel very bitter at the way I have been treated. It was a terrible shock I received yesterday.

I see the premises have been raided and Lenin's pamphlet taken away, so you will be having enough worry.

I wish you good luck.
Agnes MacLean.

5

Working-class education and the Scottish Labour College

A plea for a Labour College for Scotland
(Pamphlet published in February 1916, co-author J. D. McDougall)
Every reader of the press sees that the manufacturing, commercial, and financial class is preparing for the commercial war that will succeed the present one. This coming conflict will be fiercer and more merciless than the trade rivalry of the past. Each government will act in as close co-operation with this class as the British government is acting with the railway and shipping magnates and the manufacturers of munitions. Hence the demand for a Minister of Commerce. Political problems are going to be essentially economic problems. The government will have to pay interest on the War Debt, and, in consequence, will be compelled to interfere in the economic life of the nation more than ever before. The imperial government will impose tariffs on all enemy nations, and develop the agricultural and raw material resources of the empire. These and multitudes of other vital questions are being discussed at present, and plans are being prepared for post-war industrial developments.

We can be sure that these coming changes will affect the workers even to a greater extent that those already established by the war. House rents will rise, prices will rise, dilution of labour and lowering of wages will be attempted on a vaster scale than most anticipate at present, and American machinery, division of labour, and feverish hustle will come like an avalanche into industries not already affected. It is surely advisable to prepare in time for the coming stir, as the capitalist is doing.

We all know that to get mass action and make it effective in the interests of the workers we must have preliminary agitation, education, and organisation. Well might we do so, for are we not assured that the master class intends to spend more money on technical and commercial education in the hope that British products, made with the utmost expedition and at the minimum of cost, may hold their own in the markets of the world? Scientific education undoubtedly leads to efficiency, and that the propertied class of this country now fully realises.

It is my hope that you delegates will become just as aware as the masters are of the need for specific forms of education. The state provides an elementary and higher education that certainly needs purging and overhauling; the state may now be willing to enforce a technical or commercial training on every boy and girl not intending to enter the professions; but the state, because it must be a capitalist state so long as capitalism endures, will not provide a full education to equip workers to carry on the working-class movement or to fight for the ending of capitalism itself.

In consequence, I am firmly convinced that the workers must establish and maintain their own colleges to equip themselves for their own specific tasks as a class. I am heartily in favour of one or more co-operative colleges to train employees and administrators alike. That I specially mention lest some might imagine I wish to forestall the efforts of the Co-operative Union and the Adviser of Studies, my friend, Mr Hall. I can assure you that I am keeping Mr Hall in touch with all I am doing, and the committee convening the conference gave a special invitation to Mr Hall who, in reply, wished us every success.

But, rightly or wrongly, I attach even more importance to the establishment of a Labour College, in which workers must be trained for the industrial and political struggle which will become keener and sharper as time proceeds.

If the standard of living is lowered and the conditions of toil and employment are worsened for huge masses of the workers, the uprising of the rank and file is going to be greater and more threatening than during the three years preceding the outbreak of war.

Many of the older trade-union officials and leaders may be dubious as to the need for the establishment of a college lest there should emerge from it rivals for the positions they hold. But a slight consideration of the vast problems and difficulties that the resumption of peace will raise for solution ought to show the need for a rapidly growing number of men able to defend the rights of the workers and enable them to proceed towards the full control of industry in a thoroughly disciplined fashion.

More and better-trained organisers of the industrial workers are absolutely necessary in the future. I have no desire to belittle the ability and capacity of men who, like Mr Robert Smillie, have received their training in the rough and tumble of hard experience. But I believe that he would be the very first to admit that, with a sound working-class education, he could have rendered even greater service to our class than we all too gladly admit he has given in his strenuous and eventful career.

Training and experience are both increasingly necessary for the full equipment of a trade or industrial official, for training and experience have to be met in the opposite camp.

Multitudes of trained men will soon be more necessary than ever to assume positions on public bodies and carry on the fight there until the

117

duties of these bodies are co-extensive with the full industrial and social life of the whole community. The trade unions are irrevocably committed to political as well as industrial action, and necessarily the duty devolves on them of fitting men and women for political working-class activities.

More and better working-class papers and magazines are needed, if the people are going to get facts instead of fiction, working-class instead of capitalist leading articles. The men to conduct and write for these papers must likewise be trained.

The workers in Germany have already accomplished all that we are anxious to see done for the full training and equipment of our class, and surely we in Scotland, with all our educational traditions to urge us on, should not only bring ourselves abreast the German workers, but, if possible, give the world a lead as our fathers did of yore.

The next source of opposition to a Labour College will be the curriculum. In the city where Adam Smith discoursed on *The Wealth of Nations* a full century and a half ago, it should hardly be necessary to insist that the principal study ought to be Economics. At a Labour College economics must be taught fundamentally from the labour standpoint. Otherwise we ought to send our students to the capitalist universities. Our students must make the writings of Marx and marxian scholars the basis of their studies; otherwise the College becomes an expensive tragedy. This does not imply the exclusion of the study of Marshall, the pontiff of present-day capitalist economics, or the other great writers who have influenced or are today moulding economic thought.

Many people are horrified to hear it said that the working-class standpoint in economics is bound to be different from that of the capitalists. These tender beings dream of a certain "impartial" social science bringing about the reconciliation of the hostile classes, as if it were possible to avoid taking sides on economic questions in a society in which the interests of the workers are sharply opposed to those of the employers, the needs of the tenants conflict with those of the house-owners, and so on. True, the professors of political economy in the universities claim to be impartial men of science. But nobody believes them; their attitude is recognised as a necessary, professional pose. Their teaching has become a mere system of apologetics, by means of which they reveal the moral reasons that justify the plundering of the working class. In this respect it is as different as night from day, when compared with the work of the economists of the classic school from Smith to Ricardo. These truly great men earnestly sought for the hidden forces operating the mechanism of society; they tried to discover the tendencies that introduced a semblance of regularity into the chaotic anarchy of manufacture and commerce. They classified economic facts, and, in doing so, discovered and defined some of the principal categories of political economy. The classical economists, in seeking to grasp the influence of economic laws, were actuated by a desire to bring about an increase of national wealth.

They could afford to be quite frank, for in those days there was no need for hypocrisy, because the working class, as we know it, was hardly in existence and where it had appeared was devoid of consciousness. And so the economists in their researches into the nature of value had no class prejudices to obscure their vision, any more than has the chemist of today when he carries out an experiment. They proclaimed labour to be the source of value. But very soon the working class had developed and had even secured literary champions — such as Thomson, Hodgskin, etc. — either from its own ranks or from the other classes, and they asked the question: if labour produces all value, why does the labourer not receive the full value of his product? Thus they made a moral application of Ricardian economics, and severely criticised the competitive system. Then came Marx, who set aside moral considerations as out of place in such a study, and, in a strictly scientific manner, dealt with the economic facts: the same man who, starting from the Ricardian theory of value, which he criticised and put upon a scientific basis, burst through the economic concepts of the time and discovered a new category, which he called surplus value, by means of which he explained the origin and formation of profit, interest, and rent.

It was then that the demoralisation of economic science set in. When the working class was to some extent awakened and had even produced its theoretical writers, safety demanded that political economy should cease handling the real facts of capitalism, and should deal only in the vaguest generalities and sophism. Now we can read in the writings of such shining lights as Lord Cromer of "that unfortunate statement of Ricardo's that labour is the source of value".

In the sphere of economics the capitalists make no progress commensurate with that which occurs in other departments of science. In physics and chemistry, and in the application of these to industry, the progress made in a century has been little short of the marvellous. But in the social sciences there is no such advance to record, because the progress of these sciences and their progressive application to society means the destruction of capitalism, private ownership of the means of life. And so orthodox economics is barren of fruits, has no real connection with developing economic phenomena, and is incapable of explaining them. The economists of today write books, abounding with mathematical subtleties, such as have no guidance to give us so far as the control of social productive forces is concerned.

Just as economics must be studied from the working-class point of view, so must history. A Labour College must, of course, provide for the teaching of industrial history, just as has been done in the various Sunday and evening classes held hitherto. But useful as such a study may be, it is not sufficient. If we confined ourselves to industrial history our students would get merely one-sided views of the events of the past. However much we may be inclined to admire the work of the economic historians — such as Rogers, Ashley, Cunningham, Gibbins, etcetera — we cannot afford to forget that what we get from them is but partial history after all. They teach the history of the development of technique from primitive tools of rough stone to the latest modern factory, and the information they furnish is essential, but it only concerns some of the facts of life. And is there, some might be inclined to ask, over and above industrial history, a political history, say, or a history of morality? No! we would reply; there is but one history, however many aspects it may assume in our brains, and therefore no partial or abstract view can be satisfactory. The most effective method of historical explanation is undoubtedly the materialist method of Marx, whereby we rise from an understanding of the mode of production prevailing at a certain epoch, to a knowledge of the reasons for the origin and decay of classes and their antagonism to one another. The state and its functions are explained, and political struggles are seen to be at bottom class struggles. The law is found to be the expression of the interests of the dominant class in the state. Changes in the morality and in the ideas held by men are found to be due to an altered economic environment. Transformation of the methods of wealth production is seen to be the necessary outcome of the biologic will to live. By means of this method, then, we can understand history, and adequately explain it. History ceases to be a happy hunting-ground for either simple narrators or purveyors of romance. It comes within the sphere of the law determined, and no longer is looked upon as the realm of chance or accident. The writing of history today, so far as it is really scientific, is the work either of marxist scholars — such as Kautsky, Labriola, Lafargue, Plekhanov, etc. — or that of bourgeois writers, more or less under marxian influence, such as John A. Hobson, Usher, etc.

But the marxian method is more than a better way of writing the history of the past, it is also a compass whereby we can better guide the working class in the struggles of the present. Man makes his own history, but not always consciously. The results, for instance, of the French revolution were entirely different from what was expected by those who carried through the revolution. But the materialist method, the gift to us of

120

modern society and its science, enables us to consciously make history.

Naturally the curriculum would devote special attention to the history of trade unionism. And what better training could students get than to be set to do research work into the history of their own union or the particular group to which it belonged. In this way much valuable information which remains hidden in old and tattered minute books and records, of which too little care is taken, might be given to the world. Modern problems of trade unionism would fall to be considered and threshed out in a school in which the future leaders of trade unionism were being trained.

The development of the co-operative movement would require to be one of the subjects of special study. It is only in recent days, one might say, that the barriers separating the co-operative from the general labour movement have been broken down. Trade unionists and socialists are only beginning to realise what they have lost in failing to utilise the assistance of this powerful auxiliary. The position of dignified isolation, formerly taken up by the co-operative movement, is giving place to co-operation with other working-class forces. The essential unity of the working-class movement, under all its different forms, is a conception that is very prevalent today. No training for the working-class movement could be considered complete which did not include the treatment of these tremendous problems, such as the question of rising prices and dividends, upon the successful solution of which hangs the fate of co-operation.

Trade-union offiicials require to have a great knowledge of the labour code, and this would form a part of the curriculum. Not that it could be hoped to turn them out competent lawyers, which would be of little value if the strong legal trade union refused to allow them to practise, but it ought to be possible in a fairly short space of time to survey the most important pieces of protective legislation, and acquire knowledge of its general features.

In the working-class movement year by year we find the organisations growing bigger, their activities more varied, and hence their statistical reports more complicated. The importance, in organisations containing hundreds of thousands of members, of having the statistics carefully and scientifically compiled will be readily appreciated. In small local organisations each member knows at first hand and by personal touch the state of his association. But in large bodies all we have to show us how the society stands — whether it is strong or weak, progressive, stationary, or declining — is the report and the statistics it contains. But the construction of tables is not a simple matter, and, even if it were, a worse trouble lies in the interpretation of the figures once they are collected. In so many subtle ways is error possible that a special science of statistics has sprung up or issued forth from general economics, the special function of which is to guard against such errors. This is a side of education that could be provided by a Labour College with profit to the movement.

Such general educational subjects such as English, Composition and Literature, Arithmetic and Algebra, would also demand attention. Students could receive a training in public speaking and debate such as would save them much time later on, when they came to play their part in the movement.

It is unnecessary here to present again, as has been done in the explanatory leaflet, a definite financial and administrative scheme. The detailed arrangement already suggested will serve as the basis for discussion.

That there is need for a college is proved by the success which has attended the voluntary classes, handicapped as the students are by long hours of toil, and by the size of this conference today. The idea is certainly in the air. It is our hope that this meeting today may prove to be the beginning of a movement which will bring that idea down to earth, and have it embodied in reality. The capitalists feel the need of theoretical and scientific training for themselves, if they are successfully to compete by greater exploitation of the workers against America and Germany when the war is over. The workers, if they are successfully to resist increased exploitation, and to make progress towards freedom, can only do so if they utilise their resources wisely for the training of leaders and the diffusion of essential knowledge amongst themselves.

Independence in working-class education
(*The Call*, 20 September 1917)
Everyone now admits that Germany's marvellous resistance to overwhelming odds is due to her mighty powers of organisation, and that her ability to organise follows from her superior education. Everyone as readily admits that the remarkable output of the workshops of the USA depends on minute and thorough organisation, and that this results from widespread technical education. Hence we have renewed interest in education. . . .

Just as the Boer War revealed in the clearest manner the economic hostility of the German and American capitalist class to the British capitalist class, and led to the Education Act of 1902, and the raising of scientific and commercial education to a position above that of the old classical education, so the economic antagonism that led to the present war, and will revive fiercer than ever after the conclusion of "peace", is fundamentally responsible for these so-called "educational reconstruction" schemes already commenced or mooted.

122

The underlying motive in all the reorganisation and development of education is "increased efficiency", and this capitalist phrase simply means better wage-slaves or better producers of commodities. The test of the value of education is its power of increasing output in the workshop, and consequently its power to add to that part of each year's total taken from the workers by the capitalists. Yet we would be foolish reactionaries to oppose schemes over which we as voters have a slight control — just as foolish as those who resist improved machinery and methods in the workshop. We, as socialists, must be intensely interested in improved education along technical and commercial lines, and it is our special business to see that all public, educational institutions be used for the creation of intelligent, class-conscious workers.

In this respect we differ from the WEA, which simply has for its object the creation of intelligent workers. Personally, I wish to see all opportunities for self-development opened up to the working class. But I am specially interested in such education as will make revolutionists.

Such an education will not be given in our public schools, colleges and universities, if the capitalist class can prevent it. Part of the working-class fight must be for absolute control of all educational agencies; but in the meantime, the education of the workers themselves cannot be left in abeyance.

The very antagonisms in society that called into being the co-operative organisation in production and distribution, the trade-union movement, socialist parties, and the Labour Party, make it equally urgent that the workers should forge their own educational machine for their own class ends. It was for this supposed end that Ruskin College was for a time supported by the working class; it was explicitly for this end that the Central Labour College was established. The war has closed down both these institutions. Fortunately, their temporary cessation did not mean the demise of independent working-class education (assuming that Ruskin College was independent). Marxian classes increased in number and membership in South Wales, Glasgow, Sheffield and elsewhere, as a very consequence of the war. It was in these centres that the greatest resistance was put up against the profiteering patriots.

In August a Plebs League was formed in London, and various agencies are at work to establish an organised network of classes in our benighted imperial capital. Yorkshire will soon outstrip Lancashire if Fred Shaw and others carry out their ambitious plans. The Scottish Labour College Committee, supported by the BSP and ILP, will be responsible for at least a dozen large classes in Lanarkshire, Glasgow and Clydeside. The SLP are holding a conference in Glasgow for the establishment of further classes in the West of Scotland. Where classes cannot be held, it is to be hoped that groups will be formed in workshops, at mealtimes and in houses or halls after work-time, to read together and discuss the smaller works of Marx and Engels, and those of well-known marxian scholars. The Russian revolution was buttressed by city workers thoroughly educated in marxism. Marxian education, that is, independent working-class education, must be the supreme effort of workers this winter.

The greatest "crime" I have committed in the eyes of the British government and the Scottish capitalist class has been the teaching of marxian economics to the Scottish workers. That was evident at my "trial"; that dictated Lord Strathclyde's sentence of three years. Nevertheless, I mean to spend every evening this winter in teaching economics. And every reader should push ahead as a teacher or as a student, and in the active organising of classes....

The war after the war
(First Scottish Labour College pamphlet, prepared for Glasgow economics class, 1917-18)
Every intelligent person now admits that the antagonism among the nations of Europe that led to competition of armaments and the present world war was fundamentally due to a universal desire to secure increased empires for the deposit of capital, the enslavement and robbery of the conquered races, and the monopoly of the oil, rubber, tin, and other products of the annexed territories. The economic rivalry of races was vividly brought before the people of Britain fifteen years ago by the late Mr Joseph Chamberlain, who tirelessly referred to the menacing growth of industry and commerce in Germany and the United States as a plea for a tariff war. The workers were asked to back up his tariff proposals as the only way to protect their jobs. The free traders used statistics and economic arguments in reply, and equally urged the workers to back them up if unemployment were to be avoided and the "prosperity of the country" maintained.

But all the time prices were rising whilst the free trade and the tariff capitalists refused even to consider a proportionate increase of wages to retain the old standard of living. Freeing themselves from the follies of tax jugglery, the workers went through a series of mammoth strikes from 1911 onwards, and were in readiness for others when the war broke out in August 1914. A growing knowledge of working-class economics gave them strength of argument to justify their proceedings. This same knowledge enabled the Clyde engineers to keep their head on the outbreak of war, so that when the "profiteers" and the patriotic house-owners raised prices and rents, and the government initiated dilution, strikes broke forth, always to retain the pre-war standard of living.

Britain has had conferences with her allies to prepare for an economic war against Germany and her supporters when "peace" has been attained, and even already the governing class of this country is appealing to the workers as did Chamberlain half a generation ago to hang on to their jobs by backing up their government's future economic proposals for kicking in the stomach those "brutal Germans". To establish "harmony" between the employers and the employed, attempts are being made to side-track the revolutionary shop stewards' movement by applying the suggestions of the Whitley Report to the establishment of industrial councils, industrial parliaments, or industrial guilds, the main object being continuity of work or avoidance of strikes, increased output, with a show of partial shop control over trifling though irritating details, that nowise endangers the capitalist structure of society. This meeting of workers and employers to discuss economic problems will urge the workers to a deeper and deeper study of economics, and in anticipation of this the government is taking immediate steps to supply economic "dope".

The Commissioners on Industrial Unrest have attributed the determination of the South Wales miners to their knowledge and teaching of marxian economics, or, as it is frequently called, independent working-class economics. They consequently have urged the establishment of Workers' Educational Association classes in South Wales as a counter-agent. A like attempt is being fostered in Scotland, but in the Clyde area this has so far been a miserable failure owing to marxism having too deep roots. Nevertheless, big attempts will be forthcoming to use the WEA to muddle the minds of the workers, as the secretary's interview with King George is the conventional cue to the capitalist class.

Recognising this we make no apology in coming forth into the arena on the side of marxism, in the hope that this brief sketch of the fundamentals of marxian economics may get into the hands of hundreds of thousands of workers, and induce them to dig deeper at home, form study circles, or start classes on marxian lines. The fact that the capitalists and their government are deeply distressed over the growth of working-class students of Marx ought of itself to induce all workers to begin this fascinating study.

In shop windows we see millions of articles for sale, all at different prices. We are puzzled to know how these prices are arrived at, and so we watch the reports issued by the Food Controller. We find that he starts with the price to be charged by the producer or manufacturer, then he adds so much for the wholesaler, and finally some more for the retailer.

125

We, too, go back to the capitalist manufacturer and seek to find out how he arrives at the selling price of the commodity his workers produce for him, a pair of boots let us suppose. He may have to pay 10s for the leather, thread, and other materials needed to make the pair, and the selling price on the market may be 20s, an addition of 10s to that paid for the raw material.

How do he and his fellow boot manufacturers arrive at the 10s they add? He may offhand tell us that he allows 4s for wages, 1s for depreciation of property and plant, 1s for rates and taxes, 1s for rent, and 3s for profit, or something to that effect. That settles the matter for him as a "practical" man, but not for us who wish to get deeper. We wish to get down to the reason for the 4s for wages, and the 3s for profit.

Why do not he and his friends add 20s, and sell the pair at 30s? He might thus on the average pay 8s in wages and have 9s as profit? His reply would be quick and businesslike. It would be folly to pay out 8s instead of 4s in wages, as he can always get a plentiful supply of boot and shoe operatives at 4s. Since the men and their union seem to be satisfied why need he bother to throw away 4s in increased wages on every pair of boots? He would go further. He would show that the enlarged wage would raise the earnings of the operatives so high above those obtained by other grades of workers that there would be as great a rush from other industries into boot production as to Klondyke when gold was discovered on the borders of Alaska and British Columbia. The law of supply and demand would then begin to manifest itself by the men offering themselves for less and less, until the employer could even get them at an outlay of only 3s wages per pair.

Similarly with the profit. There are always hosts of keen businessmen anxious to invest money to the best advantage. As soon as these alert fellows heard of the huge profits "in boots" they would at once start companies to make boots. They would flood the market with boots, more than might be demanded in all likelihood. There would be a scramble to sell, and the same old law of supply and demand would make the price tumble even below 20s per pair. A reduced output would in the end bring prices up again to 20s. The employer knows that there is a normal price that enables him to obtain the normal profit after paying the normal wage.

The problem is to find out why the boots sell at this normal price of 20s, or at a sovereign which weighs about a quarter of an ounce of gold. We can better approach the subject by comparing the boots with a hat likewise selling at 20s. There surely must be something common to the boots and the hat, giving them each the same exchange value. Both are

126

useful, but we are not entitled to assert that they are equally useful since we have no means of measuring and comparing their respective uses. Practical experience shows us that frequently the price of an article is reduced the more of it that is used; and surely no one would assert that the increased use of an article implies that it is less useful than when less of it was in demand; for rather are we inclined to maintain that the demand increases with the usefulness of the article. In every article produced in the workshop, extracted from the mine, or grown in the field there is something else locked up, and that is *labour*. All must admit that the articles most easily produced are the cheapest, hence that there must be a closer connection between labour and price than between usefulness and price.

We assert that the labour spent in producing a hat constitutes the *value* of the hat. If a hat on the average takes four hours to make, then the hat has four hours' value; so also with the pair of boots if made in four hours. They have the same price, and exchange for one another because each contains the same amount of value.

It will be noted that the value is simply the labour locked up in a commodity, and is measured by the hour. Under normal conditions ten hours' worth of bread will exchange for ten hours' worth of any other commodity, gold included. If 120 loaves contain ten hours of labour, and half an ounce of gold contains ten hours of labour, then under normal conditions 120 loaves will be worth the half ounce of gold or £2; or a loaf will sell at 4d.

We here include the money commodity, gold, in the same category as other commodities and subject to the same law of value. If the loaf sells at 4d, we call the 4d the price of the loaf. It is quite clear that the normal price of the loaf or any other commodity is its value expressed in the money commodity rather than in labour-hours.

The term "normal price" is used advisedly, as everyone is aware that the price of all articles may suddenly rise or as suddenly fall without any visible change in the time taken to produce them. In 1910 the price of rubber rose from 3s 9d to 12s 6d per lb owing to the great demand for rubber for motor tyres and the covering of electrical plant. The profits of some rubber companies rose to 200 per cent per annum as a consequence. This attracted the attention of financiers and company promoters, and very soon millions of capital were thrown into the rubber growing industry in plantations in South America, Central Africa, India, Ceylon, etc.

In time the rubber output increased and the price has fallen to the old level and even below it to 2s 6d. The same happened in the case of oil for motors. It ought to be noted that this rush to the torrid zone for raw materials was one of the many economic factors leading to the feverish secret diplomacy that ultimately landed Europe in the present world war.

The point is that new capital enters those industries yielding the largest profits, that the output is increased, and that by the operation of the law of supply and demand the prices fall to and even below the normal prices, agreeing with the time taken to produce them.

The money market is the central market and all other markets are knit up with it. The masters of the money market see that each industry tends to get its proportion of capital, and it is this regulating factor that keeps prices swinging above and below the normal prices. In the game of "see-saw" the boy on the middle of the plank can regulate its ups and downs by throwing his weight now to this, now to that side. He influences the plank in the same way as the masters of the money market influence prices. Although prices seldom or never touch the normal we are as entitled to use the term normal price as the term sea level, although the surface of the sea incessantly rises and falls with the flow and the ebb of the tide.

Statements without proofs are often valueless, so that to gain acceptance of the labour-time theory of value the following suggestions are given, as well as to enable workers to discover proofs within the range of their own experience.

Every well-regulated firm has a costing department. If the estimated cost of a machine has to be made, the costing clerk finds out the time taken to do each part of the work, and then calculates the cost per part, allowance being made for on-cost. On-cost includes part of the wages of foremen, clerks, managers, outlay on heat, light, material used, and depreciation. The point is that the cost is based on the time estimate of the job.

"Scientific management" is the resort to any and every scientific expedient to increase output, or, to put it another way, to reduce the time taken to do a piece of work or turn out the completed commodity. Scientific management was undoubtedly more thoroughly applied in the United States than in the British empire prior to the war, the hindrance in the empire being largely due to the conservatism of the capitalists and the "ca' canny" policy of the powerful trade unions.

The war was not long started when the British capitalists realised that they had miscalculated the war strength and capacity of Germany. They got engineers, shipbuilders, boot-makers, clothes-makers, and other war workers to agree to long hours of overtime, and they at the same time appealed to them in the name of Kitchener, Roberts, French, Jellicoe, Lloyd George, and others to turn out more per hour. The willing slaves of Britain, ever ready to oblige their masters, tried their best, but failed. Long hours and increased output cannot go together for any length of time; fatigue

128

breaks both spirit and health, the essentials for increased output. The government had to set up a Health of Munition Workers' Committee and now Dr Addison, the Minister of Reconstruction, is urging the capitalists to reduce hours as a means of increasing output. He is citing the now famous case of women whose hours per week were reduced from 66 to 54.8 and to 45.6, and whose output per hour rose from 100 to 134 and to 158. These women are turning out in 45 hours 9 per cent more than in the 66 hours. A reduction of boys' hours from 72 to 53 per week has resulted in the output per hour rising from 100 to 129; and of men's (at heavy work) from 58 to 51, resulting in a rise from 100 to 139.

Taking these and similar results, Lord Leverhulme (Sunlight Soap) is now accepting Tom Mann's six-hour day proposal as a method of further increasing output in mechanical industries. No one can doubt the ability of this soap lord to exploit the workers. The government is now experimenting with a 50-hour week in a munition factory.

The whole object of the "welfare work" organisation is to help in keeping the workers up to the highest pitch of "efficiency"; and "efficiency" is now coming to be understood as meaning "the output per hour".

Just as the employers pressed the workers to toil harder, the government forced the trade-union leaders to abandon all trade-union restrictions for the war, after which pre-war conditions would be established. Now, however, we are being told that the economic war on the return of the peace will preclude all possibility of returning to pre-war methods. As a matter of fact, the government has adopted and is beginning to apply the Whitley Report proposal of joint meetings of workshop committees and owners, of district committees and representatives of owners, and of national councils or parliaments representative of the masters and their wage-slaves, for the purpose of establishing "harmony" and "increase of output". The "harmony" in theory means that for the complete abandonment of all trade-union restrictions and taking an interest in the industry the masters may reduce hours and increase real, as well as money, wages. In other words, the government intends to use the workshop movement in the interests of the capitalist class. The government has no alternative in the matter, because it is a capitalist government. The war debt is increasing and may easily rise to ten thousand million pounds. At 5 per cent, this means that the government realises that to save British capitalism from bankruptcy it must have the workers turn out far more wealth per hour, and therefore per year, so that from them can be taken the increase to pay its extra liabilities, if not by direct taxation of wages at any rate by taxation of "normal" or "surplus" profits.

The solution of the question "Eclipse or Empire?" does not only depend on the application of the Whitley Report and scientific supervision. Capitalists are being urged by the government to adopt any system of "payment by results", or, as it has been called, "ability pay". Among such expedients are the individual piecework, the collective piecework, the departmental contract, the premium bonus, and the profit-sharing systems. To make a higher wage than under the time system the worker toils harder under all these others: his "efficiency" is increased. The piece rate or the time allowed may be broken, and under the profit-sharing system the books can be manipulated so as to show decreased profits, or the capital may be watered to absorb more of the rate of profit on capital, in order to still further speed up the output at a lower outlay in wages. It is the donkey and the carrot applied to Mr Henry Dubb, the highly respectable working man found everywhere. In *The Efficiency Magazine* for October 1917, the docile Henry is not even compared with the donkey, but with the cow. "If cows can be developed so as to give three times as much milk, is it not possible to train employees so that the output will be multiplied by three?" But the artful writer, knowing his Henry, suggests to his fellow capitalists to write these words over the doors of their shops and factories:

"Every man who enters here
Must earn 'high wages' every year"(!)

Increased efficiency does not depend solely on the "live machines", the "human cows", but on increasing sub-division of labour, the use of better machinery, applied science, use of waste material, trustification, improved office and business methods, etc. By their superiority in this respect the Americans could in 1909 turn out about three times as much per worker as we here in Britain. For some of the comparative statistics read Gray and Turner's *Eclipse or Empire?* These writers prove that in many industries American machinery is better than British, and that each American worker uses three times the horsepower handled by his British brother. Huge companies and trusts have a vast output and can therefore afford to carry sub-division of labour to an extreme extent, if accompanied by standardisation of parts and of the finished commodity. It is asserted that in Chicago each bullock passes through the hands of about a thousand workers before it is packed up in cans for the soldiers at the front. The pace of the operators is regulated by the rate of motion of the chain from which the live animal is suspended. In the assembling of motor parts to form the completed motor car the Ford Company fixes the chassis on a travelling platform, and in its journey of $3\frac{1}{2}$ hours a succession of fitters put on and screw up the various parts needed to finish the car.

Along with division of labour goes adaptation of tools and specialised automatic machines. One feature of the revolution inside the munition factories is the introduction of American single-purpose automatic machines enabling unskilled male and female labour to turn out twice or thrice as much as was formerly done by skilled artisans using less efficient methods and machinery. Besides, continual improvements are being made with labour-time saving effects. A worker informs me that he was turning out 45 copper bands for 18-pounders per day, when, by the introduction of a "forming tool", he turned out 80 per day. As an incentive to effort his wage was reduced from 15s to 11s per day! A friend of his was tracing holes on 4-inch shells and put 50 through his hands per day. By the introduction of a "combination tool" he was able to handle 100 per day. This worker's daily wage fell also — from 15s 7d to 13s per day! . . .

To encourage and hasten the dilution of labour by the introduction of women into munition works, the government in October 1916 started the *Dilution of Labour Bulletin*. In the issue of November 1917, attention is drawn to a "record" in assembling no. 101 fuses at the rate of 105 to 110 per hour in a West Midland factory; also to the fact that in a London and South Eastern district aeroplane shop "five women are now doing the work of scraping (propellers), formerly done by six men, with an increase of 70 per cent in output". . . .

The following words form part of an advertisement by Alfred Herbert Ltd, Coventry, in the issue of the firm's *Monthly Review* for August-September 1917: "Today's problem is how to turn the work out in less time." This is a conscious recognition (in big type, too) of the marxian theory of value, that labour-time is the all-important element in production, and constitutes the value of each article produced. . . .

That there is no finality to the application of science or the invention of labour-saving machinery and appliances is now so well recognised by the capitalists that we find their government organising research and experimental departments, preparing for improved technical training of apprentices and journeymen, and encouraging the capitalists to do the same individually and collectively. The government is also urging trustification of industries, as this unification is a prerequisite of improved output in every way. Its appeal is: "Capitalists of the empire, unite! You have nothing but an empire to lose, you have a world to win!"

The labour-time theory of value applies to the worker's commodity, his labour-power. Note carefully that the worker does not sell his labour, but his ability, force, or power to labour — his labour-power. Labour is the using of labour-power. To understand the difference let us take the case of the watch. The wound-up mainspring has a stored-up energy or power. This we may compare to labour-power. The mainspring keeps the wheels and hands of the watch in motion; the energy stored up in the spring is being used up in keeping the mechanism in motion. This motion we may compare to labour.

The capitalist class is conscious that it purchases labour-power and not labour, although its defenders in public would have the workers imagine it pays for every hour of labour worked or every commodity created.

Dr D. Noel Paton, introducing a *Report upon a Study of the Diet of the Labouring Classes in the City of Glasgow* (1911-12), says: "Under natural conditions of trade, the working man brings into the market his energy — his power of doing work — and obtains for it the most favourable price he can secure. . . . Food is the fuel — the source of energy — of the human machine. . . . An abundance of cheap and good food is the first essential for a productive working class." The object of the *Study* is put thus in the report proper: "Do the working classes get an adequate and suitable diet, and, if not, can any improvement be suggested without unduly increasing the cost?" The problem is one of "scientific management" in the home to enable the producers to get the maximum of energy at the minimum of cost so as to enable the capitalists to purchase their supplies of labour-power at the minimum price, the lowest wage; for wage is the price paid for the commodity called labour-power. The value of one labour-power is determined by the time taken to produce the food, clothing, shelter, education etc., needed to keep the average family of five. This, translated into ordinary language and money, is called the "cost of living".

During strikes for increased wages capitalist flunkeys rush into the papers with letters showing how little a family can live upon, and urging therefrom that the workers ought to be content with the old wage rates. During the unrest prior to the war, *Cassell's Magazine of Fiction* published an article by Mr F. J. Cross entitled "How to Live on 3d or 4d a Day". Other flunkeys urge that if the workers got more they would become drunkards, "immoral". The argument in the latter case is that the capitalists are justified in maintaining wages at the "cost of living" level to keep the workers "good".

That many families do not even get a "subsistence wage" has been proved by investigations made by Booth in London, Rowntree in York, Noel Paton in Edinburgh, and Dorothy Lindsay in Glasgow. Adults getting less than 3,000 calories of energy are living below subsistence level, below the minimum "living wage", are in fact not getting the value of their labour-power. It has been demonstrated that one in three of the working class is on or below the "poverty line" — the "poverty line" meaning the lowest level on which the workers can normally live and work. The Glasgow

Report states that "of the families whose weekly income is under 20s or irregular, 62.5 per cent have a diet the energy of which is less than 3,000 calories"; and that "not one of the families in which the wage is regular and below 20s has a diet the energy value of which reaches the minimum of 3,000 calories".

The rise in the cost of living since 1896 and especially since the start of the war has tightened the corner in which the capitalists keep the workers. As illustrative of this increase the following instance will suffice. The Board of Trade found that the average food outlay of 1944 families was 22s 6d per week in 1904, 25s at the start of the war, and 52s 3d in September 1917. It would not be exceeding the truth to say that not one in ten working-class families has added 30s to the weekly income in normal wage increases since 1904. Undoubtedly, overtime has come to the rescue of many, and increased wages due to excessive work have staved off the acuter forms of starvation. However, this but serves to accentuate the evil of wages that fall below the subsistence level.

Skilled workers, well organised in trade unions, have undoubtedly in the past had a margin over and above the bare animal living, but much of this margin has vanished with increased prices during the war period. From facts gathered I conclude that skilled workers' wages have not increased in the same proportion as labourers' wages, it being necessary to give the labourers a greater percentage of a rise to prevent actual starvation. The tendency for the living of the organised workers to fall to the bare animal level has been largely responsible for the "unrest" prior to and during the war.

To crush the arguments of the trade unionists and other working-class fighters of the first half of the nineteenth century, capitalist professors of economics tried to prove the "wages fund" theory. They showed, to the satisfaction of their capitalist paymasters, that out of each year's wealth product only a fixed amount could be given as wages. Worked out in detail, this meant that if the workers got 5s on to their wages, the cost of living would rise 5s too, and so no gain would be derived by the workers. This was called "the iron law of wages" or "the brazen (brazen-faced) law of wages". Although abandoned in theory, it crops up continually during every strike in the assertion that prices rise when wages rise; in other words, that prices depend on wages.

From about 1875 till 1896 prices tended to fall whilst wages tended to rise, and from 1900 onwards prices have risen enormously whilst wages tended downwards until the huge strikes and tremendous agitation generally checked the drop. That should kill the lie that prices depend on wages. As a matter of fact the application of "scientific management" shows that wages can be increased, prices reduced, and yet greater profits can be realised by the capitalists.

Whilst the tendency is for wages to fall to the bare animal existence level, yet hosts of workers get above this by organisation and fighting the "huns at home". The better the organisation, and the stronger the fight, the greater the chance of the workers to keep their standard of living above the animal level.

Some capitalists have found out, e.g. Cadbury, Rowntree, and Lord Leverhulme, that a certain standard of comfort above the animal level increases efficiency, and is therefore advantageous to them. These are urging their class to adopt the policy of "enlightened capitalism" to save capitalism from the establishment of a socialist republic.

We are justified in concluding that the workers are paid for their labour-power and not for their labour. The workers create far more wealth than they possibly can get in the form of wages, despite all the fighting that ever could be put up by them, because of the operation of the law of value. Statistics prove this difference between the wealth created and obtained by the workers. The government's Census of Production taken in 1909 shows that 6,936,000 workers (roughly, seven million) created £712,000,000 worth of new value; in other words, each worker, young or old, male or female, created on the average more than £2 a week. The government's Census of Wages, taken in 1906 and 1907, shows that 7,277,056 workers got a rate of wages of from 9s 3d to 27s 4d per week, these being averages for all kinds of workers from the worst paid industry (agriculture) to the best paid (metal). The general average is certainly below £1 a week, when all broken time is taken into consideration. The difference between the estimated value created per annum and the part taken by the income-tax-paying class gives further confirmation of the extent of the gulf between the value created by labour and the value of labour-power (see Chiozza Money's "Riches and Poverty").

An American census of production in 1909 reveals that the value created per worker is between two and three times as great as that created by the British worker. Hence the universal urge now on in Britain to adopt every German and American method that will increase the output, in order to enable the difference between what the worker makes and gets — the surplus value — to be all the greater. The greater this surplus value, the easier will it be for the capitalists to pay the heavier taxes needed to meet the war charges, and yet live more luxuriously and invest more capital than ever before. This can be accomplished whilst the workers get higher wages and work shorter hours, if they but settle down to toil continuously and obediently under the industrial councils or parliaments suggested in the treacherous Whitley Report and approved of by the government.

Suppose a worker makes 200 commodities in a ten-hour day and these sell at 10s, that the worker gets 5s as his wage. The surplus value would be 5s, on the assumption that nothing is allowed for the cost of raw material, depreciation, etc. If, however, the output be doubled, the worker could turn out 360 commodities in a nine-hour day, and these might sell at 18s. The worker might get 6s a day, so that still the surplus value would be 12s. If the capitalist arranged to keep his plant going continuously, then he could easily run three shifts at least instead of two, and so gain 36s instead of 24s, a greater surplus value than ever before. A knowledge of this is actuating Lord Leverhulme to urge with Tom Mann the six-hour day.

Workers may now be able to grasp the full meaning of the chorus of the platform and press — living gramophones, *harmony* and *efficiency*.

The increased output of commodities, and especially of that part called capital, will necessitate larger markets abroad, and hence a larger empire.

The same will apply to other capitalist countries. This must develop a more intense economic war than led up to the present war, and so precipitate the world into a bloodier business than we are steeped in just now. The temporary advantage the workers may get in shorter hours and higher wages with higher purchasing power will then be swept away in the destruction of millions of good lives and fabulous masses of wealth.

We see preparations for this economic war, this war after the war, in the establishment by the government of a Commercial Intelligence Department, partly connected with the Board of Trade, and partly with the Foreign Office, which shall work hand in hand with the growing industrial trusts for the monopoly of markets outside the empire. Every other capitalist country is doing the same, especially the United States, which has now definitely passed from being a borrowing to being a lending country. It is getting a foothold just now in South and Central America, and is manoeuvring with Japan for a firmer grip over the economic life of China. It will not take long for China to become a fully equipped capitalist country, entering the world's competitive market with floods of surplus commodities.

It is perfectly obvious that to avoid a recurrence of the present world crash on a more huge scale than before, the need for dumping each nation's surplus on undeveloped countries must be avoided by eliminating this surplus. As this surplus is due to the workers having to sell their labour-power as a commodity to the owners of land and capital, it is necessary that the need to sell labour-power to anyone must be abolished. This can

135

solely be accomplished by the ending of the class ownership of land and capital, by the people taking full possession of the whole means of living and using them co-operatively for wealth-creative purposes. Under such circumstances alone will it be abolished, and for national antagonism and world wars to be stamped out for ever. The Bolsheviks in Russia have given the world the lead.

If this brief, elementary and preliminary sketch of the fundamentals of economics demonstrates the all-importance of the subject in connection with the vital affairs and issues of life, and incites the reader to dip deeper into the subject privately, in study circles with kindred spirits, or in independent educational classes organised by working-class bodies, then it will have achieved its primary purpose.

III

The post-war struggle

With the end of the war came a new era in world politics, described by MacLean as "the class war on an international scale", that is, "the capitalist class of the world and their governments joined together in a most vigorously active attempt to crush Bolshevism in Russia and Spartacism in Germany". This meant that the main preoccupation of the revolutionary movement, especially in Europe, was the defence of the young Soviet republic, by means of native revolutions or at least by "keeping capitalism busy at home".

This emerges especially from "Now's the Day and Now's the Hour", where MacLean's post-war strategy for an offensive against capitalism was outlined for the first time — a general strike for shorter hours led by the miners, which would hopefully spark off revolution, which in those "days of hope" seemed very near.

A strike for the forty-hour week did materialise, but it did not turn out as MacLean planned, and ended with Glasgow like an armed camp surrounded by tanks and soldiers armed with machine-guns. It had been led by the Clyde Workers' Committee, whose wartime strength had rested on the urgent need for munitions. Now that was gone, and the government was only too glad to have an excuse to victimise the shop stewards. Writing later in **Revolt on the Clyde** Gallacher, who was at the time of the strike still chairman of the CWC, admitted regretfully that they had been leading a strike when they should have been leading a revolution. It was the miners who were now in a strong position, all kinds of fuel being in short supply. They had also undergone the same "revolution in psychology" as the Clyde men, and in addition had been under government control during the war. Now they were determined not to go back to private ownership. That was why MacLean wanted the CWC to wait until the miners were ready, but that was not to be.

Unfortunately, not only was the strike ignominiously defeated, but also it alerted the government to the nature of the attack being planned by the revolutionary movement — a general strike to paralyse industry, and not the armed insurrection which cabinet records show they had been preparing to crush — and the government now proceeded to undermine the militancy of the miners by organising the Industrial "Peace" Conference and by forming the Sankey Commission on the nationalisation of the mines.

Another aspect of the tremendous changes was the rapid rise of American imperialism, and we see the increasing rivalry between the world powers featuring more and more in MacLean's writings, as America takes the place of a defeated Germany. MacLean had already seen the inevitability of the clash when he noted in "The War after the War" that America was changing from a borrowing to a lending nation, and in his 1918 trial speech he had enlarged on America's imperialistic ambitions.

Accepting, as all marxists did, the correctness of Clausewitz's famous axiom, "War is politics continued by other (i.e. forcible) means", it was only logical for him to assume that war between the two rival empires of the USA and Great Britain was practically inevitable. He recorded later in part of his 1922 election address* just how much more powerful America was becoming, for by that time America's world trade was greater than that of all the other capitalist countries put together. But he did not foresee that America would become so strong that Britain would be beaten without a military struggle, and would become in a very short time "a vassal of the Almighty Dollar" (see the pamphlet **John MacLean** by Tom Anderson, 1930).

In "The Coming War with America" he notes that "the big banks of New York have been co-operating to lend to European nations supplies of food and other necessities of life", and it seemed to him "obvious that Germany and other countries economically dependent on America will back up America in the event of war with Britain". What he did not foresee was German capitalism being built up so successfully that it became a kind of Frankenstein's monster which turned on its creators — for later on Britain also helped to build up Germany as a bulwark against the Soviet Union.

All MacLean's works were inspired and permeated with marxist ideas, but in 1919 and 1920 he did write articles dealing explicitly with marxist theory. During the late summer of 1919, he was involved in a controversy over a book by an American writer named Kahn, **The Collapse of Capitalism,** in which the suggestion was made that "under its vast accumulation of credit and paper money and bills capitalism is rapidly staggering to its doom". This seemed to MacLean to be another form of the old "inevitability of socialism" trend of the Second International, which ignored the dynamic role of the working class as "the gravediggers of capitalism". He pointed out that "if capitalism is to be 'sent west' it will only be the result of the delivery of the greatest knock-out blow ever given." He maintained that capitalism in Britain, America and Japan was stronger than ever before.

However, he did enlarge on currency problems, particularly inflation, in "Burn Bradbury and Down with Prices" in **The Call** (27 November 1919), where he pointed out that the cure for contemporary inflation was the withdrawal (or "burning") of the paper

*An essay called "The First Great 'Pacific' Conference of Powers", originally written for **The Socialist** and issued along with the election address.

money which had flooded the market during the war. This was actually to be done by the government later on, when the post-war revolutionary upsurge had been quelled and when unemployment was at such a level that wages could be reduced with impunity.

What might be called one of the contradicitions of socialism was featured in a very important article "Capitalists Everywhere Accept Marxism", in which he pointed out that a knowledge of marxian economics could be a weapon in the hands of intelligent capitalists — while many Labour leaders and other so-called socialists took pride in announcing that they had never read Marx.

"The class war on an international scale" was further illustrated by the rise of nationalist movements after the war, manifested in the break-up of the great tsarist, Austro-Hungarian and German empires. Even the mighty British empire was beginning to crack. Ever since the Easter Rising there had been muted revolt in Ireland, culminating in the enormous Sinn Fein majority for an Irish republic in the 1918 election, as well as the growth of the movement for independence in India.

The majority of marxists had always supported the right of nations to self-determination, even when it meant support of "bourgeois nationalism" against feudal imperialism; but there was not the same unanimity about the support of national liberation movements against modern capitalist imperialism. Lenin, however, had no doubt about where he stood. "Imperialism", he wrote in 1915, "is the period of an increasing oppression of the nations of the world by a handful of 'great' nations; the struggle for a socialist international revolution against imperialism is, therefore, impossible without the recognition of the right of nations to self-determination. . . . No proletariat reconciling itself to the least violation by 'its' nation of the rights of other nations can be socialist."

This was a comparatively simple question in the days of small-scale industry, when political and territorial secession might have guaranteed almost complete independence. But as modern capitalism advanced and pushed out the tentacles of large-scale industry everywhere, it relied more and more on economic domination rather than military might. By MacLean's time political independence had no meaning without economic independence, but that could not now be attained within the framework of capitalism: "Scottish independence means economic as well as political independence, and that can only be assured by the co-operation of all under communism" ("The Highland Land Seizures" in **The Vanguard,** September 1920).

In the British socialist movement there has always been a great deal of confusion between the nationalism of an oppressed country and the "nationalism" of an oppressor country. Especially since the days of Nazi Germany the tendency has been to lump both kinds together as fascism. Lenin had the answer in 1915:

"The socialists cannot reach their great aim without fighting against every form of national oppression. They must unequivocally demand that the social-democrats of the **oppressing** countries (of the so-called 'great' nations in particular) should recognise and defend the right of the oppressed nations to self-determination in the political sense, i.e. the right to political separation. A socialist of a great nation or a nation possessing colonies who does not defend this right is a chauvinist.

On the other hand, the socialists of the **oppressed** nations must unequivocally fight for complete unity of the workers of both the oppressed and the oppressor nationalities."

There is little evidence that MacLean took the question of Scottish independence seriously until the last months of 1919, when he became a member of the National Committee, which had been organised by Stuart Erskine to press for Scottish interests and, in particular, for Scottish independence. His association with Erskine began during the 1918 general election, when the latter had petitioned all candidates to support the Scottish TUC's demand for separate Scottish representation at the Versailles Peace Treaty. It seems to me that this new concern for Scotland had three sources. The first was the fact that his hectic campaign for a general strike during the first months of 1919 had taken him all over England and Wales, as well as Scotland, and he became increasingly convinced that the tremendous leftward swing which had taken place in Scotland and produced a near-revolutionary situation had not taken place to anything like the same extent in England. This situation was described many years later by Naomi Mitchison in her preface to the pamphlet **Labour Record on Scotland 1945-49** by Professor Douglas Young:

"I believe Douglas Young makes an important point in the fact that there was violent revolutionary socialist feeling in Scotland a generation ago, which has been largely thwarted, since it needed a vehicle for its expansion. Instead of a Scottish Parliament or Assembly, all it got was the Glasgow Corporation."

The second factor was his visit to Dublin during the summer of 1919, described in "Impressions of Dublin" (**The Worker,** 23 August 1919). This made a great impression on him. He began to realise more fully the pernicious nature of "English" imperialism within the British Isles, and just how much it was detested by most Irishmen. Finally his reaction to the changes which were going on behind the scenes in the BSP during 1919, and which came to a head towards the end of the year, was to oppose dictation from Russia as channelled through dictation from London.

The year had begun with tremendous "Hands off Russia" rallies in London and Manchester, at which MacLean had been the chief speaker; during his travels over the country he was popularly regarded as Russia's unofficial ambassador wherever he went. When the Third International was founded in March, he was one of its most enthusiastic supporters, having declared for a new interna-

140

tional as early as 1915. The invitation to affiliate to the Comintern came directly to the John MacLean section of the BSP, and when in October a large majority of the branches decided by referendum to affiliate, it was his triumph. On 23 October he was so pleased with the way the BSP was shaping that he wrote in **The Worker** (23 October 1919): "Events this year have proved that no organisation in Britain has a greater influence than the BSP on the policy of the working class."

It therefore seems surprising to hear that MacLean was, by his own testimony, secretly expelled from the BSP only a few months later. I believe Walter Kendall was right when he wrote in **The Revolutionary Movement in Britain 1900-21:**

> "After Litvinov's deportation in September 1918 Theodore Rothstein became chief Bolshevik representative in Britain. Instead of experiencing a direct political struggle for power between Fairchild and MacLean [i.e. between right and left wings] the BSP, through Rothstein, now became increasingly dependent on Soviet financial aid, and came ever more under Russian influence."

In respect of financial aid from Russia, MacLean knew that "the man who pays the piper calls the tune". In his case this was manifested by the strong pressure brought to bear upon him by Rothstein to become a full-time worker for the Hands off Russia Committee, with a good salary, on condition that he gave up all his other activity. Now MacLean at this time was not very sure of Rothstein (a Londoner whose family had been Russian immigrants), even though he had played an admirable part in the anti-Hyndman fight before the war. During the war he had worked as an interpreter in the War Office and had played no active part in the anti-war movement. This latest move aroused MacLean's suspicion, because he was quite convinced that Russia could be defended only by the kind of revolutionary work that he had been doing and not by meetings organised by the HOR Committee.

When Rothstein brought Lieutenant-Colonel Malone as a speaker to HOR rallies, MacLean became even more suspicious. Malone, now a Liberal MP, had been an officer in the Royal Navy during the war and on the Executive Committee of the bitterly anti-socialist and anti-soviet Reconstruction Society. MacLean spoke alongside him at a Glasgow rally, and became convinced that he was a government agent "soothing the socialists while the government was preparing for a spring offensive against Russia". Both were billed to speak at another HOR rally in London in the spring, but only Malone appeared. Apparently MacLean had refused to speak on the same platform as Malone, and, according to the new concept of party discipline, MacLean had to go. This new concept was outlined to the Second Congress of the International in 1920 by its president, Zinoviev:

> "The Communist Party must be strictly centralised, with an iron discipline, with a military organisation. Yes, with a military

organisation. In England we have four or five separate communist groups. . . . This must be stopped."

However, it must have been embarrassing for the new leading lights of the BSP to attend the Second Congress of the International without MacLean, about whom Lenin had written in such glowing terms and whom the International's Executive Committee in their document dated May 1920, "Moscow's Reply to the ILP", had held up as the example for the ILP to follow. It is therefore not surprising that Rothstein should have tried to heal the breach before the founding conference of the British Communist Party. MacLean was told, according to Gallacher in his **Last Memoirs** (p.141), that the Russians were anxious that he should take a leading part in the formation of the new party.

But Malone was still very much to the fore, having been elected to the Executive Committee of the BSP at Easter; and, as MacLean put it in the article "A Scottish Communist Party", "to ask me to work with Malone for revolution is a joke. A man like that ought not to be allowed in a revolutionary marxian party. . . . To allow a Malone to lead a revolutionary party after a record such as his is high treason to communism. You might as well appoint Churchill Honorary President of the Russian Republic!"

The "Home Rule for Scotland" kind of nationalism prevalent at that time was not anti-imperialist, but meant simply a Scottish Parliament for Scottish affairs within the framework of imperialism, leaving foreign affairs and other important matters to be dealt with by the imperial Parliament at Westminster. This could be regarded as typically reformist, compared with the revolutionary demand for an independent Scottish Workers' Republic which MacLean made public in August 1920, when he issued ten thousand leaflets entitled "All Hail! The Scottish Communist Republic!". Later he was to change the title to "All Hail! The Scottish Workers' Republic!" when he reissued the same leaflet along with his 1922 election address, having by that time failed in his attempt to form a Scottish Communist Party affiliated to the Comintern, and having become alienated from the British Communist Party.

There are several noteworthy points about this leaflet. It is obvious that what MacLean meant by "communism", and indeed what all marxists meant at that time, was very different to the kind of society which developed in Russia out of a backward, semi-feudal, peasant country, almost completely ruined by civil war, foreign intervention, famine and (most important of all) by the failure of the western revolutions. With its tiny working class decimated in battle, the Communist Party had to take its place. Thus the "dictatorship of the proletariat", which in an advanced capitalist country meant the "dictatorship" of the vast majority of the people, became the dictatorship of the Communist Party; and eventually soviet rule, which originally meant industrial democracy as well as the political democracy of capitalist countries, became Communist Party rule.

142

Lenin did not envisage that Russia would have to "go it alone", and neither did Marx and Engels. In their preface to the 1882 Russian edition of **The Communist Manifesto,** they had aired the problem which was later to bedevil the Russian marxist movement. At that time more than half the land was owned in common by the peasants: could the Russian peasant commune "though greatly undermined, yet a form of the primeval common ownership of land, pass directly to the higher form of communist common ownership? Or, on the contrary, must it first pass through the same process of dissolution as constitutes the historical evolution of the west? The only answer to that possible today is this: if the Russian revolution becomes the signal for a proletarian revolution in the west, so that both complement each other, the present common ownership of land may serve as the starting point for a communist development."

The "Mir" mentioned by MacLean in the leaflet was the assembly of this traditional Russian peasant community, and so he was merely following the example of Marx and Engels when he made a connection in Scotland too between primitive and modern communism — "We can safely say then: Back to Communism and Forward to Communism."

In view of present-day developments in the north of Ireland, I have included most of MacLean's writings on the Irish struggle. It is necessary at this point to make clear that none of his writings are being reproduced because of their literary quality. Most of his writing was done hurriedly while travelling by train to speak at meetings, and Harry McShane remembers that he wrote the pamphlet **The Irish Tragedy: Scotland's Disgrace** in this way. At that time socialist propaganda was done by word of mouth, mainly at open-air meetings. Although there was a high standard of literacy in Scotland, the working day was so long and the work so hard that most working men were too tired during their leisure hours to do any kind of serious reading. Meetings were regarded as a form of entertainment and relaxation, and a high standard of oratory and ready wit were demanded from the speakers.

It is very obvious that MacLean felt passionately about what was happening in Ireland. He wrote in **The Vanguard:**

"This is the greatest question confronting Scotland today, for if speedy action is not taken a horrible tragedy will be enacted, and Scotland will be disgraced for ever. This is more important than protesting against higher rents or the high cost of living. It is acquiescing and participating in the murder of a race rightly protesting its own right to rule itself."

While noting in passing MacLean's careless use of the word "race" when he meant "nation", it is important to note also that it was to push this idea that in September 1920 he attended the 600th anniversary celebrations of the famous Declaration of Arbroath, as he explained in **The Vanguard:**

"Why did I visit Arbroath on Saturday, 11 September, but to

143

protest the hollow mockery of the sex-centenary celebration of the Scottish Parliament's Declaration of Independence to Pope John XXII, whilst Scottish boys dressed in the garb of the English government were then and now daring the Irish to set up a free and independent Irish Parliament elected by the overwhelming vote of the Irish people."*

MacLean was convinced ever since the beginning of the "troubles" that the real reason for Britain's apparently puzzling determination to hang on to Ireland was the emnity between Britain and America. In his pamphlet **The Coming War with America** he had written:

"In case of war Ireland would be a fine naval and air base against Britain. . . . This explains Britain's madness in suppressing the Dail Eireann (the Sinn Fein Parliament)."

In 1920 he found himself triumphantly vindicated by a speech made by Lloyd George at Caernarvon, in which he announced the government's firm intention to hold on to Ireland:

"And we are to hand over Ireland to be made a base of the submarine fleet. We are to trust to luck in our next war. Was there ever such lunacy proposed by anybody. . . . Hand our ports over to Ireland, the gateway of Great Britain."

Out of the Irish situation came MacLean's new strategy for the offensive against British capitalism. He saw Irish independence as "the beginning of the end of the British empire, for Canada, Australia, New Zealand, India, Egypt, and South Africa will push out on their own. British labour will consequently have an easier task in seizing political power."

Towards the end of 1920 large-scale unemployment hit the country with great suddenness. After the first few months of post-war disorientation, there had been a small industrial boom as the arrears of construction and repair work neglected during the war were overtaken. But once this was completed and the soldiers were absorbed into the civilian population, the technical revolution which meant that one worker could now do the work of three pre-war workers really made itself felt. The unemployment MacLean had warned against in "Now's the Day and Now's the Hour" had arrived.

MacLean immediately set about organising the unemployed. He considered this vitally necessary for three reasons. First of all, as he had advised in "Rumblings of the Revolution", he believed that "socialists everywhere, when unemployed, ought to organise, lecture and drill the unemployed, and so create a mighty menace to capitalism." The second reason he described in his 1922 election

---

*According to the Highland paper **Liberty,** he held a public meeting at Arbroath on that occasion under the auspices of the recently-formed Scottish National League, and apologised for the absence of its founder, Stuart Erskine. This confirms information given to me that MacLean was a founder member of this organisation, which had been set up primarily to fight for Scottish independence, and was thus the forerunner of the National Party of Scotland.

address: "My object was to secure the unemployed so that they wouldn't scab when the fight started". Here he meant the fight against the reduction of wages which would inevitably follow when the government deflated the economy: that is, when the government withdrew the John Bradburys in order to reduce prices. As we have seen, the Labour movement failed to follow MacLean's lead in 1919 when Labour was in a strong bargaining position. Now, with unemployment rampant, the government was in a strong position, but nevertheless MacLean was determined that there should be a fight. The third reason was a peculiarly Scottish one. The unemployed were in a particularly vulnerable position in Scotland. Because of the big bureaucratic backlog in verifying the mass of claims for the small national "dole", there was often a delay of several months before the "dole" could be granted. Meantime the unemployed were destitute. In England parish relief was given, but under Scots law it was illegal to give relief for unemployment. That was why there were no workhouses in Scotland, only poorhouses, which were for the chronic sick, disabled and old people who could not work. Stiff penalties could be imposed on any authority which flouted this law. It was not until the end of April 1921 that emergency regulations were passed empowering poor law authorities to grant relief to the destitute unemployed. Until that time, as we can see from MacLean's writings, the main priority for the Glasgow Unemployed Committee was to obtain food and shelter for the destitute. After April, enormous demonstrations were organised to bring pressure to bear on the different parish offices to implement these new powers by granting relief at least equal to that granted in England.

A unique feature about this Glasgow movement was the huge meetings held twice a week in the large City Hall, as described by MacLean in his "'Open Letter to Lenin".

As unemployment grew there came the expected huge fall in wages, the failure of the Triple Alliance to support the miners, and the miners' lock-out. Something of this troubled situation is conveyed in "Scottish History in the Making", published in **The Socialist**, organ of the SLP which, since the majority of the members had joined the CPGB, was now hardly more than a sect.

Expecting the inevitable showdown with the miners, the government had passed an Emergency Powers Act late in 1920, and MacLean was only one of many who were jailed in the spring of 1921 to prevent "trouble". He had not long been released when he was arrested again in October, and on 25 October was sentenced to one year.

An interesting sidelight on these two imprisonments was that, as the result of merely threatening to hunger-strike, he was granted the privileges of a political prisoner, something quite novel in Scottish prison history. Among the various welcome concessions was the permission to write a letter once a week. Many of these letters have been preserved. The majority of them were to his old friend

James Clunie, who was at that time a member of the SLP. He continued to write to Clunie from time to time until his death. All these letters were preserved and were published many years later in Clunie's book of memoirs **The Voice of Labour,** as proof that the allegation that MacLean was mentally ill at this period was "completely untrue".

Many other letters written by MacLean during this period have also been preserved, including those to my sister and myself, and to my mother. Not only is there no indication of mental illness, but on the contrary most of the letters show a sense of humour and an outgoing interest in all that was happening which seems incompatible with mental illness — unless his dedication to the revolutionary socialist movement is regarded as the sign of an unbalanced mind.

By the time MacLean came out of prison for the last time in October 1922, revolutionary fervour had all but died away, so he changed his tactics accordingly and plunged into electoral activities. He contested Kinning Park ward in the November municipal elections, and actually beat the Labour or "Pink" candidate, with almost as many votes as the Moderate victor. He stood for Gorbals in the general election which followed, and I have included most of his rather remarkable election address, omitting only a long section on the Honolulu Trade Conference, in which he traced the tremendous strides being taken by American imperialism in the Pacific.

Two important points emerge from the address. One is that his anti-imperialist strategy has not changed ("the break-up of every empire, including John Bull's, will make more easy the world revolution from capitalism to communism"). The other is his hardened attitude to the CPGB and to Russian financial aid. While nobody could have foreseen the bloody counter-revolution which took place round about the time of the Moscow trials in 1936, when thousands of the men who had led and taken part in the 1917 revolution were murdered and imprisoned, he certainly saw disaster ahead. The intention to remodel the British party on Bolshevik lines announced by Zinoviev in 1920 was carried out in 1921. In the very first issue of **The Communist International,** organ of the Comintern, Lenin had expressed a foreboding that the new International, in the event of the failure of revolutions in the west, would become dominated by the Russians. This foreboding was expressed again in 1921:

> "At the third congress in 1921 we adopted a resolution on the structure of communist parties and the methods and content of their activities. It is an excellent resolution, but it is almost exclusively Russian, that is to say, everything in it is taken from Russian conditions. . . . My impression is that we committed a gross error in passing that resolution, blocking our own road to further progress."

MacLean in the election address was much more emphatic:

> "I haven't got to Russia yet. I'm not going there underground. I must go openly. . . . In spite of my keen desire to help Lenin and the other comrades I am not prepared to let Moscow dic-

tate to Glasgow. The Communist Party has sold itself to Moscow, with disastrous results both to Russia and to the British revolutionary movement."

While he was in prison the Unemployed Movement built up by MacLean and his comrades had been taken over by the CPGB, which was in a position to pay the leaders £4 a week to carry on the work. But MacLean was not disheartened. He now set about organising the Scottish revolutionary party he had been thinking about for more than two years, as he reported to Clunie when writing to tell him about his election campaign:

"I urged a Scottish Workers' Republic. My business is to create a keen desire for it, and so lay the basis for a Scottish Communist Party or a Scottish Workers' Party. The CP is going 'rocky' and as it fades the ground will be cleared for a real fighting party independent of outside dictation and finance."

The last year of his life was spent building up the Scottish Workers' Republican Party, which was formed in the spring of 1923. By May Day, held on the first day of May for the last time, there was a large contingent headed by MacLean with the banner "All Hail! The Scottish Workers' Republic!" out in front. The new party fought all the available municipal by-elections, carrying out the leninist policy of using the conventional political machinery as a platform for revolutionary propaganda. But he always pointed out, as he did in the November municipal election address (which was issued by all the SWRP candidates), that "nothing we can do in the town council will materially alter the general condition of our class."

By the autumn of the year he had, according to Sylvia Pankhurst who had come up from London to support one of his campaigns, gathered round him again a mass movement. In his 5 October letter to Clunie he reported that he was getting crowds of about three thousand every Sunday night at his open-air meetings at West Regent Street, "the biggest crowds ever held Sunday after Sunday in Glasgow".

He died one week after writing the last election address, and although it was a plea for Scottish separation, the last sentences show quite clearly that he retained his marxist world outlook to the end:

"Your only course now is to back me up for the complete change in the ownership of the world. Every vote cast against me is one cast for world war and the further starvation of the world's workers. Every vote cast for me is for world peace and eternal economic security for the human family."

6

Revolutionary struggle in Britain

Now's the day and now's the hour
(*The Call*, 23 January 1919)

We witness today what all marxists naturally expected, the capitalist class of the world and their governments joined together in a most vigorously active attempt to crush Bolshevism in Russia and Spartacism in Germany. Bolshevism, by the way, is socialism triumphant, and Spartacism is socialism in process of achieving triumph. This is the class war on an international scale, a class war that must and will be fought out to the logical conclusion — the extinction of capitalism everywhere.

The question for us in Britain is how we must act in playing our part in this world conflict. Some are suggesting a general strike to enforce a withdrawal of British troops from Russia and, I suppose, from Germany as well. That, to some of us on the Clyde, is too idealistic. Were the mass of the workers in Britain revolutionary socialists they would at once see that their material well-being depended on the peaceful development of Bolshevism in Russia and would, in consequence, strike for the withdrawal of British forces, at the moment attempting the downfall of Russian's social democracy. But the workers are not generally of our way of thinking, and so are unable to see that their material interests are bound up with Bolshevist stability in Russia. It necessarily follows that we will have no success in urging a strike on this issue, especially as the government has the majority of trade-union leaders in the hollow of its hand, and can easily manipulate them against us — with comparative safety to the leaders at that.

Some of us on the Clyde, therefore, think that we must adopt another line, and that is to save Russia by developing a revolution in Britain no later than this year. We socialists know that the capitalists can only realise their profits by selling a great part of their goods abroad. We know that America is in exactly the same predicament as Britain, and we further know that America intends to assume the economic position in the world that Germany has just failed to attain. If it is true, as well-informed commercial papers assert, that in 1918 America built more ship-tons than Britain, we may take it that America is in a position to lick Britain in the "navy race".

In five years' time such will be the glut of goods on the market that

148

fear of revolution through unemployment and hunger may force these two powers into war. If capitalism lasts, then war is inevitable in five years; yes, and a war bloodier than the present war. Humanity is in a very tight corner, and so those who will be called on to kill in the next war will have to make up their minds or fight capitalism to death this year. . . .

The next question for us is the start of the fight. How can we get the mass on the move and pulled onward by the young, who wish to save their lives? We have the opportunity at hand. The demobilisation has already created a menacing unemployment problem. We can get the support of the unemployed if we can suggest a means whereby they can get a living. The only possible solution is a drastic reduction of hours per week. This reduction will appeal to the employed if they are assured of at least a pre-war standard of living. Here we have the economic issue that can unify the workers in the war against capitalism.

The Miners' Reform Movement in South Wales and Scotland, in view of this, adopted as their minimum programme the six-hour day, five-day week and one pound a day. I place my services primarily at the disposal of the Miners' Reform Movement and am recognised as one of their spokesmen. I am as proud of that honour as the one conferred by our Russian comrades. My first campaign was amongst the Lothian miners, and as the result of a week's mission, we have there now a powerful unofficial committee and movement. Shortly a Lancashire County Conference will be held at Bolton, when the movement will spread like wildfire.

On the Clyde and amongst the miners the cry was "All eyes on Southport". It should be borne in mind that the Clyde Workers' Committee has issued a leaflet urging the thirty hours' week, and pledging its support to the miners. The Miners' Reform Movement decided that, if the Miners' Federation at the conference at Southport on Tuesday and Wednesday, 14 and 15 January, did not make up its mind to have the programme enforced, they would call a strike about the middle of February. Thanks to the advance guard, the MFGB has at Southport agreed to the six-hour day. The government is asked to enforce it by amending the Eight Hours Act. My good old friend, Bob Smillie, at the Conference pointed out that "we can produce enough in less than a six-hour day if we were not producing to make millionaires".

The Executive Committee has now to interview the Prime Minister and the government and, failing satisfaction, must convene another conference. From our point of view that is all to the good. The onus for the strike is thus thrust on the government, and will add to the fierceness of the fight when it comes off, as we know the government will never concede the miners' demands. This will also give the Reform Movement time to

149

expand their propaganda in the various coalfields and knit up more closely than ever. Let all miners who read this article buckle to and build up a powerful group in their own area. . . .

To convince the simple-minded worker who believes his master ought to have a profit, I am providing my audiences with the following illustration. Shortly since, the chairman of the Darracq Motor Company at the annual meeting stated that since August 1914 their employees had increased fourfold, but that their output had increased sevenfold. That means that one worker now in four hours is producing as much as formerly in seven hours. Seven sevens are forty-nine. Add two and that makes fifty-one, a very common pre-war number of hours per week. Seven fours are twenty-eight. Add two and that makes thirty. So that in thirty hours the Darracq workers are doing as much now as formerly in fifty-one hours. Once we get the mass on the move on this issue, we shall be able to take control of the country and the means of production at once, and hold them tight, through disciplined production under the workshop committees and the district and national councils. Through the co-operative movement we shall be able to control the full distribution of the necessaries of life, and so win the masses over to socialism.

All revolutions have started on seemingly trifling economic and political issues. Ours is to direct the workers to the goal by pushing forward the miners' programme and backing up our "black brigade".

The condition of the army, the navy, and even the police strengthens us in the fight. Capitalism is in the last ditch. Let us this year cover over this dripping monster and prepare the way for human solidarity on a sound world-wide workers' owned and controlled economic solidarity.

Rumblings of the revolution
(*The Call*, 30 January 1919)
The strike on the Clyde has been precipitated by the general discontent with the forty-seven-hour week expressed at hosts of shop and union meetings, and by the anxiety of the union officials not to let the matter slip out of their hands lest trade unionism be supplanted by one-class unionism. Never was industrial appeal so widespread and never so quickly have the workers organised such a vast venture, and it is to be hoped that workers everywhere will unhesitatingly enter into the conflict right away. Into it then, comrades, as you never did before. Let this be the class war started at last.

As I indicated last week some of us would have preferred the miners to lead off and then other workers to line up with the same programme. As we all ought to know, historical events never start and shape themselves as we plan them, and so our desire is not to be exactly realised on this occasion. And yet it is, too. For the Fife miners have led the way this last week on an hours question for pithead workers, and now the whole coalfield is idle and determined to get the six-hour day. . . . I have had four splendid meetings in Lanarkshire after a grand tour by comrade Cook of South Wales. . . .

The Lanarkshire men assured me they would come out with the Clyde men and hinted that they should not return till they got the six-hour day for themselves. Now that Fife has led the way, as she formerly led for the eight-hour day, Scottish and Welsh miners will come out, and if our knowledge of the other coalfields is correct, all the miners will come out before the Federation ceases negotiations with the cabinet.

The miners will thus eventually take the lead, and other workers will be forced to accept the miners' immediate charter — six hours a day, five days a week, and £1 a day as a minimum wage.

Comrades must remember that socialists will all be "fired" if unemployment persists, and so it is in every socialist's interest to plunge fearlessly into the fight if for no other reason than to make the job a little more secure. Socialists everywhere, when unemployed, ought to organise, lecture and drill the unemployed, and so create a mighty menace to capitalism. Then the masters will see that it is safest to keep the socialists employed. The best preparation is obviously playing a bold part at this critical juncture in the history of British wage-slavery.

With mutual confidence and self-reliance, then, into the fight, comrades, and make it a real revolutionary one. I know that socialists in the Scottish industrial belt can be relied upon. Are our brothers across the border going to funk it or fight as the Yorkshire miners have done, even though on a trifling issue? If the Midlands can be paralysed for a 20 minutes' meal hour, surely England ought to be paralysed for a drastic reduction of hours of labour. England, arise!

Sack Dalrymple, sack Stevenson: the forty-hour strike
(Pamphlet, Autumn 1919)
A terrible blow was struck at the working class of Scotland on Bloody Friday, 31 January 1919. A mass movement was started on the Clyde on the Monday prior to reduce the working week to forty hours. The movement rapidly spread over the industrial belt of Scotland. A strike for a forty-four-hour week was simultaneously proceeding in Belfast, where the stoppage was almost complete. The Tyneside also had its strike on the meal-time question. . . . Had the strike feeling spread the whole country might have been involved, and in the temper of the people at the time the

government feared a revolution such as had swept Germany into the hands of the "right" socialists.

The movement had to be nipped in the bud, and the opportunity presented itself in the move of the workers, who appealed to the Lord Provost of Glasgow to force the employers to grant the shorter working week.

On the Wednesday the Lord Provost told the strikers' deputation to call at the City Chambers on Bloody Friday. Meantime, acting under instructions from Bonar Law, the Lord Provost made preparations to trap the people. The tramway services provided the authorities with the required provocation on the fatal day. The strikers had calculated that the tramway workers would join them, and so disorganise the transport to and from the works.

The failure of the tramwaymen to respond to the strike call embittered the strikers, who on occasions became very nasty to them. This was known to the authorities, who in consequence planned that cars should run through George Square as usual on Bloody Friday, although the Square was packed with as immense a crowd as had ever gathered there before.

The man immediately responsible was the general manager, James Dalrymple. Of course, he was acting in conjunction with the police under Chief Constable Stevenson; and the latter was carrying out the instructions of the capitalist town councillors led by the magistrates and the Lord Provost.

Had no cars been sent through the Square, packed to excess with strikers who were provoked by the treachery of the tramwaymen and [tramway] women, no riot would have been started and the Chief Constable's "gallant" men would have got no excuse to crack the skulls of defenceless, innocent people. . . .

The tramway workers were not entirely to blame for being at work. On their side, the major part of the blame rests on the shoulders of their then union (Municipal Employees' Association) organiser, the brave soldier, Bailie A. Turner. . . .

Of course fine profits were being made out of the trams, profits that largely ought to have gone to improve the lot of the employees. Dalrymple's salary went up all right. When the war broke out, Dalrymple used the car system and the profits, not only to help recruiting and other war work, but to get a knighthood as well. That is why I nicknamed him "Sir" James Dalrymple from early on in the war, a form of ridicule that probably played some part in turning people against him and preventing him attaining the desired goal.

He used his spies effectively at the depots, and by that means stampeded men into joining the army without any show of force or open threats on his part. . . .

Naturally amongst those remaining on the car system in January 1919, there was a feeling of complete despondency and demoralisation. Turner had been away fighting the enemy in France when he should have been fighting them in Glasgow. The women, who had been introduced on to the cars for the war period, had neither interest in the union as a rule nor in any fight for a shorter working week.

Under these conditions it would be very wrong to hold the car workers absolutely responsible for the scabbing during the forty hours strike. The above explanation shows clearly enough to the usual member of the working class who has seen the spy system and the victimisation system in operation, that the essential blame for the cars being out during the strike of January 1919 must be placed on the shoulders of Mr James Dalrymple. . . .

The tramway system of Glasgow has been boasted of all over the world as the triumph of municipal socialism. From the standpoint of profit-making efficiency I have no objection to raise. But socialism implies security, comfort, and happiness for the people who actually run the cars.

Victimisation is the opposite of security, and spying is degrading both to the spy and the one spied upon. Spying implies that it "pays" to hold your tongue; it spells ruin if you speak your mind. Socialism means that your bread and butter are secure no matter what you think. Socialism means that you are free and entitled to speak your mind.

Under socialism the making of profit will give place to the comfort of the employees. . . . From a labour standpoint the "municipal socialism" of the Glasgow trams is a ghastly blank. . . .

Onward, ever onward
(*The Worker*, 12 April 1919)

. . . *The Worker* unified the forces that led to the January strike, Scotland's first attempt at a general strike. Though the strike itself was a failure, due more to the lack of working-class ripeness than to batons, tanks, and machine guns, it forced on the government expedients to stem the spread of the strike fever. . . . Alarmed by the monstrous majority of miners for a strike and by the prospect of support not only from the other members of the Triple Alliance, but also from other sections of the organised workers, the government established the Industrial Peace Conference as well as the Coal Commission.

The result has been enough to gladden the heart of the very last·

ditchers of the capitalist class. The miners' paid officials and unpaid delegates have accepted the immediate offer of the seven-hour day and 2s a day extra, and have advised the rank and file to vote for acceptance of the offer. The NUR leaders also advise their followers to take the government compromise without even the farce of a Commission. And now Bob Williams justifies the capitulation of the Triple Alliance on the ground that it is not strong enough to successfully face the organised forces of the master class, and suggests that to gain real successes the next offensive must be made by the whole working class. With him we all agree that only by a general offensive of the working class as a whole can any effective gains be obtained, but we cannot accept this is a justification for the collapse of the Triple Alliance. It was the business of the Alliance to start the fight, and then call in all other sections of the workers to the rescue.

While the Coal Commission was openly performing its part and giving us stale statistics and staler thrills of horror about miners' slums, the Industrial Peace Conference committees were secretly deliberating, and let us know their principal findings the day J.H. Thomas accepted the compromise for the railwaymen. The principal finding was the forty-eight-hour week, one good enough for ten thousand years ago, but hardly adequate to satisfy a revolutionary working class. The betrayal of the workers by the leaders' agreement to this working week, even as a maximum, is cynically brought into relief by the immediate announcement of Lord Leverhulme that his workers at Port Sunlight and elsewhere were going to be put on a six-hour working day with a free dinner thrown into the bargain, not as a piece of philanthropy, but as a business proposition. One may legitimately ask what is the use of trade union leaders when they accept forty-eight hours as a working week, when a capitalist is determined to make handsome profits on a thirty-six-hour week. It was the intention of Lloyd George to use these men to hold back the rank and file by offering, or seeming to offer, concessions; and they have for the time being succeeded in earning the confidence of the "Welsh wizard" and the capitalist class. These latter realised that if the workers made a united lunge at capitalism for a shorter week they would not only gain their immediate objective, but might also be urged forward by events towards the establishment of a Bolshevik republic. Their own safety lay in gaining the men's leaders to their side, and these they easily got over.

My own desire for an immediate onslaught of labour was induced by a desire to so engage British capitalism that it would be unable to vigorously pursue the policy of attempting to crush the working class republic in Russia as a means of preventing the spread of triumphant socialism. Could peace at home be maintained by manipulating the labour leader to stem the strike movement, then Britain would be free to carry on the war with the workers of Europe. The capitulation of the leaders of the Triple Alliance and of the other unions represented at the Industrial Peace Conference was followed by the announcements in the press that the allies must now commence a vigorous offensive against Bolshevist Hungary and Russia. And the events of the past three weeks have shown the preparations now being made to crush our working-class comrades on the continent.

Ours is to forge ahead with our propaganda and our workshop organisation. The very move of Lloyd George in summoning the trade-union leaders together to settle an economic compromise for all the workers gives us the cue to our next propaganda offensive.

The Clyde and Belfast failed because the strikes were limited in area and numbers. The Triple Alliance failed because the leaders felt their joint forces were inadequate to meet the forces Bonar Law gathered to back up his threat, and Bob Williams, in expressing his colleague's feelings, urges a united attack. Lloyd George provides us with the necessary precedent. If for his purpose he summoned the union leaders to act as a unit in conference with the employers and the government, we for our purposes are equally entitled to urge the rank and file to unite as a class and press forward with the same demands at the same time, and compel the union officials to fight unitedly for these demands or clear out. To achieve the necessary cohesion of forces, it must be the duty of the unofficial movements everywhere to organise every work, yard, and pit as a whole, irrespective of sex, grade, or craft. Get down to work, comrades, and quote Lloyd George's move as justification.

As a preliminary canter in the exercise of the workers of Scotland at least in class solidarity, let me suggest that a tremendous effort ought to be made to stop every worker on the first day of May to protest against the baton charges in George Square, Glasgow, on 31 January 1919, demand a public enquiry, and prepare for further action if the government condemns the twelve men at present on trial in the High Court at Edinburgh.

Should the sentence be adverse, it ought to be the duty of the rank and file to force the officials of the unions existing in Scotland to summon a special conference to discuss ways and means of releasing our comrades. If joint action can then be attained, it will pave the way for joint British action for shorter hours, a higher standard, and workshop control.

These suggestions ought to enable the rank and file to find other means of keeping the workers on the move, pressing ever onward to the great goal — the industrial commonwealth, under the full and absolute control of the workers.

The miners' next move

(*The Call*, 23 October 1919)

Events this year have proved that no organisation in Britain has a greater influence than the British Socialist Party on the policy of the working class. We in the end are going to triumph because we apply the materialist interpretation of history to events as they occur, and use it to find out what next great events are liable to take place, so that we may suggest to our class the tactics to be pursued. The British governing class as represented by the permanent officials supervised by cabinet ministers are materialists, too, and adopt tactics similar to those we apply....

The coalition gang in December stemmed the political ambitions of Henderson, MacDonald and co., expecting thus to stagger Labour. This but cleared the way for "direct action", prepared for by the Miners' Reform Committees and the shop stewards' movement. The forty hours' strike set the ball rolling in January, with the miners threatening action immediately after. The BSP members played their part in the conflict to save Russia and thus pave the way for the revolution here.

The government was forced to offer the Coal Commission and the Industrial Peace Conference in order to prevent a general strike, until the Bolsheviks and the Spartacists were crushed and the peace treaty moulded in favour of Britain. By this means it prevented strikes whilst it set itself by victimisation and sabotage to break up the unofficial rank-and-file movement. To continue the miners' negotiations on nationalisation the government threatened to put an end to the Coal Commission if the miners struck against the first Sankey award on hours and wages. Only till the peace terms had been almost agreed upon did the government sweetly submit to Smillie's lunges at dukes and capitalists. Then came the attack on Smillie, the attack on the miners' alleged ca' canny policy, and finally the 6s on the ton of coal — as a prelude to the government's proposal to trustify the mines.

People, however, rallied to Smillie and the miners, who are bent on united working-class action on nationalisation, skilfully rolled up inside withdrawal from Russia, conscription, and military intervention in strikes. ... To sicken the miners of direct action the government induced the Yorkshire miners' strike over the 10 per cent increase on ton rates with lavish praise of Herbert Smith, MP. This the government followed with a rumour of a general election this year.

But all this failed to prevent the miners carrying the day at the Congress....

I am aware that in the meantime there is a magnificent rush in the oil industry. It looks as if the government and the trust-capitalists are buying up spot and future supplies of oil in case of a miners' strike. This is probably a move to hustle the miners on to precipitate action. Can the miners afford to wait a month or two, until March if need be? I believe they can, if they apply the ca'-canny policy and are backed up similarly by other workers.

Time tells in our favour. The miners are rightly starting off on a publicity campaign. Let them perfect their organisation, and see to it that a Central Committee of Labour is at once established, whilst the unions amalgamate along the lines of industry.

Let the unofficial movement also play its part in furthering the workshop committees with appropriate district and national committees. Let them also adopt a united programme round which all workers can rally.

At this stage we of the BSP can play a supremely important part. We can call into being workshop committees with a right class bias; we can provide them with a programme identical with that of our South Wales comrades for the mining industry.

Let us urge full socialisation of mines and other trustified industries, full industrial control by the workers involved, though modified to permit of the use of the co-operative movement, control of the education of the workers, a thirty-hour week, fifty per cent increase in wages, communally produced houses, withdrawal of British troops and aid from all parts of the world, the abolition of the army and the navy and the establishment of a workers' defence force, and the transfer of the functions of Parliament to Labour's Central Committee.

Labour's commissariat department
(*The Call*, 30 October 1919)
The "London Letter" writer to *The Scotsman* (18 October) says: "It is doubtful whether the advanced wing of the Labour movement will be at all grateful to Mr Fred Bramley for his disclosure that in future strikes affecting the community as a whole it is being arranged to introduce the machinery of the co-operative societies for the support of the striking trade unionists threatened with a shortage of supplies. The idea is to ensure the distribution of food supplies and the payment of benefit by issuing through the various branches of the co-operative movement food coupons or loans from the Co-operative Wholesale's Bank on the security of trade-union assets."

Why the left wing should deprecate Bramley's disclosure puzzles me. We of the BSP are of the left wing, and we have insisted that such should be Labour's policy. Our only regret is that the co-operative organisations were not long ago made Labour's Commissariat Department. We, therefore, cannot but be pleased at Bramley's disclosure, because it will hearten us to push the scheme everywhere, especially after the scabbery of the Middle-Class Union, which is mainly composed of the shopkeeping class or the high-paid flunkeys of the capitalist multiple distributive companies. The fight of the future centres round food and the armed forces. If by publicity we can win the armed forces and thus get access to the food, the co-operative movement can help us to ensure that our class is regularly and properly fed during the crisis.

Labour in Scotland is not going to rely exclusively on the growing entente of the trade unions and the co-operative agencies, for this Saturday (25 October) a great conference is being held in the Good Templars' Hall, Glasgow, "to discuss the construction of industrial and social committees in each area". The summons to the conference declares that "Labour's great fight with capitalism is drawing near. There can only be one result: Labour must win! It is essential, therefore, that the workers must have the necessary knowledge and machinery to 'carry on'."

The Scottish workers' committees, who are responsible for the conference, are determined to project plans fitted to enable food to circulate freely for the benefit of the workers (and the social committees will see that the food is rationally distributed when the crisis comes). It is to be trusted that the rank-and-file movement everywhere will follow suit — or go one better, if possible. That will stimulate the official movements in production and distribution, and will guarantee greater security when the enemy try on the game of the economic blockade of the working class. I have no desire to stimulate opposition between the official and unofficial movements. I want to ensure success one way or the other.

To revert to the official entente. *The Scotsman* truly asserts that in many areas the co-operative movement is non-existent, or is so weak as to be useless in time of crisis: and that in these places co-operation has an almost impossible task to gain footing owing to the spread of the multiple shop system.

Some years ago I pointed out the full significance of the multiple system and the trusts producing for the multiple companies. As a result of my suggestion, the Co-operative Union appointed a committee to investigate the trusts and their power to apply limits to the growth of co-operation. That good work is still proceeding, as I see that co-operators have been given the main power in the Committee on Trusts appointed by the Labour Research Department. Where some years ago co-operation had to depend on dividend advantage in competition with multiple shop price-cutting in the frightful struggle of individual families to make ends meet with stationary wages against rising prices, and therefore had to discuss agencies likely to win in the fight, nowadays the problem is changing in view of the growing intensity and extent of the class struggle.

I am of opinion that in London and other areas where co-operation is still weak, the movement could be quickly rushed into a position of supremacy if organised labour used its funds and its machinery to establish and strengthen the movement.

Let Bramley and others in responsible positions take up the matter at once. It ought to be quite easy to use the Miners' and the Labour Party demonstrations to get new members for existing co-operative societies.

Now, then, London comrades, you set the pace. Permit me also to suggest that the three great Labour organisations ought now to set out jointly to map Britain into areas, and send the best speakers everywhere to organise demonstrations and work-gate meetings to see that every worker is in a union affiliated to the Labour Party and that every worker is also in the co-operative movement.

Let Labour earnestly now spend its hundreds of thousands on a thunderous publicity campaign. Spread and knit up must be the policy, for now the day of victory is at hand.

7

Ireland

The James Connolly birthday celebrations
(*The Worker*, 21 June 1919)
As the capitalist press in Scotland, as usual, has given a distorted statement as to the shooting of policemen the evening of the celebration of
Connolly's birthday, it is only fair that *The Worker* retaliate by publishing
the statement I have received from the Countess Markievicz, although she
did not ask me to thus make it public. Readers should particularly note
that the splendid Connolly souvenir programme states quite clearly: "Proceeds devoted to the establishment of a Connolly Memorial Workers' College."

The argument has incessantly been used that Ireland is under catholic priests whose game it has been to keep the Irish workers in ignorance.
But here are the accusers, the British capitalist class politicians, openly
trying to suppress a concert, the profits from which shall help to establish
an Irish Labour College similar to the Central Labour College and the
Scottish Labour College. It is apparent that the priests of capitalism (British and Irish alike) fear the spread of real education amongst the wage
slaves, since they understand that an educated working class will fight
capitalism with its robbery and "continuous reign of terror" to the death.

This attempt to nip the Irish Labour College in the bud is in line with
the attempt to crush Scotland's aspiration for a Labour College. Readers
may remember my dramatic removal to Edinburgh Castle in February 1916,
just six days before the first SLC conference in Glasgow. I had to read the
paper outlining the scheme. It was calculated that delegates would stay
at home and the scheme burst. But thanks to Scottish dourness that
gathering was a brilliant success, described ultimately in the Labour press
of the world. Our last one in May proved even more successful, and with
the workers' united monetary assistance our college will be the envy of
the workers of the world. Let this Dublin deed of darkness fire readers
up to a more generous response to our cry for help. And once we have
enough in Scotland we shall send help to Ireland to establish her Connolly
College, bedad we will!

This, Ireland's most noble method of perpetuating the name and
fame of Connolly, has suggested to me that the Keir Hardie Memorial ought
to be associated with the Scottish Labour College in the form of a perma-

nent college building or bursaries called the Keir Hardie bursaries. . . .

Impressions of Dublin

(*The Worker*, 23 August 1919)

Never having been in Dublin before, I was naturally desirous at the most suitable opportunity of visiting it to see the results of Easter week 1916 and the fighters who participated in it for Ireland's freedom from Britain and for Labour's emancipation from capital. On Thursday, 17 July, I managed to penetrate into the sacred precincts of Liberty Hall, and there spring a surprise on an old friend, Joseph MacDonnell, manager of *The Voice of Labour*, the organ of the Irish Transport Workers. He at once introduced me to Thomas Johnston, W. O'Brien, J.J. Hughes, Joseph McGrath, John O'Neil, and other prominent persons in the Irish Labour movement. In the middle of our conversation we were joined by a Gorbals contest friend, Cathal O'Shannon, editor of *The Voice of Labour*.

I at once desired to know what was going to happen on Peace Saturday, and how Irish Labour would respond to the Russian appeal for a world protest against allied intervention in Russia. I learned that the workers were asked to boycott the peace celebrations, and wisely so; for especially since May Day, when the Countess Markievicz visited Glasgow, the British government had done everything possible to incite the Irish people to rise in revolt. . . .

In my walk around I saw that Dublin and neighbourhood had many large dwelling-houses packed with soldiers apart from the thousands occupying the various barracks, obviously in preparation for eventualities. On Peace Saturday round the neighbourhood of College Green were thousands of policemen in plain clothes and spies galore brought in for the occasion to support the soldiers, and the police openly armed with revolvers. Apart from these and women, very few (mostly incomers like myself) witnessed the solemn farce of 15,000 soldiers with bayonets fixed, machine guns and tanks marching through the streets to celebrate peace. . . .

I learned further that no protest demonstrations inside the city or in County Dublin were allowed, so that no organised protest against the "peace quackery" or intervention in Russia was possible. . . . This little bit of news convinced me that Britain really had fought the war for democracy and freedom, and that the wicked socialist cynics were guilty of slander against Churchill, Law, George & Co. in their allegations that the war was fought to intensify British forms of slavery. However, meetings were arranged for me. . . . I spoke on Sunday, 20 July, in the Irish Workers' Hall, Langrishe Place, at the request of Delia Larkin. . . . There I urged that Ireland alone could never gain her own freedom, that her republic

161

depended on the revolt and success of British labour, and that therefore the Irish workers ought not to antagonise the soldiers of occupation in Ireland, but should try to win them over to the Irish point of view; further, that Irish labour would not be free under a Sinn Fein republic, but only under a socialist workers' republic, and that consequently Irish labour should support British labour in the campaign against intervention in Russia, and should be prepared to play its part in the worldwide establishment of Bolshevism, or socialism, as it is better known. Although the meeting was attended by a large number of the men who participated in the Easter Week rebellion, no objection was raised to my suggestion as to the attitude to be adopted towards "Tommy". In personal conversation, I found that these men fought not against the soldiers as enemies of Ireland, but just as the interposed tools of British capitalism, and that they had no hatred of the soldiers but of the government that foully used the soldiers in Ireland, although they were prepared to fight again for Ireland should occasion arise. They clearly comprehended the position I urged, and the ultimate advantage of it from the world workers' point of view.

On the Monday I was the guest at an informal reception, and there met for the first time Madame Maud Gonne McBride whose husband helped the Boers, and played his part during the Easter Week; L.P. Byrne of the Co-operative Union; Darrell Figgis, editor of *The Republic*, and many other outstanding dramatis personae of the great "Irish tragedy". Again I had the pleasure of a chat with Mrs Sheehy-Skeffington, now brightly hopeful that she shall see her murdered husband avenged in the coming Irish workers' republic. At this gathering I again suggested the above policy, but met with keen criticism and opposition from those only aspiring towards a republic. My lax use of the term "home rule" and my reference to Britain as the "mainland" provoked good-natured correction, since "home rule" signifies Redmondism and that of course is dead, whilst to Irishmen Ireland is obviously the "mainland".

Even more bitter and outspoken was the opposition to my proposals on the Tuesday in the garden of the Socialist Party of Ireland. The Lord Mayor had granted us the use of the Mansion House, but when we approached the entrance we found the police, at least two hundred strong, in possession and the meeting barred. The Inspector obdurately refused to listen to my plea that I had come on a mission to civilise Ireland! Such is humour in Ireland! We consequently adjourned to the garden in North Great George's Street. Although in the circumstances the audience was not large, it was quality undiluted, William O'Brien being in the chair. One man desired to know why the Gordons came to Ireland after refusing to go to India. Hot stuff like that was poured into me, and through these manifestations of the Irish mind at home I began to realise the spirit that nine hundred years of oppression had failed to subdue. Once the workers develop a similar hatred of capitalism things are going to move on avalanche-like. However, Cathal O'Shannon neatly and effectively supported me from a socialist standpoint, whilst Sean McLoughlin, who fought through the rebellion, urged the international position as a true supporter of Jim Connolly must. . . .

I have since received a letter from Madame McBride in which she frankly states that as a consequence of my Irish case from the international revolutionists' point of view, she had been compelled to modify her outlook as an Irishwoman earnestly loyal to the best interests of Ireland. A little more of this frank interchange of viewpoints will undoubtedly help forward downtrodden races and classes.

I had the pleasure of meeting George Russell, better known as "A.E.". I can now understand W.P. Ryan's growing appreciation of perhaps Ireland's greatest intellectual. Never have I met one in whom so nicely are blended the idealist and the realist. In him Ireland is seen at her best. Attached to the Irish Agricultural Organisation Society and steadily working towards a co-operation of equals in Ireland as a good socialist should, he nevertheless retains the poet's outlook on the healthy aspect of nature and mankind. More power to your pen, George! . . .

On the Wednesday evening I was favoured with an opportunity of addressing the shop steward movement inside the Transport Union, and from the applause I received and the sentiments expressed after my address, the Irish workers understand clearly the international role of the working class. The motto of the Transport Union, as their neat little flags show, is "one big union". That indicates their allegiance to the policy of industrial unionism. They, therefore, are not enamoured of America's "sympathy" with Ireland, since Mooney, Debs, Haywood, and thousands of industrial unionists are still kept in prison after the signing of the "peace" treaty. They discount "Labourism" in Australia as long as Pete Larkin and his comrades are kept in prison for industrial agitation. They know that Irish labour can only gain freedom when British labour leads the fight against capitalism. . . .

The Irish fight for freedom
(*The Vanguard*, June 1920)
No international worker can afford to leave out of his calculations the success of Irishmen in slowly crushing British rule out of Ireland, for that success is not due to the Irish intellectuals or to the Sinn Fein members of the propertied class. Ireland's new fight started in 1907 during the

Belfast dock strike, after which James Larkin commenced the Transport Workers' Union to embrace all Irish workers not in the old craft unions or attached to British unions. Liberty Hall in time became the centre of Irish activity in the great fight against Boss Murphy.

With Larkin was associated Jim Connolly, the brain centre of the Irish working class. Naturally so, as he got his early training in the Scottish socialist movement where Marx's marvellous book *Capital* was the inspiration of all thoughtful socialists.

On Larkin's passage to America, Connolly assumed power at Liberty Hall, and here he found most of the men who fought with him during Easter Week 1916. His murder by the British government roused the latent fires in Irish breasts, and every subtle and unscrupulous move since made by Ian MacPherson and his minions at Dublin Castle but added fuel to those fires, fires that never again will be quenched, even by a general massacre, until an Irish republic has been established.

The restraint imposed by the war gave way to savage fury after the general election when about four-fifths of the Irish voters voted for a republic, and returned 73 Sinn Feiners, who at once set up an Irish Parliament, or as the Irish call it, the Dail Eireann. Then came the army of occupation, later the arming of police with bombs. Everything conceivable has been done to stir the Irish to open rebellion. Meetings, sports, concerts, fairs, exhibitions, and newspapers have been suppressed wholesale, houses innumerable have been searched, 67 of the Sinn Fein MPs have been jailed, numbers of the local councillors elected by proportional representation have met the same fate, and even such prominent leaders of labour such as Wm. O'Brien and Cathal O'Shannon have been incarcerated without a trial. The Lord Mayor of Cork was deported to an English prison and the Lord Mayor of Dublin was murdered in his own house.

From May 1916 till December 1919, there have been 59 murders, 2,084 deportations, 575 armed assaults on unarmed civilians, 15,153 raids on private houses, 5,041 arrests, 2,038 sentences, 369 proclamations and suppressions, 53 suppressions of papers, 506 courts-martial — a total of 25,378. This year the situation has grown worse. . . .

These facts are not published in the capitalist press, which dilates solely on all the supposed misdeeds of the Irish. . . . Britain believes in self-determination for the races under the heel of the late tsar, but not for the races under the sway of his kinsman, George "Windsor". Britain's fear is that Ireland might ally itself with America in the next war — if we are silly enough to let capitalism last another five years.

Those very fears lead Britain to disaster. Ireland is clearing the police out first and then will follow the army — with the help of British labour, let us hope. The Irish workers' recent strike to get comrades out of Mount-joy Prison, and their successful threat to stop exports if prices of bacon and butter were not reduced, show clearly that, if the Irish workers remain united, Britain must go. That is the beginning of the end of the British empire, for Canada, Australia, New Zealand, India, Egypt and South Africa will push out on their own. British labour will consequently have an easier task in seizing political power from the decrepit coalition misfit as a preliminary to the breaking up of the propertied class's economic power.

Ireland cannot stop at a republic; Ireland's one big union will before the republic has been really started convert it into a socialist republic, despite the imprisonment America has given to Jim Larkin. The world socialist movement must demand the release of our great comrade Larkin, so that he may return to his native land to be Ireland's first communist president, for his present sentence is due to his assuming a position on the executive committee of the Communist Party of USA. Up, Ireland! Up, Larkin!

The Irish tragedy: Scotland's disgrace
(Pamphlet, June 1920)
Let me address myself to Scots people particularly at this critical juncture in the world's history — just as critical as in August 1914 — to save Ireland from a tragedy that is bound to come if a stop is not put to the bloody career of the present coalition gang of unmitigated scoundrels.

My plea is that Britain has no right to dominate Ireland with constabulary armed with bombs, and with an army and navy considered foreign by the Irish. We Scots have been taught to revere the names of Sir William Wallace and Robert Bruce because these doughty men of old are recorded as championing the cause of freedom when Edward I and Edward II tried to absorb Scotland as part of English territory. All Scots must therefore appreciate the plight of Ireland, which for over seven centuries has chafed under the same English yoke, and now ought to stand by Ireland in her last great effort for freedom; the last because triumph is bound to be hers very soon.

Right through the war the British government justified its prosecution of the war on the ground that it was a war of "democracy" against Prussianism, and that the war would guarantee the rights of small nations if the allies won.

The allies have won — or at any rate, America has won. Has democracy been recognised? Have small nations had their rights? The piteous plight of Ireland gives the lie direct to those profound prevaricators called the coalition government. The allies saw to it that a faked plebiscite was carried through in Alsace-Lorraine and Slesvig to take away parts of the German empire, and that all the small nations round the Russian territory obtained their independence as a first step to bribery and use against Russia herself.

But to let Ireland have independence is a different story. Despite Ireland's wonderful unity and solidarity on the issue of separation from Britain, the coalition government violently persists in keeping its hold on Erin.

Nothing but loathing and disgust must animate any straight-thinking person when he or she recalls the continuously repeated cry that Britain must release German democracy from the blight of Kaiserism and Junkerism and Prussianism, and recollects the lying bleat that the Bolsheviks, in deposing Kerensky, had overridden the principle of democracy, and that, though a minority, they held the reins of power in rustic Russia. As a matter of simple fact, the alleged "dictatorship by terrorists" was the stock argument used all last year by Winston Churchill and his press puppets to justify the spending of close on two hundred million pounds in the direct and indirect attempt to overthrow the vast Russian Communist Republic. Even yet Britain is chary about trading with Russia because of Russia's alleged repudiation of the principle of democracy.

To any right-thinking person Britain's retention of Ireland is the world's most startling instance of a "dictatorship by terrorists", as Britain rules Ireland against Irish wishes with policemen armed with bombs and a huge army equipped with over 40 tanks and as many aeroplanes, machine guns galore, and all the other beautiful manifestations of Christian brotherhood, love and charity.

Democracy in Britain means rule by a clear majority vote, although in some cases trade unions insist on a two-to-one majority. How did Ireland vote at the general election in 1918?

Sinn Feiners and Redmondites polled 1,211,516 votes or 79.3 per cent of the total votes, the Unionists polled 271,455 or 17.8 per cent; and the Independents and Labourists polled 45,939 or 2.9 per cent. Obviously, the vote shows that by 4 to 1 the people in Ireland wish to look after their own affairs. That overwhelming vote satisfies the most stringent demands of democracy inside trade-union and co-operative circles.

This Irish decision was reaffirmed in January 1920 at the municipal elections, when 95 per cent of the townships outside Ulster fell into the hands of the republicans under a system of proportional representation. Even Derry and Lurgan in Ulster were taken from the Unionists, and in Lisburn, Dungannon, and Cookstown the Carsonites have only a bare majority.

The complete statistics of municipal elections show that in Leinster 36 out of 38 towns were won by republicans and nationalists, in Connaught 9 out of 10, in Munster 32 out of 32, and in Ulster 21 out of 47.

That is not all. The republicans are now controlling and policing 21 counties, and news has just arrived that in Ulster the Sinn Feiners and Nationalists combined have captured County Tyrone with 11 against 9, and County Fermanagh also with 11 against 9. Great gains have also been registered in the other four of the special Ulster counties, although the final results are not out at the moment of writing.

If all these decisions do not clearly indicate the mind of the majority in Ireland, then elections will never establish any definite verdict.

Britain has obviously no excuse for the flooding of Ireland with troops, and it must be British labour's bounden duty to see that these soldiers, mainly boys of 18, be withdrawn and let the Irish settle their own affairs. If the minority cannot stand up for themselves, let them emigrate. That is what Lord French and the coalitionists wish 200,000 young Irishmen to do. They are trying to starve these youths out of their native land. That is why Clyde capitalists gladly engage the Irish. The government tells them to do so, as Irishmen in Scotland are less dangerous than in Ireland; whereas Scotsmen will submit to unemployment and starvation and even commit suicide rather than annoy the government or the bosses. Instead of blaming Irishmen for stealing their jobs, Scotsmen should blame the government and the capitalists, who are responsible for the influx of Irishmen to the Clyde and the west coast of England. If Ulstermen cannot tolerate an Irish republic, let them take a taste of emigration.

The government defends its persistent policy of retaining Ireland by alleging that it is its sacred duty to protect the Orange protestants, who would have a rough time of it if the Irish catholics held full sway in an Irish republic. This line of argument was good bluff in 1914, but cannot hold water today with clear-headed people, who are nimble-witted enough to put two and two together.

Just remember Britain's excuse for entry into the war. Was it not to defend poor little Belgium against Germany? Even Lloyd George tried on that "wheeze", on Xmas 1915 in St Andrew's Hall, Glasgow, when he came to persuade the Clyde workers to accept dilution of labour. But everyone ought to know that the Belgians are catholics and the Prussians protestants.

Does anyone really believe that Britain fought the greatest world war to protect catholics against protestants on the Continent, and now is preparing to turn the Emerald Isle red with catholic blood to protect protestants?

Sir Henry Wilson, Field Marshal, in the middle of May 1920, blew the gaff on the Belgian bluff at the Union Jack Club when he blurted out in indiscreet military fashion that Britain entered the war to save her own skin.

For saying the same, in other words of course, I was sentenced to three years and then to five years' penal servitude. Sir Henry obviously ought to be sent to Peterhead quarry for the rest of his natural!

Sir Henry is perfectly right in saying that Britain entered the war for selfish ends — the preservation of British capitalist predominance in the world. May not the same reason explain the stubborn insistence that Ireland shall not get independence?

I think it does. Britain murdered men to steal Egypt because of the Suez Canal, and is going to keep Egypt, although no Ulster exists there. What is the motive behind the retention of Ireland? I think the real reason is not the Ulstermen, whom the government loves as ardently as the citizens of that Indian city called Amritsar, where General Dyer (or Killer) wiped out over five hundred to prove to the poor people of India the abounding love of Britain towards the poor heathen!

What, then, is Britain's real motive for its bulldog grip of Erin's Isle? Ireland stands between Britain and the Atlantic Ocean, on which British ships must freely sail, in case of war, to preserve the people's food supplies. If Ireland were an independent republic and formed an alliance with America, which Bottomley in *John Bull* now calls "Britain's Next Enemy", then in the event of a war (which is coming on much faster than the late war with Germany) Irish ports would be the base of operations of the American fleet, and Irish soil would be the base of operations of the American army. Britain might thus be bottled up by America and Ireland combined, as Britain bottled up Germany and starved her into surrender. . . .

Lord Leverhulme has bought up some of the isles off the west coast of Scotland, Lewis and Harris particularly, not only to catch fish but to make harbours, roads, houses, stores, railways etc., for the British navy in case of war with America. For the same reason Stranraer is being also made a big fishing centre. So, also, are necessary precautions being taken in the Bristol Channel, south of Ireland.

Last year I calculated that this war was bound to come in five or six years' time; but recent events show that the fight may burst out at any moment. The five big bully-beef trusts of Chicago, helped by the bankers, are trying to corner the world's food supplies; so also is Britain. The Standard Oil Trust of America, backed by all the big interests of America, is making desperate efforts to corner the oil supply of the world; so also is Britain. Both sides are accusing the other of greedily trying to monopolise the world's oil resources. America is in process of stealing Mexico to use Mexican oil in her navy in case of "eventualities"; Britain has stolen Egypt outright now, and is in process of stealing Mesopotamia and Persia to secure the Anglo-Persian Oil Company, which dominates the oil and mineral resources of those countries and in which the British government has millions of pounds.

Britain has determined to run her naval and merchant fleet with oil to get out of the clutches of the Miners' Federation, particularly the revolutionary South Wales miners. Hence the need to control the oil resources of the world. Hence the present bitter fight with America to get a controlling grip over these resources.

This delicate situation, admitted by Sir H. Wilson to be as critical as the one in July 1914, explains why Britain allowed comrade Krassin to come to London and see Lloyd George. Up till the present Britain has blockaded Russia, refused to see Russia's trade representatives, and refused to trade with that vast communist country. Why has she so suddenly reversed her policy? The only feasible explanation is that she fears the American situation, and wishes to secure food and raw materials, particularly Russian oil, in case of a breakdown of good relationships with America. Do not be deceived into believing that Britain's new Russian policy is dictated by humanitarian motives. It is her selfish ends that dictate her policy all the time and every time.

Her brutal treatment of Ireland, more blatant today than every before, indicates that quite clearly. Immediately the armistice was signed more troops poured into Ireland, not as a precaution against a possible rising but as an irritant. Meetings were deliberately suppressed with brutal arrogance, then football matches and other sports were stopped and the spectators and players scattered with violence, concerts and entertainments were forbidden — even a concert run to provide money to establish a Labour College in Dublin; in fact, the social life of the people was calculatedly interfered with to create an open rising that would give Britain the chance of having an "Amritsar slaughter" in Ireland to settle the Irish for another generation at least.

Those of us who are conversant with the irritating methods adopted in prisons, at socialist meetings, and in Ireland can readily realise that the people of Armritsar were irritated by British army provocateurs into the jeering at General Dyer that afforded the excuse for the most cold-blooded butchery ever perpetrated by any conquering race. If the Irish had shot down and wounded as many Orangemen in the streets of Belfast, what a hellish howl the prostitute pressmen, politicians, and pulpiteers of Britain would have set up!

The Irish only escaped a "bloodbath" by calmly and meekly submitting to every calculated effort to arouse them to violence. Senator Walsh and others from America visited Ireland, got the drift of affairs, and then returned to America to place the plight of Ireland before America. America was only too pleased to find some excuse for blackening Britain, so Americans say that the world learned all about Britain's brutalities in Ireland (and India, Egypt, and the West Indies, too, I daresay). British patriots cannot complain of America doing this, as Britain has similarly blackened the Turks for massacring Armenians, Germans for massacring women and children, and Russians for running the whole gamut of social crime.

Thereafter, De Valera went to America to get funds to help the Irish Parliament or Dail Eireann. Appeals for funds also appeared in the Irish press. Then followed suppressions right and left, as Britain was determined to stand no rival parliament in Ireland:

Sept. 20 The entire republican press in Ireland was suppressed.
Oct. 21 Weekly meetings of Sinn Fein Central Club suppressed.
Nov. 21 Military and police raid headquarters of the republican government and arrest and imprison the staff.
Nov. 27 Sinn Fein and republican organisations suppressed throughout Ireland.
Dec. 10 Sinn Fein and republican headquarters ordered to be closed.
Dec. 12 Sinn Fein leaders, including the secretary of the Sinn Fein organisation, arrested in Dublin and provinces and deported without trial. Republican headquarters again raided and literature confiscated.

During 1919 and the early months of 1920, 66 of the Irish MPs elected in 1918 were sent to prison after farces of a trial or without trial at all. Only 7 escaped prison by leaving Ireland shortly after their election in 1918.

Since the municipal elections in January 1920, 35 councillors have been arrested, and attempts were made to arrest at least 36 other councillors.

On 3 March, armed military raided the Women Workers' Club, the Irish Workers' Union, Liberty Hall, the Socialist Party of Ireland headquarters, the Grocers' Assistants' Union headquarters, and the Irish Drapers' Assistants' headquarters — all in Dublin. At the same time Alderman William O'Brien, the leader of the Irish labour movement, was snatched away and smuggled into England, where he was kept in prison without trial.

Immediately after that it was learned that on 1 March 1920, Mr Alan

Bell had commanded high bank officials to appear at the police court, Inns' Quay, Dublin, with all books and documents used in their banks, so that they might be examined by government officials. The purpose was to trace all Sinn Fein monies, and also to know all the business of prominent supporters of the Sinn Fein cause so as to crush them down to poverty.

Bell issued the summonses as resident magistrate for the County of Dublin. He first appeared as an assistant to James E. French, chief of the English Secret Service in Ireland. As a result of Wm. O'Brien's exposure in 1884 of Dublin Castle immorality, French was convicted of unnatural crime. Bell acted as his agent-provocateur in the West of Ireland in the Land League times, one of his exploits being the arrest of Henry George, author of *Progress and Poverty*, during his visit to Ireland in the eighties. Bell was the secret agent of the London *Times* during the Piggott forgeries' case, in which Piggott confessed he had been bribed to forge the handwriting of Parnell so as to involve Parnell in high treason. But for the confession Parnell might have been shot. Since then Bell carried on his dirty work as an English spy in Ireland.

He is the scoundrel dragged in broad daylight from a Dublin car and shot. What self-respecting man or woman can blame the Irish for ridding the earth of such a foul skunk? Who ever was sorry for a Judas?

When even the first suppression in September failed to draw the Irish into open revolt, the British government had to do something to justify its base, brutal, and bloody occupation of plucky Ireland. My opinion is that it, through Dublin Castle, arranged the assassination of detectives and police and then blamed the Irish. The culmination came when it arranged the attempt on Lord French near the spot where Cavendish and Burke were killed in the eighties. French was in an armoured motor. Unfortunately for Britain, few sensible people pitied the Flanders' failure, and doubtless many who lost sons under French would not have been at all sorry had he crossed the black stream. It is certain that the day the Irish wish to put his lights out, off he goes.

The government seized the excuse to arm the police with bombs and convert police stations into barracks. Then the Irish began those attacks on the police system that have absolutely demoralised it, in fact have virtually broken it up altogether. The government now seeks by faked statistics to show that the Irish have done this for ordinary criminal purposes.

As a matter of fact there is no crime the government has not incited the police and the soldiers to perpetrate in this war to the knife with Ireland. . . .

The following letter was sent on 9 March 1920 by Major Erskine

Childers, DSC, to the General Officer Commanding-in-chief, General Head-quarters, Dublin. Childers is the son of a former Chancellor of the Exchequer. His famous novel *The Riddle of the Sands* warned England of the German menace. He has also written one of the volumes of the London Times *History of the War*:

"Sir, I received the honour of a visit last night from a tank belonging to your command at the somewhat inconvenient hour of 1 a.m. I do not demur to this. War is war. But I suggest that it might be in the ultimate interest both of the visitors and the visited on these occasions if a code of etiquette or deportment were imposed upon the former. It would, perhaps, be unreasonable to complain of bayonets being flashed in the eyes of my small boy in his cot, and of similar means of impressing the household generally with a proper awe of the forces under your command. But it is a matter of legitimate complaint that a young subaltern (of by no means attractive appearance, if you will forgive me) should on entering the house stroll into my drawing-room in my presence puffing a cigarette, and should continue to refresh himself in this manner after I had invited him to desist. The trifling scene which ensued was ended by the intervention of another officer of no less polished breeding, who decreed an ingenious compromise under which the cigarette was to be thrown unextinguished upon the carpet. 'Upon the carpet' was the express injunction delivered with studied insolence by this young carpet-knight.

Thus I was to win my point about the consumption of the cigarette, and he was to save his dignity by burning a hole in my carpet.

The point may seem trivial, but is it so? When armies are eventually withdrawn from occupied territory — and may I, without the least offence, express the hope that yours will be eventually withdrawn from ours? — it is of the most vital importance that an army should leave behind it a record for civility and humanity in the performance even of its most obnoxious duties. Surely none can be more obnoxious and more easily provocative of exasperation than these midnight raids upon civilians' houses, about 19,000 of which have taken place, I understand, in the last two years, often, as in my case, on false information, and often resulting in indignities and hardships infinitely worse than anything I experienced.

Though I am no longer a member of the British army, long service in it during the war, and the regard which I still retain for the best among its traditions, encourages me to address these remarks for your consideration.

I have the honour to remain, Faithfully yours, ERSKINE CHILDERS, late Major, RAF."

That the attacks on the Irish are continuous, widespread, and numerous is proved by the statistics issued by the Sinn Feiners themselves. Here is a typical 1920 week's work by Dublin Castle, ending 17 April: raids, 1,135; arrests, 260; sentences, 2; proclamations, 2; courts-martial, 2; armed assaults, 16; deportations, 92; murders, 4. This information is carefully suppressed by the government, so that ordinary people are forced to come to entirely wrong conclusions as to the real situation in Ireland.

Acts of aggression in Ireland, 1919:

Feb. 12   Pat Gavin shot dead by soldiers at the Curragh Camp.

Apr. 6   Robt. Byrne shot dead by police in Limerick Hospital.

Apr. 26   M. Walsh shot dead by police at Dungarvan.

Apr. 29   Two men shot by police at Longford.

June 5   Matthew Murphy, Dundalk, shot dead by soldiers at Dundalk.

June 16   Michael Rice (60 years) and his son Martin shot dead in his house by police.

Aug. 14   F. Murphy, Glan (15 years), shot dead by soldiers firing into his father's house at midnight.

Sept. 9   Fermoy sacked by soldiers.

Oct. 10   Boy shot at Banbridge by police.

Nov. 6   Kinsale sacked by soldiers.

Nov. 12   Cork partly sacked by soldiers.

Nov. 20   Motorists shot by police at Sligo for not halting.

Nov. 24   Civilians shot at Tipperary by police.

Dec. 29   Laurence Kennedy murdered by police at Phoenix Park, Dublin.

1920:

Jan. 6   Dr Keane, Ennismyon, shot by police while on his medical rounds.

Jan. 19   Civilians at Enniscorthy shot by police.

Jan. 20   M. Darcy, Cooraclare, drowned while police held off would-be rescuers.

Jan. 22   Thurles wrecked by soldiers.

Feb. 4   Man and girl shot dead in Limerick by soldiers and police.

Feb. 14   Jas. O'Brien shot dead at Rathdrum by police.

So I might continue itemising the bloody butchery right down to the time of writing this pamphlet were I not sick of the whole murderous business.

To expect the Irish to accept crushing and blackening both is to stretch expectation and endurance beyond the limit. So the Irish have naturally replied by laying low policemen and detectives. Policemen are

173

now resigning by the hundred. Police barracks have been blown up and policemen driven from whole stretches of the country. The Sinn Feiners are, however, establishing their own police and their own courts, which now control 21 of Ireland's 32 counties. Britain's police system is virtually destroyed in vast stretches of Ireland, never again to be re-established.

Naturally, also, Irish dockers and railwaymen have followed the example of the London dockers, who took their cue from *The Daily Herald* and refused to load the *Jolly George* with ammunition for Poland. Irishmen now refuse to supply the army of occupation with the ammunition that may be used to kill themselves when off industrial duty. This is surely the most sensible thing Irishmen have ever done in their history of toil and trouble. Irish labour may call an Irish general strike to force the withdrawal of troops from Ireland. Meantime, Irish railwaymen have asked the executive committee of the National Union of Railwaymen (NUR) to take action to prevent ammunition being sent to Ireland. The NUR has put the responsibility on to the shoulders of the Triple Alliance (Transport Workers, Miners, and NUR), and the Triple Alliance in turn is slipping the responsibility on to those genial old fogies who constitute the Trade Union Congress Committee. By the time these benevolent old gents make up their mind to deputise the Prime Minister, Ireland will have established a republic, and have then passed on to a Socialist republic herself!

Britain is pouring more and more troops into Ireland, and now the navy is being called into play. A terrible tragedy may be perpetrated by Britain before labour has realised the full gravity of the situation. It is therefore essential that drastic action be taken very soon.

The real centre of the Irish fight is Liberty Hall and the Transport Workers' Union, founded by the mighty Jim Larkin, now doing ten years in an American prison because he was an active member of the Communist Party, and carried on by the martyred Jim Connolly till Easter Week 1916.

Should Ireland get a republic the class war will then burst out and be fought out till Irish labour wins and establishes communism finally again in the "Ould Counthrie".

This new phase in Irish life ought to be the inciting influence to British labour, for labour everywhere must ally against the common enemy, capitalism, and destroy it to make way for world communism.

The victory of British and Irish labour will pave the way for American labour, the triumph of which will eliminate the possibility of the threatened war with America.

Ireland's victory is obviously the undoubted prelude to labour's triumph throughout the world, when robbery shall give place to justice in the mighty communist commonwealth, and when, with the scrapping

174

of armies and navies, mankind can live in peace to enjoy the fruits of their labour.

A general strike, then, for the withdrawal of British troops from Ireland, and the demand of the release of Jim Larkin (America) and his brother, Pete Larkin (Australia).

PS. Since writing this pamphlet *The Glasgow Herald*, in a leader on Tuesday, 8 June 1920, entitled "The Army in Ireland", gloats over the fact that Scots regiments are pouring into Ireland and others are held in readiness. It seems the Scots are being used to crush the Irish. Let labour effectively reply.

Scotsmen, stand by Ireland!
(The Vanguard, July 1920)
On Tuesday, 8 June, there appeared in *The Glasgow Herald* a leading article entitled "The Army in Ireland", in which it virtually stated that Britain with blockhouses and wireless apparatus intended to crush the Irish into submission as Britain crushed the Boers twenty years ago. Readers should note that this declaration of war on Ireland was made after a deputation from the NUR headed by Mr J.H. Thomas met Mr Lloyd George at 10 Downing Street on Thursday, 3 June, to explain the obvious to anyone — why the Irish railwaymen refused to handle ammunition.

Mr Lloyd George told them that submission to the Irish railwaymen would be a "complete abdication of government". Then he explained the position from the standpoint of the British government. "In Ireland we have had within a very short time 48 murders of police and 128 attempted murders that failed. The men were shot down in the street, men of the same race, men of the same religion, leaving wives and children behind them, who were simply carrying out the elementary duty of any force of that kind — the preservation of order. The police have nothing to do with the rights or wrongs of the controversy."

Policemen have to do with every political controversy and struggle, as they are used as government agents against any class, faction, or nation opposing the government and the class and nation it represents.

The Irish police have been particularly active against movements for Irish political independence and Irish police have raided Irish houses innumerable in the British government's fight against the Irish race. Such police are scabs and traitors to their race, and are treated as such. Irish secret societies have disposed of some of the forty-eight killed, but Dublin Castle has had its toll as well to justify the army's occupation of Ireland. . . .

Lloyd George expects too much when he imagines that a high-spirited

175

race like the Irish are going to carry ammunition to the men who will murder their own comrades or even themselves in their off-duty time. If refusal to handle ammunition in such circumstances is a breach of "good government", then all good men and true will be against "good government".

The Irish are not against "good government", but against bad government. British government to them is bad: Irish government is good. Bad government ought to be always resisted, and this the Irish are doing.

Three times since 1918 the Irish, by "democratic" vote, have agreed to the principle of Irish independence by a 4 to 1 vote. Instead of getting independence from the "world's greatest democratic country" Ireland has got an army with aeroplanes, tanks and other blessings of civilisation and an armed police. Irishmen have been and are being murdered. From a communist point of view the greatest murder was that of Jim Connolly, and Jim was worth an army of Irish police traitors. Lloyd George need not whine over the dead 48 policemen when he, with Asquith, is responsible for the murder of a wounded man, a man who fought openly for his race and his class, the wage-slave class. . . . Murders committed by Irish patriots are but retaliation, and are as justifiable as the murder of Germans to save the independence of Britain, to say the least of it. Lloyd George and his government played their part in overthrowing Bela Kun and giving free scope to that "butcher" Horthy, who has already wiped out thousands of good communists or people suspected of being communists; Lloyd George and his government are responsible for the blockade of Russia and the wars on Russia from within as well as from without, leading to the death of thousands of men, women and children through starvation and disease; Lloyd George and his government are responsible for the cold-blooded murder of over 500 people at Amritsar and hundreds in Egypt during 1918 to terrify races we are not fit to govern. . . .

Mr J.H. Thomas absolutely accepted Lloyd George's position; in fact, even before he went. The visit but served as a means of placing the responsibility for treachery on the government and of bluffing the members of the NUR. He seems to have been able to persuade his executive committee to advise his Irish members to return to work and to advise that they ought to handle ammunition for Ireland, Poland, and Rumania. Naturally, the Irishmen refused to accept the EC's advice. They cannot be expelled as they would at once join the Irish Transport Workers' Union, the proper place for them in the long run, especially now after Thomas's speech at Battersea on Sunday, 6 June. He is reported as follows: "Nobody could accuse me or my colleagues of want of sympathy with Ireland, but I for one would never condone the murder of innocent soldiers and policemen who were doing their duty."

The government has seized hold of the NUR advice to its members to assume that the British workers will condone any bloody deeds in Ireland. As *The Glasgow Herald* acknowledges, it is rushing troops into Ireland and is holding others in readiness. The *G.H.* seems proud of the fact that Scottish troops mainly are being used as the tools of the government as they can be relied on to pay strict attention to "business".

To every Scottish lover of freedom, to every Scotsman who has felt proud of Scotland's political and religious fights against England for freedom, the blush of shame must come when we learn that Scottish boys are to be used to prevent by murder the Irish race from attaining that very freedom we have been taught our fathers fought to preserve.

It remains to be seen whether the Lanarkshire miners will agree to a one-day strike for Ireland, and if that will be the signal for a general Scottish strike to force the withdrawal of Scottish lads from the cold-blooded murder of the Irish.

This is the greatest question confronting Scotland today, for if speedy action is not taken a horrible tragedy will be enacted, and Scotland will be disgraced for ever. This is more important than protesting against higher rents or the high cost of living. It is acquiescing and participating in the murder of a race rightly protesting its own right to rule itself. . . .

Up, India!
(*The Vanguard*, August 1920)

Once more attention is being drawn to India. We make no apology for filling our front page with the Connaught Rangers' cartoon as it ought to concentrate the workers' minds not only on Ireland, but also on India. It was a gloriously stupid piece of folly for the War Office to send Irish soldiers to India as it is now learning to its cost. No better place could this dramatic and significant incident have happened in.

The incident itself is pregnant with great historic results. That typically capitalist rag *The Manchester Guardian*, stimulated by the "down guns" of the Connaught Rangers, wrote a "leader" pointing out the coming disaster in Ireland. It warns the government to be cautious, since Irishmen in large numbers are to be found in every regiment and battleship. If a civil war starts, the *M.G.* sees the possibility of every regiment being rent in twain and a mutiny in every vessel of the navy, as well as an Irish outburst all over the Empire.

We see, further, that other soldiers will learn the C.R. lesson and refuse to shoot their class when called upon — and even take labour's side. That happened in Russia and elsewhere on the Continent, and is bound to become an increasing practice the more revolutionary the workers become in thought and action. The Irishmen in the bosses' army and navy will be the centre of such revolt. The Irish situation, obviously, is the most revolutionary that has ever arisen in British history, but unfortunately lads who fancy themselves the only revolutionaries are too stupid or too obsessed with some little crotchet to see with sufficient clarity the tight corner the Irish are placing Britain in.

The Irish Sinn Feiners, who make no profession of socialism or communism, and who are at best non-socialists, are doing more to help Russia and the revolution than all we professed marxian Bolsheviks in Britain — Smillie, Mann, Williams even being included in the "we".

The Russians have undoubtedly largely benefited by the Irish situation; the British are afraid to send too large forces against the Turks; and their blessed Connaught Rangers have done more to wipe out the discouragement ensuing on the massacre of Amritsar than all the meetings the Hindoos ever could have held.

Every Indian heart will have been uplifted, every Indian inspired to act as the Irish are acting. The Indians must and will break up the native police force, a force of Indians established by Britain to keep Indians under Britain's bloodstained heel.

Then the Indians may inspire Indian soldiers to do more even than the Connaught Rangers have done. They may incite them to leave the British Army en masse, and thereafter form the nucleus of a genuine Indian Army.

After that they may propagate the "down guns" idea amongst the other British Tommies. . . .

And, last of all, they may invite the co-operation of the Bolsheviks who now are rightly entitled to break up the British empire since Britain has done her level best for two years at least to overthrow Russia.

Should the Russians help the Indians, it would not be an attack on the British people, but a fight to help a vast people to gain national and racial independence.

The only atonement Britain can make for the slaughter and injury of perhaps more than three thousand people at Amritsar is self-determination for India. It is very cunning to give a report of the Amritsar massacre more than a year after the bloody deed, dismiss the murderer, General Dyer, and then discuss him in the House of Thieves. The Thieves have confirmed his dismissal (with a very fat pension and probably secret gifts galore for "saving India") and expect the world to believe that this compensates for the cold-blooded massacre. It won't do. The only reparation is independence for India, and nothing less. . . .

Stray straws
(*The Vanguard*, November 1920)

. . . The government seized the occasion afforded by the miners' strike to let the hunger-striker Fitzgerald die in Cork prison. Now Lord Mayor MacSwiney has been killed in Brixton Prison after a torture of seventy-four days. The government kept him alive by feeding him whilst unconscious, kept him alive to prolong his tortures, and probably drugged him into the delirium he experienced immediately prior to his death. They thought they could conveniently let him die when people's minds were focused on the strike, and when no labour stoppage of protest could manifest to the world labour's wrath against the calculated brutality of Lloyd George and his devilish government. Perhaps they calculated that now the Irish may come into the open and be slaughtered. At any rate they have planned well their satanic feast on the blood of the Irish race. First Lloyd George at Caernarvon says that his devil's brigade have been justified in taking "reprisals" on the Irish and that England will never lose grip of the Irish ports. Then Greenwood on the opening of Parliament says he will comb Ireland to run to earth the extremists. After that the strike is used as an excuse to cut Ireland completely off from the world — to prevent the inflow of arms and ammunition to the Irish. Everything is ready for the match. The Lord Mayor of Cork is allowed to die when all is ready. Will the Irish strike the match and let Macready wreak his bloody will on a great race? Ireland! Keep cool, hold tight. . . .

Comrades, champion Ireland's cause with trebled energy and thus avenge the martyred Lord Mayor. Never in all our reading of history have we read of a slower and more cruel torture than that practised in Brixton Prison. No cruelty perpetrated by the Belgians on the Congo rubber plantations, no cruelty perpetrated by the Spaniards and other Europeans on the natives of America, no brutality of the slave-snatchers of Central Africa, no torture by the merchant princes of Europe ever excelled in refinement of cruelty this deliberate slaughter of a hero who will rank beside the greatest martyrs of the world. Down with the bloody government that attempts to do such deeds in our name! Down with the system of greedy capitalism that develops blood-mania in its dominant class!

Are we to condone the murder of Irishmen on their own soil that England might retain hold of Irish ports as a prelude to a fiendish fight with American capitalism? Never, comrades, never!

The Irish tragedy
(*The Vanguard*, November 1920)

. . . The work, however, must turn against the hell-born scoundrels now

179

comprising the "British" cabinet, for Lloyd George at Caernarvon gave away the reason for all the trouble in Ireland. Thus spake the oracle:

"And we are to hand over Ireland to be made a base of the submarine fleet. We are to trust to luck in our next war. Was there ever such lunacy proposed by anybody? . . . Hand our ports over to Ireland, the gateway of Great Britain? They might starve us. No!"

There you are now, Christian brethren. Lloyd George and his friends are getting ready for "the next war" with the next rival in the world markets — Uncle Sam, poor chap. Some of Lloyd George's murderers-in-chief (pardon, generals) tell us that in "the next war" towns must be continuously bombed for at least ten days. Lloyd George may have practice over Dublin as a preliminary canter before beginning "reprisals" on the erring Irish race. . . .

We people of Scotland must now realise the shameful depths to which our race has fallen when boys from our homes are being used by the English cold, calculating capitalists through the mad Welsh lawyer to slaughter, under the madman's cunning guise of "reprisals", the Irish people on their own soil to keep the Irish ports in bloodstained English hands.

Has not this been my warning all summer? . . .

Why did I visit Arbroath on Saturday, 11 September, but to protest the hollow mockery of the sex centenary celebration of the Scottish Parliament's declaration of independence to Pope John XXII, whilst Scottish boys dressed in the garb of the English government were then and now daring the Irish to set up a free and independent Irish Parliament elected by the overwhelming vote of the Irish people. . . .

8

American Imperialism

War or socialism! Which?

(*The Worker*, 17 May 1919)

Mr Woodrow Wilson is being applauded in Britain as elsewhere for his League of Nations proposals, but there are those of us who view him and his project with as much loathing and suspicion as we do Mr Lloyd George and his Industrial "Peace" Conference. How should it be otherwise, as long as Wilson and his capitalist masters retain in prison Mooney, Haywood, Debs, Berger, and the hundreds of rank-and-file champions of labour in the United States. We realise that his League of Nations is but a momentary League of Capitalist Governments for the suppression of Bolshevism and Spartacism in Europe and the further robbery and enslavement of the world's wage-earners, and that if this end can be attained the world once more will become a battlefield on which to decide whether America or Britain will dominate the trade and profits of the world. . . .

Britain's vast war debt of close on eight thousand million pounds, involving an annual interest payment of about four hundred millions, is forcing the capitalists to adopt and improve American machinery, taylorism and trustification for the increase of output per worker. It is clearly stated by the London financial top-notchers that through increased output the workers' standards may be raised, and yet permit of vastly swollen profits from which the government may directly take the taxes needed to keep Britain going as a solvent concern. These same London bankers have bought up banks and similar institutions all over the world as well as the industrial banks of Ireland, Scotland and England itself, and have united to establish the forthcoming British Overseas Bank, the object being to help the sale of British-made goods carried on British-made ships. The bankers well know that the greater the volume of goods produced the greater must be the need for imperial and foreign markets; hence their preparations.

Industrial and commercial capitalists have been forming associations to mutually aid one another in marketing their goods abroad and now we learn that the British War Cabinet is in process of overhauling the whole Consular Service. The number of posts held abroad is going to be raised from 200 to 404, and each consular agent is going to be paid such an increase as will enable him to devote his whole time to British interests —

mainly commercial.

The British capitalists know that the same economic urge towards world markets manifests itself in America. Before the war America was economically dependent, i.e. she had to pay interest to foreign investors, largely British. Now America is independent, having bought up to a large extent bonds held by British and Frenchmen out of her war profits, and having lent largely to the Allies. She has seized markets formerly dominated by British and German investors and intends to keep them. She is still making immense profits, part of which at least must be invested in South America, China, or some other part of the world. But these are the very markets Britain has her eyes upon. Hence there must be the keenest rivalry. . . .

The coming war with America
(Pamphlet, Winter 1919)

Some people foolishly believed Lloyd George and his friends when they assured the country that the recent war was one "to end all war", and others as stupidly fancy Woodrow Wilson's League of Nations will avert war.

The marxist contention is that war cannot be avoided if capitalism lasts, and many marxians are of the opinion that the principal antagonists in the next war will be Britain and America; hence the urgent need of helping the Bolsheviks today and Bolshevising the world tomorrow.

We marxists knew the war with Germany was coming, as both Germany and Britain were conducting a life and death struggle to dominate the world and its markets. From the Boer War onwards Germany began to build a fleet, whilst Britain enlarged hers and constructed naval bases on the North Sea; Germany perfected her army whilst Haldane gave us the Territorials; Germany built up the Triple Alliance whilst Britain brought off the Entente with France and the Alliance with Russia; each riddled the other's territory with spies; J. Chamberlain urged a tariff war against Germany, whilst Lloyd George imported German insurance and other expedients to gain Labour support in case of war. . . .

In a speech in Glasgow early in May 1919, Sir Douglas Haig warned Britain not to rely on the League of Nations, but to make "adequate military preparations". In a later speech at St Andrew's University on Wednesday 15 May, he warned the students of the danger of the Chinese and the Indians flooding the world's markets to the exclusion of European-made goods, as a result of the lower standard of living of the yellow men. To avert the danger he urged the raising of the eastern civilisation to the level of that prevailing in Europe.

Then he used an expression that justifies our view of the European War and of all wars under capitalism: "Only thus can the terrible pressure of economic competition be prevented from driving whole continents into war." Here he clearly and undeniably traces war to competition for world markets and thus supports our contention as to the cause and motive of the late war. . . .

As the Germans had as high a civilisation as the British and both fought, we must disagree with Sir Douglas when he thinks that raising eastern civilisation to the level of western will in any way prevent war. We also disagree with him when he anticipates a yellow menace. We calculate that America holds the field. So popular is this view in political "high-class" circles that *John Bull* utters on a poster the pitiful cry: "Is America to Boss the World?"

Some may protest that a war between English-speaking peoples is impossible. Perhaps: but let them recollect that the bloodiest war of last century was the American Civil War, 1861-5, over an economic question — the extended use of black chattel slavery. May not another economic question drive Britain and America to war? We would remind sceptics that from 1910 onwards the oil interests of both countries have been responsible for the Mexican Civil War; Lord Cowdray financing one side, Rockefeller the other.

In the February 1919 issue of an American magazine *The Arbitrator*, Henry L. West urges universal military training and service, because he is convinced that "as long as human passions remain unchanged, as long as lust of power or love of land or greed for commercial expansion exists, so long will there be war". This American holds war an inevitable consequence of the rush for markets and imperialism without the qualification stated by Sir Douglas, and advises America to have "her adequate military preparations". In 1915, the American Professor R.G. Usher, issued his *Pan-Americanism* and in 1917 his *Challenge of the Future*, and in these he urged the immediate policy adopted by Woodrow Wilson when the latter got America into the late war, and the ultimate policy of absorbing all North and South America. These writers but express the prevailing view in capitalist circles in America; hence the importance of their utterances. . . .

Many people may imagine that, since we know the cause of war and since we have just gone through the pains and devastation of war, we should avoid the clash for markets and so escape another war. That is impossible. Britain has incurred a war debt of £8,000,000,000 and must pay every year to bond-holders £400,000,000. This outlay, with that on pensions, army, navy etc., will mount to at least £1,000,000,000 a year.

Financiers and politicians have seen that this can only be got out of increased profits, and that these can only be realised by increased sales on the markets of the world — i.e. increased pressure on the markets, increased competition, increased speed headlong into the next war. Lloyd George showed this to be the capitalist policy in his Commons speech, Monday 18 August 1919; and Austen Chamberlain shortly before him urged the same policy in order to save the government from bankruptcy. . . . Lloyd George in the same speech urged increased exports along with decreased imports to restore the exchange with America. . . . At present for a pound note a moneychanger will give you four dollars instead of four dollars eighty-six cents; in other words, you lose eighty-six cents or 3s 7d out of every pound note. What Lloyd George suggests is perfectly correct, but it involves increased exports, the very evil that plunges us into war.

Again, it is well known that America's foreign trade has trebled during the war period and this year has rapidly risen. The Americans now own over 6,000,000 ship tons instead of 1,000,000 in 1914, whilst her 200 shipyards with their 1,000 slips are now constructing over 4,000,000 tons in place of 140,000 in 1914. Britain's foreign trade is again expanding and she still has over 15,000,000 ship tons; but her yards have only on stock a declared weight of 2,500,000 tons. No wonder the press recently had an "inspired" advertisement headed: "Shipping Supremacy — American Shipyard Competition".

The New York bankers have united forces to finance exhausted Europe. The loans, of course, will take the form of foodstuffs, raw material, and machinery to re-establish economic life. This will give America a grip on European markets and on European people in the event of war with Britain. America is naturally seizing the opportunity, too, to get a grip on other world markets, especially on those of South America and China.

To counterbalance that menace, Britain, by the mandatory power camouflage of the Peace Treaty, is adding a million and a half square miles to her empire, is in process of absorbing and digesting Afghanistan and Persia, and will "protect" huge slices of Siberia if Russia perchance be crushed; whilst to counteract American influence in Europe France has just been granted £10,000,000, and Lloyd George tells us £26,000,000 must be spent on capturing the trade of Roumania, Serbia, and other southeastern countries. (Now also the trade of Finland, Latvia, Estonia, Lithuania, Poland and South Russia.) All this despite the so-called bankruptcy of Britain.

The latest phase of British policy is resumption of trade with the "hated Hun". A press campaign prepared people's minds for this resumed relationship with Germany. Toy-makers and other British manufacturers

184

may whine at the flood of German imports now penetrating into British markets, but if German imports are not tolerated then Germany will take no British manufactures or raw materials. America will get into Germany, and economic contact will lead to military alliance against Britain. This double danger explains the sudden change of British policy towards Germany.

British banks are amalgamating with banks all over the world in the hope of freezing the Yankees out of the markets and they have just started a British Overseas Bank with a nominal capital of £5,000,000 to speed up this process. To meet America Britain knows that the fundamental is "increased output" by every worker, and increased exports.

A London moneylending firm, Eldridge & Morris, in a booklet to capitalists, puts the matter concisely and logically: "It is necessary that we recover our wealth by ever increasing our individual efficiency, our productive power and collective national output — the production of merchandise for export, far beyond what we have hitherto accomplished, as the great, not to say the only way of discharging in adequate amounts our tremendous national responsibilities" (paying back the war debt).

"Our national productiveness must dominate the world's markets" (the Hun policy!), "our Empire trade must be protectively conserved for ourselves" (imperial Sinn Feinism!).

To keep our own markets and dominate the world's markets is a challenge to America, Usher's "Challenge of the Future" from a British standpoint. Thus we see the conditions of today are evolving a trade rivalry of monstrous dimensions urging mankind onward pitilessly and helplessly to the next war. . . .

Both combatants know that the country that can sell cheapest and yet make immense profits is the one that is able to create its wealth in the least time. The less the time to do a job, the less the cost. To produce in less time the worker is now being urged to work harder and harder, to increase his production. The gospel is *work hard! Harder! Hardest!*

That explains the government's press campaign against the workers who are being accused of lazing or "ca'ing canny". It is not surprising, either, to find that the trade union leaders who rushed their members into the army are now intent on hounding them on to produce more goods to save the empire. . . .

[*Here follows a section illustrating methods of "increasing production", under paragraph headings: The Profit-Sharing Traps, Welfare Work, Scientific Management, Improved Machinery, Scientific Research and Education, Trustification. This repeats essentially parts of "The War after the War" —* N.M.]

The British government was from the start of the war apprehensive of the advantages the United States would derive from its freedom from direct participation in the war, and hence the sneer at America's plea of being "too proud to fight". It kept pegging away at America, however, until by its clever collapse camouflage in the spring of 1918 it brought not only the Bolshevik revolution into ill repute, but also the USA into the maelstrom of murder; not, however, before America became the supreme economic power in the world.

The economic developments and the mind-evolution in the States are well known to the British government through its intelligence department, and so we find it accordingly moulding its own policy, as well as urging the capitalists along the lines just indicated.

The government is setting aside millions for scientific research, is doing its utmost to force the capitalists to bring their plant up-to-date, and has powerfully appealed to them through Lloyd George to adopt profit-sharing and other methods of baiting the workers to increase production. It is also backing up the trustification policy by its coal proposal of unifying all coal companies in each coalfield, by keeping united the railway system and docks, by forcing to a head the unification of shipping and ship-building, and by projecting an electrical power-station scheme involving the electrification of all industries in the country; cheap power and cheap transit to enable cheaply-made goods to be thrown in ever-increasing masses on the markets of the world.

One obstacle to the cheapest possible production of goods is the vast number of John Bradburys issued by the government. These paper notes must be largely withdrawn and burned, and as they disappear prices will inevitably fall until they rest on a gold basis again. But before such a step be taken the government must make sure that wages can be reduced as prices fall, so that the purchasing power of labour in Lloyd George's "future" will be no higher or only very slightly higher than it was in 1914.

The government knew it must break or tame labour again. So it made its preparations this year, and chose what it thought the proper time and union to make the offensive against. When Parliament was grouse-shooting in the Highlands a fortnight after the miners' triumph at the Glasgow Trades Union Congress, the government forced a fight on the National Union of Railwaymen, expecting that the locomotivemen would scab after receiving their bribe and that J.H. Thomas would collapse, or that the use of soldiers and sailors, the Middle-Class Union, and the calling into being of the National (Black) Guards would frighten the railwaymen into surrender. Had the railwaymen not been solid and had not all workers shown determination to fight with them (soldiers and sailors, too, if Dame Rumour speaks true) the government would have won and then would have had a free hand to reduce prices when convenient in the trade offensive against America.

We may take it as an opinion that the government will feverishly mature other plans to accomplish its end. Prices must come down by reducing paper currency, but labour must be tamed beforehand. It behoves the working class to prepare as well by forming a Central Committee of Labour for organising, educating, agitating and fighting purposes; since our object must be not the capture of foreign markets but the capture of Britain itself.

The NUR strike for the first time in British history brought a section of the workers right up against the capitalist class as a whole through its coalition cabinet; and this shows that the main government functions are now economic, and that the primary motive of the government's action was the breaking of labour's power. . . .

The big banks of New York have been co-operating to lend to European nations supplies of food and other necessaries of life, and to this end have been working along with the Meat Trust, or the "Big Five" — Armour & Co., Morris & Co., Wilson & Co. and the Cudaby Packing Co. It is obvious that Germany and other countries economically dependent on America will back up America in the event of war with Britain. America is using the differences between France and Britain over the peace terms and Syria to win France to her side. . . . Americans are buying up works in Europe as well and these will be centres for the radiation of American influence.

Britain's loans to European countries, especially those on the Baltic, are dictated by a similar policy. . . . If Britain can crush the Bolsheviks and establish an autocratic government in Russia under the thumb of Britain then she will have access to raw materials without needing to cross the Atlantic at all. Hence Britain's present policy in Turkey, Persia, and Afghanistan, and her support to Denikin and Kolchak. She is encouraging Japan in North China against America; and in East Siberia for the same reason.

America is exploiting Ireland's distress and this explains the mighty reception given to De Valera, backed up by loans in due course. In case of war Ireland would be a fine naval and air base against Britain. Britain could be kept out of the Atlantic, and if cut off from the continent by a ring of opposing powers her course as the Mistress of the Sea would be run. This explains Britain's madness in suppressing the Dail Eireann (the Sinn Fein Parliament) and Irish papers, and the imprisonment of Irish patriots. America is exploiting this all right. She is showing herself as the "righteous democracy" whilst at the same time she is absorbing her own little Ireland — Mexico, to wit.

To back up the British Overseas Bank and the British Empire Producers' Organisation, which is an adjunct to the Federation of British Industries devoted mainly to meet foreign competition in any area and in any industry, and similar organisations of a purely commercial character, the government has this year brought into being the British Overseas Trade Department under the joint control of the Board of Trade and the Foreign Office. The Foreign Office is supposed to deal with political matters and to determine when war must take place. Its connection with the Overseas Trade Department is therefore very significant especially when we couple with it the appointment of Grey as ambassador to America, the very Grey who was at the Foreign Office and who rushed Britain into war with Germany.

The consular system is being re-cast. Now Britain will have over four hundred full-time consuls over the world instead of about two hundred on half-time as before. That means more trade and political spies everywhere — the prelude, surely, to another war.

Of course, America's touts and agents are also swarming the world with the camera and cinema journalists to boot.

America is witholding her signature to the Peace Treaty as long as possible to prevent British capitalists settling down to peace-time production, and at the same time the Meat Trust is attempting to corner foodstuffs everywhere in the world, to limit supplies to Britain at enhanced prices, to prevent British aggression economically and militarily. At the same time America is proceeding with an Army Bill that will enable her to keep an army of over half a million, and a reserve of a million and a quarter, while she shall be empowered to give three months' training to every lad who reaches the age of nineteen. That is the first step towards conscription when necessity arises. Is this the reason why Britain still clings affectionately to her conscript army? I think so. Britain means to leave nothing to chance in military or any other preparations unless British citizens and soldiers vigorously raise opposition. This opposition partly explains present demobilisation. . . .

After the armistice America urged Britain to reduce her navy as a step towards freeing the seas and towards a real League of Nations. Winston Churchill in *The Sunday Post* clearly replied that Britain would do no such thing. Americans then began to boast that in three years' time the United States would have as large a navy as Britain. This was followed by a vote for their navy of about £50,000,000 (in dollars, of course). Britain's budget reply was a similar sum for the British navy for the year

1919-20. This equality of the sums voted for navy purposes is surely a startling indication of the conscious preparations of both sides. The press has admitted that the Admiralty early this year made a thorough examination of the Hebrides to find out all port and store facilities for the navy. The buying up of Lewis and Harris and other Western Islands by Lord Leverhulme for fishing and fish oil purposes suggests that he is working with the Admiralty in organising industries that will not only breed sailors and provide food, but lay that basis of economic organisation without which the navy would be comparatively helpless. We are also just beginning to learn that the British and Australian governments jointly intend to spend at least £68,000,000 on the laying down of a Pacific fleet with Australia as its base of operations. This new development on the Atlantic and on the Pacific is leaving nothing to chance. As merchant vessels play a vital part in naval warfare as well as in commercial rivalry we can more fully comprehend the keener and keener interest that is being taken in the development of American shipbuilding.

The transatlantic flying last summer is but a complement to the other preparations and explains the tremendous effort made by the government to get the world to realise Britain's superiority in this field. The fact that both countries were making trial flights at the same time, that the British government rewarded her successful aeronauts, whilst America placed her fleet at the disposal of her fliers, clearly indicates the true purpose of the great flying feats. It is not surprising to find Britain following this up by sending the Prince of Wales to Canada, whilst De Valera pays a visit to the United States and receives a more than royal reception. . . .

The recent war has shown the horrors and the futility of war, victors and victims suffering alike. It will be an unpardonable crime if organised labour permits human society to go through the same a few years hence for lack of warning on the part of socialists or for lack of heed to that warning.

It is perfectly clear to us socialists at any rate that capitalism breeds antagonism leading to war and that the only way to avoid war and waste is to end capitalism.

The characteristic feature of capitalism is the ownership of land and the means of production by a small class. The motive of ownership is not the material comfort and well-being of the whole community, but getting rich quick at the expense of the non-owners. It is this economic cleavage which has brought into being the class war with class organisations for its prosecution. The working class has been forced to bring into being the co-operative movement, the trade-union movement, and the socialist and labour movement for defensive and offensive purposes.

189

The class antagonism fortunately affords the way of escape from capitalism and war by prosecution of the class war until labour gets into supreme position in every country, as in Russia. However labour may attain power, it must do as the Bolsheviks are doing; it must get full possession of land and all means of production in order to use these co-operatively by the whole community in the creation of wealth for the advantage of all. That this would have been done peacefully and fairly in Russia but for the venomous intervention of British capitalism, aided more or less by world capitalism, must now be admitted by every fair-minded man. It can be done everywhere without bloodshed unless the propertied class in devilish glee prefer the course of social destruction to that of reconstruction along the lines of socialism.

It is the duty of workers to get into one big union along the lines of industry right away and not wait for the snail-like movements of the Parliamentary Committee of the Trades Union Congress; and to fall into line with the miners, who have conducted a great and growing campaign, not only to benefit miners, but the rest of the workers as well. The programme must be widened so as to make the objective not mere nationalisation of trustified industries, but the complete socialisation of production and distribution. Nationalisation implies the payment of rent and interest; socialisation means the payment of neither rent nor interest.

It is most encouraging to note that the great Canadian strike, induced by the Scottish forty-hour strike, has stimulated American labour to burst into what looks like a general rank-and-file strike in defiance of the government, which has tied up the workers' funds and terrorised the union leaders. The programme of the United Mineworkers and the Railway Brotherhood is similar to that of their comrades in Britain, so that we may assume with confidence an American labour bid for political supremacy of labour if Britain gives the lead again. And there is no doubt Japanese workers will fall into line in due course.

To avoid another world war, then, labour in America and Britain must move swiftly towards full political control as the first step on the road to the complete reconstruction of the forces and agencies of production on a communal basis. . . .

The cutting out of market rivalry will lead to transatlantic co-operation, abundance and leisure for all. The rest of the world must fall into line at once, and so prepare for the time when mankind shall as a unit rule the world as a whole and extract from it copious supplies to furnish the every need of every citizen.

Choose, reader, world Bolshevism now or a few years hence another world war.

America's shame

(*The Worker*, 25 October 1919)

I read in *The Voice of Labour* (USA) that an attempt is being made to get a day's strike in America on 8 October to protest against the continued imprisonment of more than 2,000 workers, who are in jail because of their activity in the labour movement. *The Voice* adds that many have died of illness, many have committed suicide because of intolerable tortures, and others again have gone insane. From these bald statements it is apparent that the prison methods of America differ in no way from those of Britain; and that it is the business of British labour to press for the release of our American comrades as labour pressed for the release of British COs — it is to be hoped that the workers' committees will take the first step in this direction.

The worst sufferers in America have been the members of the Industrial Workers of the World, and not unnaturally huge sums are required to maintain the dependants of the imprisoned, the maimed, and the dead. I have just received from William D. Haywood an appeal form for funds to help the release of all "class-war prisoners"; and in view of the developing antagonism between the British and American capitalists for the domination of the world's markets . . . I make no apology for inviting class-conscious workers to show their solidarity by forwarding to me at their earliest sums collected inside workshops and in labour circles.

Thousands have been arrested without warrant and held without charge. The report of the Commission on Industrial Relations admits that 900 men and women were thrown into prison without warrant or trial during the textile workers' strike at Lawrence, Mass., and that 1,900 men and women were treated similarly during the silk workers' strike at Paterson, New Jersey. . . .

Amongst hosts of IWW men tarred and feathered by gangs of prominent citizens, bankers, businessmen and hired thugs, are specifically mentioned Frank H. Meyers, D.S. Dietz, and J.L. Metzen. The "constitution" must have changed since Washington's time, for the "Stars and Stripes" must have given way to "tar and feathers". . . .

Amongst men left with scars due to whipping are mentioned Joe Marks, James Rowan and John Avila, the last being hanged almost till death before being beaten and jailed for three months. . . .

IWW men have been denied the privilege of defence through the postal authorities stopping appeal circulars to working-class organisations. . . .

An IWW member under arrest at Birmingham, Alabama, was taken from prison and exhibited at a fair, twenty-five cents being charged to view him.

The fire department at Fresno, California, turned a jet of water on IWW prisoners in that town, one comrade having his eye thus torn out. . . . Property has made fiends of men. But moralising is a waste of time.

9

Capitalist crisis, inflation and unemployment

Will capitalism collapse?
(*The Call*, 28 August 1919)

Many comrades seem to have been carried away by Kahn's *Collapse of Capitalism* and by the alarmist "leaders" and speeches of British journalists and politicians, and believe that under its vast accumulation of credit and paper money and bills capitalism is rapidly staggering to its doom. My impression is that capitalism is more vital today in Britain, Japan, and America than ever it was and is preparing for expansions such as have never been made before, that if capitalism is to be "sent west" it will only be the result of the delivery of the greatest knock-out blow ever given, and that this blow must be given by a united, revolutionary working class.

My contention is that capitalism is not based on credit or paper but on production of commodities for surplus value in the form of interest, profits, and rent. The conditions are sources of raw material, machinery, and organisation, skilled labour, and markets. The war has opened up new sources of raw material and coming railways will vastly extend these sources, and the war waste affords vast demands for goods and the seizure and opening-up of the world by the League of Thieves means markets vastly exceeding past experiences.

It is admitted that the big companies of Britain have extended their plant during the war and installed the latest and best machinery laid down in scientific manner. Much of the war expenditure has involved the vast extension of this "fixed capital" inside Britain. The general skill and aptitude of the working class has been rapidly improved by war adaptation, and the labour-power resources have been swollen by a mighty new army of women workers. In Britain alone we have therefore today, now that war production has been transformed into peace production, the conditions of a production perhaps double that of pre-war times and thus the possibilities of a surplus value realisation treble that prevailing in 1914.

What applies to Britain applies more or less to the United States and Japan. If more gold be needed to back up the paper media of commodity circulation, that can easily and plentifully be obtained from industrial sources and the gold mines; or silver can be used as unlimited legal tender

193

as in Britain in the eighteenth century.

The secretly planned campaign of the London bankers and the government finding expression in the alarmist whine about credit collapse, and most recently given voice to in the Commons by Austen Chamberlain and Lloyd George, is part of the settled policy of inducing the working class to increase production by toiling harder than ever. Compulsion through scientific management and inducement through bonus, profit-sharing, and similar payment-by-result methods will supplement the alarmist appeals to the workers to save the empire by reducing the time and cost of production. (By the way, everyone now adheres to the labour-time theory of value except J. Ramsay MacDonald, some capitalist economists, and the mass of the trade-union leaders and labour men such as William Adamson, MP, PC.)

The agitation to increase production has, as the usual bait for Mr Henry Dubb, an increased standard of life, such as is enjoyed by some workers in America — the intention cleverly being to divert the workers away from revolution. The accomplished increase of output will mean cheaper goods for the market and success against American competition throughout the world.

If Britain can extend her world market, her increased sales will realise increased profits. On those profits depends the safety of British capitalism, for out of them the propertied class will be able to make a fatter living through dividends and interest directly, and indirectly through £400,000,000 interest on the £8,000,000,000 national debt.

From this swollen income the propertied class will be enabled to put by vaster sums than ever before to invest abroad, in governments to buy their allegiance in the event of another war, and in industries everywhere to extend the direct robbery of the world's workers.

Britain's every economic preparation at present — improved machinery, industrial research, trustification, and standardisation, scientific management and applied industrial psychology and physiology, bank amalgamation and world extension, state unification of mines, railways, electricity production and supply, slightly and economically reduced hours, capitalist industrial unionism, the Overseas Trade Department etc. — is a vital preparation for the coming trade war with America. Such is not the sign of death, but renewed life. As a matter of fact the capitalists are leaving the trade unions and the socialist leaders "light years" behind and are ruthlessly sweeping the co-operative movement aside despite its numerical expansion. Never were the capitalists more lively, more aggressive.

Politically since the armistice they have played their cards desperately well. Army and navy officers together with Bolshevism and the "ticket" won an amazing election result. This year's game has been to keep peace, i.e. prevent a revolution at home, whilst stemming the revolution in Europe, and winning the tricks at the Paris Peace Monte Carlo.

Our hopes lay first in the Miners' Federation leading the workers to battle on an immediate programme that would have ultimately involved capital and labour in a revolutionary conflict. By the introduction of the Coal Commission and the Industrial Peace Conference with its committee, Lloyd George prevented a general strike until Britain won the stakes at Paris. The Sankey worm on the coalition hook baited the miners, who realise they are now hooked by Lloyd George's utterance in the Commons on Monday 18 August against nationalisation of the mines and in favour of trustification. Horne's hooks lie behind the Minimum Rates of Wages Commission Bill, and the Hours of Employment (No. 2) Bill, the outcome of the Industrial Conference. Before his pronouncement last Monday week, Lloyd George saw that the miners were denounced for reducing the output and tried to turn the workers generally against them by the brazen-faced 6s per ton impost on coal. He has converted the miners' attack into a defence with a host of official and unofficial traitors in the ranks of the miners weakening even the defence. That is no evidence of capitalist collapse, is it?

Our hopes were then transferred to the Triple Alliance. The Triplets determined on a ballot for a strike to force the withdrawal of British troops from Russia. The Wondrous Winnie made a most audacious speech in the Commons assuring the "Labour leaders" Britain was withdrawing her troops from Russia (the wounded, of course), this despite his speech on 17 July in the Connaught Rooms, London, appealing to the League of Nations to make "one united concerted effort" against Russia. The "Triplet" leaders met and thanked Winnie for the excuse he afforded them for suspending the ballot. If Russia is crushed these "leaders" will meet solemnly and declare a ballot is unnecessary. . . .

Meantime, the press is working up the opinion behind the "Labour politicians", such as Henderson and Clynes, that "direct action" may thus be hung up this year. The capitalist class that can manoeuvre "Labour" backwards and forwards in this way shows no signs of having lost its kick.

Then once the "Peace Picnic" at Paris is over Britain sets about adding Persia and Afghanistan to the empire whilst excluding France from Syria, assuring the world all the time that these countries are clamouring for Britain's protective help. Britain also led the way to "democracy" in Hungary by installing that "direct actionist", Archduke Joseph (the recent autocratic enemy), and now has settled down seriously to bomb and batter Bolshevism in Russia to blazes. If world capitalism is to be saved the

195

revolutionary workers of Europe must be starved and killed (women and children do not matter). The fight really begins as Parliament goes on holiday for two months, and to prevent sporadic outbursts in Britain the government has brought back a huge slice of the Rhine army of occupation, leaving France to do the dirty work there. The Highland Division is camped near Mansfield, Notts, ready for the miners. Ireland, meantime, is being incited to revolt so that John the Bully may give her a long sleep.

The lesson we ought to draw is that we must agitate, educate, and organise more boldly and vigorously than before. Let us remember that although the trade union and political leaders of the working class have been afraid to be as audacious as the leaders of capitalism, have failed as ever at the critical moment and will do so again, nevertheless the mass of people are coming more and more towards our position.

Therein lies salvation. The safety of society rests not in the hands of a few (leaders or heroes), but in those of masses of mankind, conscious or unconscious. Although the events do not seem propitious, a growing mass of workers is becoming conscious of the need for a new society and is drifting our way all right. The greater the drift the more the props of capitalism will vanish, and hence the pending collapse of capitalism. Quantitative change on our side will become qualitative, in other words, newer and clearer views with higher and prouder spirits will come with numbers, and the moment will come (perhaps even this year) when the workers will challenge capitalism to the last fight and win through to the world society of a united human race, producing each for all and all for each.

On with the fight, comrades!

Capitalists everywhere accept marxism
(*The Worker*, 1 November 1919)
Now that thousands of working-class students are settling down to study marxian economics, or rather economic laws from the standpoint taken up by Marx, I may be pardoned obtruding this subject on your readers. However, it is an historic dictum that those only succeed who are impelled by a consuming conviction, a conviction that is based on a true interpretation of historic facts and historic tendencies.

The working class is developing into the conviction that it is robbed of by far the major portion of the wealth it plays the essential part in producing and distributing. That conviction takes deep root on a deep, broad, and solid foundation once the worker settles down to study economics as expounded by Marx, the kernel of whose teaching is the labour-time theory of value. That theory accepted, we can apply it to what the worker sells on the market — his labour-power — and find out that the worker is not and never will be paid "by results"; that is to say, by the total wealth or value-equivalent of what he produces. His wage is paid on "the cost of living", and his cost of living is far less than the wealth or the value he contributes to the world's stock.

Marx, then, and the working-class real conviction stand or fall with the labour-time theory of value. Is it true to fact, is it true to life? Young university prigs — and the majority are prigs — will in superior style assure you Marx was killed a generation ago; the professors said so!

Certainly, the professors have tried to kill him by every cunning sophisticated device at their command. They had to do it; they were paid to; and they are the types who are eager to come down to teach economics to the working class. The discussion with these gents was so useless and wasteful of time that many socialists, including the leaders of the ILP and BSPers such as Fairchild, pretty well avoided insistence on the study of economics, and depended mainly on capitalist-supplied statistics, or sentiments based on the wrongs and injuries suffered by the mass of the people.

But although the professors are satisfied they buried Marx long ago, some of us all along have maintained that Marx buried the professors. During the war the big capitalists realised that the professors were wrong and Marx was right, and so we find that their whole attitude is now marxian, and that all their experiments are wrought out from the marxian basis.

The Yankees, having no fear of marxism in America, long ago adopted the marxian point of view, and hence it is by no accident that taylorism or scientific management sprang up across the Atlantic. The war compelled Britain to accept and adapt the first fruits of taylorism with the necessary result of a revolution in economic outlook and thinking.

The new view was typically expressed by that up-to-date capitalist, Lord Weir, who in an address to the businessmen of Glasgow insisted that the main factor in production is man-time. Man-time is just the marxian expression labour-time, so therefore labour-time is the main factor in production — the mighty fact refuted for a generation by university dons, but now preached by Scotland's engineering capitalist top-notcher! Not only preached but practised as well, for at Weir's, Cathcart, in September *The Weir Bulletin* was issued for the first time to the workers to explain the function of the new planning department. This function will be "the gradual revision of all shop processes and methods to ensure genuinely efficient methods of production". "The (shop) stewards felt that better output would be obtained if the employees fully grasped the fact that the directors desired the men to make high earnings, and that high earnings

197

would not result in any breaking of allowances." New schemes of increased output will go from the planning department to tool drawing offices, then to the toolroom, and ultimately to the demonstration section to test the tools and jigs and to fix a satisfactory time allowance or piecework rate.

In settling the time in the demonstration department, there shall be present, if desired, a representative of the planning department, rate fixing department, an operative and his appropriate shop steward. The time analyses will be abstracted in the following divisions: actual machinery time; actual manipulative time; tool allowance, 5 per cent of machinery time, fatigue allowance, 20 per cent of manipulative time; contingency time allowance, 40 per cent of total machinery time plus manipulative time; allowance for $33\frac{1}{3}$ per cent bonus.

This practical application of the labour-time theory of value knocks the learned nonsense of the professors into smithereens — and the WEA too.

Every engineer and every student of economics ought occasionally at least to read *Engineering Industrial Management*, the new name for *Cassier's Magazine*. Every issue teems with proof that up-to-date capitalists accept and apply the man-time theory. The issue of 16 October 1919 is especially fruitful. In an article entitled "Eliminating the Stopwatch from Industry", we learn that the greatest part of industrial inefficiency is due to shortcomings of management. (That knocks on the head Mallock, who insisted that capitalists had special directive ability, entitling them to call part of their earnings rent of ability.) Better than the stopwatch is proper organisation, reliable records, production properly controlled and good working conditions.

The importance of the labour hour as the unit in measuring value is brought out more sharply than ever I have heard of or read before, and two economic terms are used as a necessary evolution of applied marxism — equivalency and equivalent.

Equivalency is "determining a fair hour's work for different operations in industry that men and equipment can turn out without injury to health or well-being or detriment to the equipment":

"This is an economic fundamental, for if we can secure increased hourly production we need not concern ourselves so much about the matter of wages or the hours of labour. It is altogether a matter of securing production by utilising every facility that can be invented and every method that can be devised towards getting out a maximum or quantity of production. The greater the hourly production the less the cost. The less the cost the greater the demand, and the greater the demand the more business there will be. The more business there is the more demand there will be for labour."

Settling the equivalent — the output per hour in a particular case — must be a matter of "give and take" between the employer and the workers involved: "In determining hourly equivalents the idea is to arrange for an average performance by an average man over an average period of time". That is almost precisely what Lord Weir intends to do in his demonstration department. This reiteration of the word "average" reminds us of what Marx says on page 6 of *Capital*: "The labour-time socially necessary is that required to produce an article under the normal conditions of production, and with the average degree of skill and intensity prevalent at the time." The definition of the "equivalent" is obviously a deduction from Marx's definition of the "labour-time socially necessary".

"The use to which these hourly equivalents are put is in planning and running and routing work through the plant so that in despatching shop operations, like despatching trains, we may know the length of time between points and arrange accordingly". A workshop time diary or schedule is quite the thing as scientific management.

Let every shop stewards' committee buy this magazine and use it to teach the rank and file. I think in every workshop there ought to be a "breather" during every spell of work when one or other of the shop stewards ought to give a little address of ten minutes on some phase of "workshop economics". This ought to be part of the technical training of every workman, and as ideas and methods are always evolving, every man ought every day to be an apprentice, or rather a student. The clerking department ought to provide a typed summary of every address. To accomplish this efficiently the scope of the Scottish Labour College will have to be extended, so that the leaders in the workshop obtain an appropriate grounding in the broader and deeper issues involved in social evolution and revolution, to adequately fit them to guide their comrades along the most accurate lines. This is necessary to balance the contents of the magazines issued by the employers.

To revert again to *Cassier's*. We are told that Dr Vernon in his report issued by the Industrial Fatigue Research Board concludes that after several experiments the hourly output during a six-hour shift is 10 per cent greater than during an eight-hour shift. If the equivalent is of more importance than hours or wages to the capitalists, it looks as if it were time for the workers to make a bid for a six-hour day.

Frank Graham in an article, "A Means of Harmonising Capital and Labour", states that he learns from Lord Leverhulme, the pioneer of welfare work at Port Sunlight, amongst other things, that the object of profit-sharing must be increased efficiency of the undertaking, implying an in-

199

crease in the equivalent, a goal more vital to the capitalist than increased wages to the worker; and that in any profit-sharing scheme the control must remain with those who find the cash capital. Capitalist tyranny, forsooth!

Major E.A. Pells in an article, "The Basis of Comparison for all kinds of Work", shows the importance of the equivalent in comparing the value of commodities by admitting that "the usual basis to consider the labour method upon, is that of the output per worker hour". That is, Lord Weir's man-time converted into man-hour and Marx's labour-hour.

An article urges the need for a National Institute of Psychology and Physiology applied to industry and commerce. The object is, of course, to so care for the body and mind of the worker under scientific conditions that the highest equivalent possible may be attained.

With the marvellous growth of trusts and the brilliant detail work evolving inside the best plant only an arrant knave would deny the truth of Marx's teachings in economics, and would stand in the way of the mighty work of the Scottish Labour College.

Away with the idle rich
(*The Call*, 22 January 1920)
Not long ago in *The Worker* I wrote an article showing that the leading capitalists, such as Lord Weir of Cathcart, accept Marx's labour-time theory of value. Every issue of *Engineering and Industrial Management* proves this. Addison accepted Murphy's pamphlet on "The Workshop Committee", and the government is consequently trying to get workshop committees established. It accepts the guild socialism notion, and foists on labour the spurious Whitleyism. Recently *The Call* quoted Dorman of the Dorman Long Group of the Teesside as urging virtually "The One Big Union" on the workers.

Why all this? Obviously to stave off real Bolshevism. The marxian theory of value applied under capitalism increases production and increases exploitation. Workshop committees, Whitley councils, and industrial unionism under the guidance of the capitalists and the capitalist coalition government means greater harmony, greater peace, inside the workshop and inside the whole sphere of production.

Because the capitalists accept our theory and the type of structure we as marxians may suggest, that is clearly no reason why we should scrap our theory and mechanism for the control of production after we displace our enemy from power. They played the same game in the old days when they stole our socialist thunder and our socialist programmes for election purposes.

The latest phase we find well put in the leading articles in *The Statist*. The tone is obviously false, and is consistent with that running throughout the business articles in the rest of the paper. It seems clear to me that the government realises that the very rapid "Labour drift" will soon bring Labour into political power. The policy will therefore be to guide it, to channel it, nay to earth it if possible, and so stave off the communist commonwealth. *The Statist* is giving the cue to a section of the business world, and it seems that Lord Fisher has caught on. Here are extracts from *The* for the present we have the worst government upon earth, and nobody knows, or at least nobody seems to know, what ought to be done to give us a good government, or even to avoid serious international danger. We *Statist* of 20 December 1919. In "The Money Market" leader it says: "But must sweep away the idle rich. That is clear."

In another entitled "The Trades Unionist", it says:

"No other class is strong enough to uproot the rule of the idle rich and the rule of the idle rich is the main enemy of the prosperity of the kingdom and the empire at the present time. . . . We would, then, earnestly appeal to the trade unions. . . . They are numerous enough and energetic enough to acquire an almost irresistible power in the state. Are they willing to establish a really bona-fide democratic government? And, as a beginning, are they ready to dismiss the idle rich, once and for all, to the idleness for which alone they are fitted, or rather to prepare the way for taking from them properties that never ought to have been given to them, and compelling them to work like other people? Is there any reason under heaven why a particular caste should be endorsed with the ownership of land, so that they and their eldest sons and their daughters may live in idleness and pretend to govern when they have no absolute knowledge either of government or of anything else?"

This sort of talk is being kept up week after week. It reminds us of Lloyd George's Limehouse speech. We know that he and Churchill are poles assunder in policy inside the cabinet in their mutual endeavour to keep capitalism on top for a time longer. We also know that Lord Fisher "loves" Churchill over the Dardanelles mess. When we see Lord Fisher writing to *The Times* urging the "idle rich" to work to increase production we naturally conclude that he is lining up with Lloyd George and Lloyd George's tools in *The Statist*.

On Monday 5 January last, I visited an office at 163 West George Street, Glasgow, entitled "Political Information Office", on a little investigation, and there had a talk with a Lieutenant-Colonel Hutchison regarding an advertisement for an organising secretary. His talk to me was confirmed by another comrade. His suggestion to my comrade was that he should help to form a new political party under Lloyd George. The organisation must break official connection with other political parties. They must oppose the class war and be against the views of Karl Marx.

If this be true (and Lloyd George's photo was over the fireplace in his sanctum) then we may expect Lloyd George in intrigue to get a grip over the most influential leaders of the Labour Party, have a dramatic quarrel with Churchill over Russia or some other world issue, break away, join and lead the Labour Party. Lloyd George's sham Russian policy, expressed through O'Grady, and Churchill's statement that Labour is unfit to govern, fit in with this conception.

The by-elections show that Liberalism is dead, and that Labour would win at a general election. Whether this conjecture be true or not, it is our business to be alive to the situation, and to do all we can to forestall such a contingency.

Let us therefore push forward with classes and colleges on marxian lines, with one political and industrial policy, and with one more detailed programme for the guidance of our class in the onslaught on the capitalist class.

"Burn Bradbury and down with prices"
(*The Call*, 27 November 1919)

The Board of Trade *Labour Gazette* has just informed us that retail prices for October were 131 per cent higher than in July 1914, a rise of 9 per cent since September. This rapid rise is likely to be continued despite government rumours that prices will fall after the New Year. In fact, we may take it that this hint is but to disarm labour so as to allow further price increases right on till Spring's return.

To this conclusion we are entitled to come when we realise that the net result of the heralded Profiteering Act has been a rapid rise in prices, whilst honest people were led to conclude that the Act would limit prices if not reduce them.

Further, we are entitled to advise the working class not to believe the government nor the capitalist class. The only way to win anything from labour's enemy is to fight for it.

Labour in September rallied to the railwaymen in the fight to keep up the money wage, and won.

Now labour must fight to reduce prices, and win.

Prices today are usually compared with those prevailing in July 1914; but to get a proper view of the real income, not the paper income, of the working class we must go back to the retail prices of the foodstuffs con-

202

sumed by the workers in 1896.

The Board of Trade has taken the retail prices of twenty-three of the principal articles of food in London since 1895. If the average price of these for 1900 be represented by the index number 100, then the number was 92 for 1896, the year we have selected as the starting point. In July 1914, the number was 116, and in October 1919, it was approximately 268.

This means that the housewife today has to spend 268 pence to buy 116 penceworth in July 1914, 100 penceworth in 1900, and 92 penceworth in 1896.

In other words, it means that she had to pay £3 today to get the same quantity of food as £1 would purchase in 1896. We must not talk of quality!

Were we to include, coal, clothing, and other articles needed to keep a family going the difference would be even greater. The Board of Trade provides us with no retail price record to cover these items, but provides us with the wholesale prices of forty-seven articles. The food section rises from 100 in 1900 to 262 in 1918, whereas for all the articles the rise is from 100 to 270. The general index number for 1896 was 88.

If the retail prices of the same articles rose at the same rate, then the housewife would have to spend 282 pence today for 92 pence in 1896; or £3 1s 4d instead of £1. . . .

Taking rates, wage-taxes, and rent into consideration as well as other household outlays, we can safely conclude that the cost of living is fully thrice as high as it was in 1896.

No one will be bold enough to assert that wages generally have trebled within the same period. On the average wages of the workers within that period have just about doubled. It follows, then, that the living of labour has fallen in the last twenty-four years despite two wars for "freedom" — the Boer war and the "Great" war.

The only course open to labour is the absolute destruction of capitalism, as is being worked out in Russia. The way to victory must be through prosecution of the class struggle; and in connection with this struggle labour must see that the living of the workers is raised either by raising wages or lowering prices, or both.

The fight for higher wages is a sectional one even inside the ranks of the five million organised wage-earners. The unorganised get little or no benefit and can therefore be pitted against the organised.

On the other hand, a fight for lower prices involves all organised workers at the same time, and favourably affects the unorganised with the consequent possibility of bringing them within the ranks of the organised. From a class point of view, then, the fight for lower prices is the better course, especially as many workers have had wages stabilised till September 1920.

Furthermore, the way to decreased prices gives less opportunity to "the increased production" stunt than the claim for higher wages.

Since the war the government has brought into being about £340 millions of paper money for ordinary circulation, mainly in the form of John Bradburys. Before the war the gold and the bank notes needed to circulate wealth amounted perhaps to no more than £150 millions. This increase in paper money above the £150 millions is the principal cause of the high prices. The same took place during the Napoleonic wars — a flood of paper money and high prices.

When gold payment was resumed in 1819 prices began to fall. Labour's cry then ought to be: "Burn Bradbury"; not the man, but his effigy composed of Treasury notes.

If these notes were burned and gold payments resumed, supported as before by the usual bank notes, prices would at once fall to half their present level. Therefore, let the Labour campaign have as its slogan, "Burn Bradbury".

If prices come down wages cannot be broken except at the risk of revolution.

Lord Milner expressed this fear in the Lords the other day, and hence favoured the keeping up of prices.

"Burn Bradbury and down with prices!" must be our reply to the Milners.

The unemployed

(*The Vanguard*, November 1920)

The report of the trial of a Finn who is alleged to be a courier between Lenin and revolutionaries in this country has brought to light a letter supposed to be written by Sylvia Pankhurst. She is supposed to tell Lenin that she got lads to create disturbances amongst the unemployed whilst Lansbury and the other London mayors were discussing matters at 10 Downing Street.

If she wrote it, then Sylvia acted as a police provocateur, consciously or unconsciously. At any rate whether she is guilty or not, the work was that of the police to head back any dangerous outburst when unemployment grows worse as the year proceeds.

We find the same in Glasgow. I start the unemployed demonstrations. All goes well till the Monday the London crowd get a smashing. On that date men, discharged from the Albion Motor Works and Beardmore's M shop at Parkhead Forge on the Saturday, meet at the Glasgow Green

Monument, and talk about seizing works as some of the unemployed did at Coventry. The Clyde Workers' Committee fasten on, and J.R. Campbell boasts at 31 N. Frederick Street that he will capture the committee established at the first demonstration convened by me.

We had at our first meeting appointed a deputation to meet the Trades Council and the Town Council and we got down to business right away.

The Trades Council was not anxious to move, but we have succeeded in getting it on the way a bit in the usual slovenly way.

The Town Council had to receive our deputation since it was the last meeting prior to the elections. A refusal meant a sure win for Labour at the elections.

We demanded food at municipal restaurants as the most urgent question of all. Then work on farm colonies at trade-union rates of pay, with representation on all committees employing the unemployed. We requested houses to shelter full families on the colonies. We urged the corporation to proceed with all available work of a new and repair character. Failing work we urged emigration to Russia, amidst the laugher of the men who do not intend to lose their slave class. Finally, we requested use of a city hall in which the unemployed might meet and comfortably discuss the situation.

The day following our deputation, Campbell and his committee met ours and wished to drive us contrary to the programme laid before the corporation. I left them in disgust, and told all to the unemployed. They followed after, and Campbell addressed the meeting. Unanimously the meeting agreed that the already existing committee proceed with its work.

Under powers from the meeting, the committee right away interviewed Bailie John Stewart, convener of the Municipal Restaurants Committee, and Bailie John Wheatley, convener of a special committee to find work under corporation auspices for the unemployed.

The committee has also urged the Distress Committee to meet it, as well as the Parish Council and the Education Authority.

We have found up-to-date every committee willing to convene a special meeting to discuss matters with us.

Bailie Wheatley's committee met our delegates and agreed to grant the City Hall three times a week and agreed to convene the heads of departments to get work under way. The next day this was done. The Restaurant Committee meets on 28 October and the Distress Committee on 29 October.

Never before in the history of Glasgow was such alacrity shown. Why? Because our committee appears every day lobbying Labour councillors and others on every issue. We wish the Education Authority to proceed with boots, clothes and food for the children. We wish Barnhill Poorhouse to be placed at the disposal of the homeless.

In fact, we mean to exhaust every constitutional method of safeguarding the unemployed of our class. Whatever happens after that we certainly will not be to blame.

To rush a work just now would mean split heads and a defeat for the Labour candidates. To use the misfortunes of the unemployed to increase those misfortunes is pitiable, but at the same time to defeat Labour is positively criminal. A Labour Town Council will respond to our pressures more readily than a bourgeois one. If labour fails then a forceful revolutionary fight is the logical next stage. Unemployment has not really begun yet, neither has the winter. There is ample time for desperate deeds before the winter is over if other and more "constitutional" means fail.

Only provocateurs would rush the situation at this juncture. Had the Clyde Workers' Committee pursued the fight for the shorter working week after Bloody Friday we might see reason for their anxiety about the unemployed at the present time. Their only desire is to undermine honest attempts to wage the class war, to keep in the public eye, or worst of all do the dirty destructive work of the capitalist class. They have done sufficient this last eighteen months to earn the contempt of every real revolutionist.

Unemployment
(*The Vanguard*, December 1920)
Since the beginning of April, wholesale prices in America and Britain have fallen about 3s in the £1, due to the shamefully high prices extorted out of a world gasping for commodities beyond the reach of impoverished peoples. The goods have been left in the hands of merchants unable to find purchasers. These merchants have stopped purchases from manufacturers who in turn have slackened or stopped production. Hence a large army of nearly half a million unemployed.

The "increased production" stunters are significantly silent on unemployment. If increased output and export are the cure of all the ills frail humanity at present patiently has to endure, then surely the half million ought to make some impression. . . .

Increased output would further glut the markets and swell the ranks of the unemployed. What the world needs is increased consumption of the glut of goods, and so provide a stimulus to trade. The wage-earners work too hard and too long; they create more than enough to satisfy all the Rab Haws God ever graced this wicked earth with.

The besetting weakness of the workers is their insistent and persistent modesty on pay-day. They readily accept a wage that but purchases back a little bit of the mountain of wealth they have so generously created. A very thick cream is left for the jolly fine bosses whose outstanding virtue is the provision of "work". It has been clear to some socialist cynics that the bosses are not christians because of this very virtue; for does the Bible not tell us that work is a curse? . . .

When we urge the needs of the unemployed we are met with the plea that work must first be found; dig holes, say the Good Government Gang in Glasgow Corporation . . . , and do constructive work, say the Labour men.

Some of the Labour men urge that if a man is fed and does no work, he deteriorates as a producer, and may never recover his old powers this side of time.

Obviously the first thing is to provide food (and clothing) to prevent his deteriorating until work of a constructional character has been found. . . .

As time goes on unemployment will increase whilst the Good Government and the Labour parties are fighting one another in the City Chambers. . . . We must pull the Labour men back to food. Let the unemployed and the sweated be fed right away. We can take it that if food is forced out of the Good Government Gang of grafters they will soon supply the workless with plenty of God's curse; whether on constructive work or not, work will be found. Part of the punishment they mete out in prison is "hard work". Let municipal restaurants be planted down in every ward. That is the most constructive work Labour men can do. That is the scaffolding needed to help build the new society. And the Labour men know it. . . .

The unemployed: will there be a general strike?

(*The Socialist*, 27 January 1921)

Keir Hardie insisted at the now dead Second International that the best way Labour might avert a world war would be by the adoption of the policy of the general strike. The respective governments in the late war saw to it that national patriotism was used to influence the minds of the leaders of Labour as the first step to using them as recruiting agents for their masters' armies and navies. It would have been better had Hardie fought for a general strike policy to raise the wages of the British workers as a preliminary to the attempt at an international strike.

Rightly or wrongly, I have been, and still am, of the opinion that his chum, Bob Smillie, in the last two years was manoeuvring for a general strike — if required — on the question of nationalisation of the mines. Recognising the narrowness of the basis of appeal to all wage-earners, he coupled with it a policy of "hands off Russia". I maintain that the government broke Smillie's health, outmanoeuvred the miners in the publicity campaign, and used the tame, insane leaders such as Clynes and Henderson to turn the workers' thoughts last March from industrial to political action. Still, the miners forced into being the new practice of special congresses.[*]

Special congresses cannot meet often without bringing to the top in workers' minds the idea of class instead of craft or industry. The idea of class leads to class action in its primary form — the class or general strike. . . .

When the London letter-writer of *The Glasgow Herald* on Monday 17 January writes that "leaders of labour are beginning to realise, no less than the captains of industry, that there must be a reduction in all standards of wages this year", the rank and file must be on the look-out. Unemployment and starvation are the methods used to bring the workers "down from the clouds" to the realities of life.

The general strike may bring starvation, but it will be the starvation of our class and not of a fraction of our class, and it will be starvation in the struggle for existence. Such starvation, even followed by reduced wages, is better than these evils unaccompanied by a fight. Solidarity of fight and solidarity of suffering will weld our class together for the final solidarity of success. . . .

If we are defeated at this juncture through defective organisation we shall be able to rectify it at the annual Trades Union Congress in September, when it is expected to abolish the Parliamentary Committee and institute in its place a full-time paid committee, with an adequate staff, with the object of bringing every wage-earner into the fold, sorting the unions out on lines of industry, and cohering all the forces for united pressure on capitalism from then onwards. Thus may be built up outside Parliament the instrument that will take the place of Parliament, that will as well take over production and exchange of wealth from the Federation of British Industries, the Chambers of Commerce and the Institute of Bankers.

That the science of society in its evolution and its functioning may guide the workers in the mighty transformation that is preparing, it is necessary that we hammer the fundamentals of marxism into the brains of our class. This can be most systematically done by the new Trades Union

---

[*]Special Congresses of the TUC began to be held in autumn 1919, and were the first step in transforming the Parliamentary Committee into the General Council (a step which MacLean had advocated for some time previously).

Congress Committee taking over the Labour College, London, and the Scottish Labour College, and making these the basis of a series of colleges and a network of evening classes all over the country. . . .

Speech from the dock, 25 October 1921 (excerpts)

. . . From the beginning of the Unemployed Agitation, [Sandy] Ross and myself said so far as we were concerned it was a case of food first, work came second, and when we met the Town Council and Labour councillors we put forward these ideas and urged the extension of national kitchens so that the unemployed could get their food from them. We went to Councilor John Stewart, convener of the national kitchens, and urged that the kitchens should be extended in Glasgow. At my meetings I said Sandy Ross was associated with me in exhausting every constitutional means of getting food for the people and keeping the people in their houses who were unable through unemployment to pay their rent.

I thought the Labour councillors might be able to get money out of the Common Good Fund for the relief of the unemployed. Money was obtained out of the Canadian Fund left to the Lord Provost of Glasgow for necessitous cases from the war, and that money was used by the Corporation to pay rents for the unemployed who were prosecuted by factors. When they finished that money the Lord Provost opened a fund for that purpose — the purpose of paying the rents and buying food for the unemployed, but that merely touched the fringe of the question. Ross and myself were on the Unemployment Committee and we explained what we wanted powers to do. Ross, myself and others on the Committee went to the Distress Committee. We had already appeared before the Town Council, prior to the November election, and made certain proposals, but the only one they granted was the use of the City Hall twice a week.

We went to the Unemployed Committee of the Corporation of which John Wheatley was then convener. We appeared before them with our proposals, and we appeared before the Distress Committee; and I myself was taken out by Mr Spence, the General Manager, and Councillor Nicol to Palacerigg to see the work done there. I came back and reported to the Unemployed Committee.

We went to the Parish Council and asked them to give us the use of Barnhill for those who had no shelter, but we were told we could not get it. We also appeared before the Education Authority and asked them to feed the children of unemployed parents, and provide boots for the children of others — those who could not afford to buy them. We had at least two deputations before the Authority, but all to no purpose.

When December came I saw that in January unemployment was

going to be very severe and thought the Corporation was not doing enough. I urged our committee to again try to see the Corporation Committee or the whole Corporation, but the Town Clerk said it was against the standing orders of the Corporation to hear the Unemployed Committee a second time, because a special committee of the Corporation was carrying out that work, and he referred us to the Unemployed Committee.

I urged that the Unemployed Committee was not working hard enough. We led the unemployed in front of the municipal buildings, but we were kept out by the policemen; every entrance was barred. I asked to see some of the labour councillors, but the Lord Provost would not grant us permission to enter as a deputation. . . .

The only time Ross and myself made any public utterance to these people was in the City Hall. We deliberately stated in the City Hall that instead of breaking up our organisation, we wanted to hold it together. Ross's message to them was that if there were any who could not hold out it was their business to go and take food rather than die of starvation. We held to this principle, and it is one I shall hold to as long as I live. It is one of the fundamental principles of my life. . . .

10

World Revolution

Foreword to "The Class State"
(September 1919)

The sham cry raised in Britain against the "dictatorship of the proletariat" established in Russia by the peasants and the former wage-earners has at the right moment brought out Tom Anderson's pamphlet "The Class State". Tom shows that Britain is under the "dictatorship of the bourgeoisie", the robbed ruled by the police, soldiers, and sailors of the robbers. These robbers control the royal family, the church, the judges, the press, and Parliament, and use these tools and clever agents to feed the people with lies as to the freedom under the "union jack".

If the wage-workers in big numbers demand shorter hours, then batons are used as on Friday, 31 January 1919 (Bloody Friday), in Glasgow; or bayonets as in Liverpool in August 1919; or soldiers and sailors are used as "scabs" as in the Yorkshire mines, July 1919. Lies were told about Bolshevism at the general election, December 1918, and most of the workers and their wives were thus frightened into voting against Labour candidates by voting for the coalition candidates, that is, the agents of the robbers. Then when the workers saw the trick played on them and struck for their rights, the coalition men these very workers sent to Parliament used the police, the army, and the navy to break their strikes and force them back to work for the capitalists. That is tyranny by a state acting on behalf of the robbing capitalist class.

The dictatorship in Britain will last as long as capitalism lasts: the dictatorship in Russia will end as soon as every capitalist and landlord becomes an honest worker. Down the British dictatorship! Up the Russian dictatorship!

On with the revolution!
(*The Call*, 6 November 1919)

6-7 November 1917 will ever be celebrated as the dawn of the wage-slaves' freedom — the birthday of the new world rising out of the ruins of the old society of robbery, tyranny, and universal murder. The down-trodden workers and peasants of Russia responded to the call of the *Communist Manifesto* of 1848, by uniting on that day and expropriating the landlords and capitalists of the Russian empire; and despite the concentrated attack of world capitalism they may hold out long enough to allow of the rest of the working class responding to the same old call: "Workers of the World, Unite!"

When France ended feudalism at the time of her celebrated revolution, the forces of European landlordism and British capitalism united to restore the old order. All that they accomplished was the delay of the day of victory of the town artisans and wage-earners. French capitalism came into being on the backs of the freed peasantry, freed at least from the blight of landlordism. View the Russian situation in the blackest light we may, then, surely we must conclude from French experience that landlordism and capitalism will never be able to take root in Russian soil again. . . .

From the revolutionary outburst of 1905 on through the Reign of Terror and right throughout the early half of the war, our Bolshevik comrades had ever kept aloft the ultimate goal of the people against the organised and secret forces of the tsar and the ignorance and illiteracy of a people widely spread and separated by wretched means of communication. When the political revolution of February 1917 was betrayed by the Cadets, and then by the Social Revolutionaries and the Mensheviks, led by Kerensky, the Bolsheviks fought to save the victory, and were in the end rewarded by the confidence of the soldiers, sailors, wage-earners, and peasants.

Once in power, the Bolsheviks not only stopped the war against Germany, but started a world campaign to stop the war itself, to let the workers of the world rise to political and economic power. Whilst Trotsky was negotiating for a hopeless peace with his class enemies of Germany, at Brest-Litovsk, his Russian comrades flooded the German trenches with appeals for class solidarity and the cessation of working-class suicide in the interests of the capitalists and landlords. This bold and noble appeal so caught the imagination of the German workers that mutinies and strikes immediately broke out. Military decay in Germany set in from that moment, and had the British Labour Party withdrawn from the coalition government at that time the war would have ended sooner than it did, and labour throughout the world might have been in power.

At any rate the Bolsheviks left organised labour in the allied countries no excuse for failing to back up peace and Russia by their wise and timely exposure of the corrupt secret treaties. We who adhere to Bolshevism feel proud at the mighty efforts made by our Russian comrades, to end both the war and capitalism at the same time. In everything they have done in world politics our comrades have carried out the genuine spirit of the International.

Their internal policy has been grander still. At once they set about the repair of roads and railways for the transport of food from the country to the cities, from the southern grain belt to the less fertile north. This led first to the German raid into the Ukraine, and now to that of Denikin. The object of the "cordon sanitaire" and the British blockade has been to prevent food, seed, and agricultural implements entering Russia, so that a slowly starving people would rise against the Bolshevik regime. Some who claim to be authorities allege that millions of children are slowly wasting away as a consequence of these devil's deeds, and from the information to hand as to the plight of Europe and India we may accept these allegations as approximately correct.

Yet withal, perhaps for the first time in history, a starving people have not turned against those in power, are not willing to sacrifice freedom for the bread the British are baiting them with in the Baltic. Why? Because the people have formed their own government and have been so soundly educated in the principles of a people's freedom, despite mountainous obstacles, that they are rather prepared to defend their country to the death than accept the slaver-poisoned bread of British plutocracy.

Allied agents and terrorists have tried to murder the Bolshevik leaders and raise a counter-revolution, and their failure is sure proof that the people are convinced that Bolshevism is good. Then the allied capitalist governments have polluted the mental atmosphere of the world with poisonous lies about Russia. They who, by blockade, are starving and killing Russian babies accuse our comrades of murder, because a few allied spies were put to death! It is obvious that this base world campaign was meant to gain support for the foreign suppression of Russia that is now reaching its height of mad frenzy. The very fact that the neighbouring states, even under British and German coercion, are refusing to attack Russia and that the fight has to be really made by the conscript and un-willing troops of the "beastly powers" amply proves that Bolshevism has deep roots, has a wide and solid foundation.

Let Britain capture Petrograd. She cannot hold it against the con-viction of the Russian races. She has failed to tame Ireland next door with a rebel population half that of London. Revolt in Ireland is rising day by day. The same revolt is also developing in South Africa, Egypt and India. Most important, revolt is raising its righteous head even in Britain. Bonar Law's refusal to discuss the secret organisation of the Citizen Guard (Britain's Black Guard) is evidence of the fact that the plunderers here are beginning to tremble at the Bolshevist spirit that has spread like wildfire since the NUR defeated the government of all the capitalist virtues. Tom Mann's success and the miners' new offensive are but signs of the spirit of revolt and freedom abroad in our sluggish land.

And American labour is menacing, too, and will move faster than British labour, because of the lack of troublous traditions and because of the dam-up of forces by Gompers and the AF of Labour. The Scottish fight in January naturally brought forth response in Canada, in which so many Scots have sought a home, and as was anticipated American labour is consequently just starting a Big Push of its own.

The driving force everywhere is the spirit aroused by Russia. The workers are linking up all over the world, are preparing and manoeuvring for the final clash of the class war. The greed of the British capitalists, fed by American competition for the world markets, is urging them to finance industry to the neglect of their duties to their government. The increase in national indebtedness is forcing the government to issue more bills and notes and withdraw the bread subsidy. Prices are rising and will continue to rise. Rents and rates are going to soar very soon. . . .

Let us then take inspiration from the mighty struggle of our comrades, the people of Russia, and the growing solidarity of a revolutionary English-speaking people, and pledge ourselves to strive unceasingly till victory caps our efforts in time for the peoples of the world celebrating the next seventh of November under the red flag of human liberty, equality, and fraternity.

May Day

(The Vanguard, May 1920)

The Socialist International in 1888 instituted the celebration of not only the coming of summer and sunshine, but also the solidarity of the working class throughout the world by stopping work on the first day of May in defiance of the master class. We are proud that the Clyde has played its part in getting the workers of Britain to hold their demonstrations on the real May Day, and we believe that millions in this island will take the holiday out of solid conviction that it is Labour Day. Countless millions throughout the world will be attending monster gatherings swearing unity with their fellow workers in other lands and protesting against the continuance of capitalism. All will be jubilating at the success of Russia to be the first to break through the chains of slavery, whilst, strangely enough, Russia will be the only country where the workers will on May Day be celebrating the occasion by ardent toil of a sanitary character, a day consecrated to social health, a day set apart to fight the fiend of fever. . . .

The Bolsheviks have asked us this year to make May Day a one-day strike for withdrawal of the murderous blockade on Russia. So we will, so we must. Britain squealed out hypocritically against German bombs killing women and children, but now Britain is trying to slowly murder a vast people she is not officially at war with by the hunger blockade. Against this black infamy let us raise out mighty cry of protest. . . .

"The Vanguard" resurrected
(*The Vanguard*, May 1920)

Irishmen say that Ireland is unbeatable; we say that *The Vanguard* is irrepressible. It is appropriate that it be resurrected on May Day 1920 to hail the dawn of the world revolution that may break out any time and anywhere. We consecrate *The Vanguard* to the cause of the workers' revolution.

Some may remember that when Hyndman and *Justice* betrayed the British Socialist Party and the International by taking the side of the British capitalist class in the "Great War", we of the BSP along with *Forward* steadied the socialist movement and prepared the way for the strikes that will ever make famous the class-conscious workers of the Clyde Valley.

We started our modest little paper in September 1915 and had just put into the hands of the Civic Press our fifth issue, January 1916, when we learned that the police had raided that Press to stop *Forward* for its fine report of Lloyd George's trouncing in St Andrew's Hall, 25 December 1915, by the nine hundred delegates from the engineering works on the Clydeside. Naturally, our paper was seized also as we had two articles on the same "Christmas pantomime" of which Lloyd George was the "knock-out". When the seizure was raised in the Commons, Lloyd George stated that *The Vanguard* was the worst paper in the country. At the time, we went to printer after printer, but were told time and again that the authorities had sent out a circular forbidding anyone to print the paper. Before this I had (November 1915) been sentenced to five days or five pounds by Sheriff Lee, and then dismissed by the Govan School Board. Immediately thereafter the BSP was turned out of the Panopticon, and on 26 December 1915 was refused entry into the Good Templars' Hall by a cordon of police drawn round the entrance. Then our Russian comrade, Peter Petroff, was arrested and thrust into prison after a farce of a trial, in which Petroff defended himself and defeated the furious old humbug of a sheriff in the interpretation of the section of the Defence of the Realm Act used to indict him.

In due course came the arrest of James D. MacDougall and myself and our imprisonment for one year and three years respectively. The government intended to so cripple us that we would be effectively disposed of as agents in the class war. The preparations in Russia and the outbreak

215

of the first revolution saved us after a degradation and drugging that we might call devilish, but for the more monstrous deeds of the war and the slow death-pressure Britain is applying to Central Europe, Russia, and Ireland.

The continuance of the war during 1917 and the issue of *The Call* by the BSP, purged of the social patriots headed by Hyndman, made it impossible and unnecessary to restart *The Vanguard*. MacDougall went to work in the mines in Lanarkshire, and started amongst the miners there the finest piece of socialist propaganda ever conducted in Scotland. *Forward* carefully suppressed references to MacDougall's work as his policy of revolutionary direct action was antagonistic to that of the editor and the fossil types inside the ILP. Nonetheless, the work was done, and that explains the fervent support Lanarkshire gave to the premature forty-hour strike, and to the policy of aggression last year that lifted the British miners into the forefront of the workers' movement throughout the world.

The skill and cuteness of the government prevented a strike of the miners, who might have received the support of the rest of the workers to the detriment of the British proposals at the Peace Conference, to the defeat of Britain's anti-Russian policy, and to the endangerment of British capitalism itself. Whilst giving free scope to Smillie and his colleagues at the Coal Commission — now seen to be a farce to stave off revolt — the government set itself to the task of breaking up the miners' reform movement and driving MacDougall out of public life. This accomplished, it then faced up to the Miners' Federation itself, and has now succeeded in driving Smillie out of the fighting ranks, has defeated direct action for nationalisation of the mines, and has isolated the miners from the other trade unions.

At the same time it has paralysed the BSP and the SLP, and may do so to the ILP as well, so as to clear the ground for a safe and sane Labourism; safe and sane, because dominated by ideas of the reform of capitalism rather than by the determination to destroy capitalism and inaugurate the workers' republic.

Dissatisfaction with the plight of the BSP, maimed by the year's onslaught of capitalism, has compelled us to resurrect *The Vanguard* in the hope that we may concentrate the minds of the workers on the revolution to be gone through in this country as well as on the one gone through already in Russia. The main use of the Russian workers' success is the inspiration we ought to derive from it for the accomplishment of a similar feat within the bounds of Britain.

11

The Scottish workers' republic

All Hail, the Scottish Workers' Republic!
(August 1920, subsequently issued along with November 1922 election address)
For some time past the feeling has been growing that Scotland should strike out for national independence, as well as Ireland and other lands. This has recently been strengthened by the English government's intention to rely mainly on Scottish troops to murder the Irish race.

Genuine Scotsmen recently asked themselves the question: "Are we Scots to be used as the bloody tools of the English against our brother Celts of Erin?" And naturally the instinctive response was — No!

Again, the land seizures by Highland crofters are arousing the blood of Highlandmen driven south to the Clyde Valley for work. Especially the filthy tactics of Lord Leverhulme (an English capitalist), who has dismissed Stornoway wage-slaves as a means of beating the Lewis raiders who seized the farms of Coll and Gress. Divide and conquer again!

Scottish students of history now realise that Edinburgh lawyers and politicians sold Scottish independence in 1707, although most blame has fallen on the Earl of Stair. Many of us are convinced that ever since 1707 the Edinburgh kings' and queens' counsels and politicians have been in the regular pay of London to keep Scotland as the base tool of the English government. These scoundrels in the eighteenth century helped to ruin Burns, the peasants' and people's poet.

The "rebellions" of 1715 and 1745 were natural reactions against the treacherous deed of 1707, but these unfortunate outbursts but gave the English the excuse and chance to subdue the Highland chiefs and then corrupt them with an English education at Oxford and Cambridge.

Since 1790 the chiefs became Englishmen in outlook, and used their clansmen to defend English capitalism against the revolution started in Paris in 1789. Since the Napoleonic wars the Highland regiments have been used to defend the stolen lands of England all over the globe, and have largely helped to extend the English empire.

Whilst doing this, the Dukes of Sutherland and Argyll and other chiefs proceeded with the English landlord policy of land clearances. The friends of the fighters were chased off their native heath into the lowlands or out to Canada and Australia.

Now the reaction is beginning — inspired by Ireland and Russia.

Scotland must again have independence, but not to be ruled by traitor kings or chiefs, lawyers and politicians. The communism of the clans must be re-established on a modern basis. (Bolshevism, to put it roughly, is but the modern expression of the communism of the *mir*.) Scotland must therefore work itself into a communism embracing the whole country as a unit. The country must have but one clan, as it were — a united people working in co-operation and co-operatively, using the wealth that is created.

We can safely say, then: back to communism and forward to communism.

The control must be in the hands of the workers only, male and female alike, each workshop and industry sending delegates to district councils and the National Council.

The National Council must be established in or near Glasgow, as half the population lives within a radius of twenty miles from Glasgow.

In the period of transition a wage-earners' dictatorship must guide production, and the adoption of the machinery and methods of production, to communist methods.

Many Irishmen live in Scotland, and, as they are Celts like the Scots, and are out for Irish independence, and as wage-earners have been champion fighters for working-class rights, we expect them to ally themselves with us, and help us to attain our Scottish Communist Republic, as long as they live in Scotland. Irishmen must remember that communism prevailed amongst the Irish clans as amongst the Scottish clans, so that, in lining up with Scotsmen, they are but carrying forward the tradition and instincts of the Celtic race.

All hail the Scottish Workers' Republic!

Irish stew

(*The Vanguard*, August 1920)

The Scottish Home Rule Association has in July issued the first number of its *News Sheet*, devoted to self-determination for Scotland. There will be no self-determination if Scotland is ruled by a handful of KCs at Edinburgh. Since the Earl of Stair sold Scotland in 1707 the Edinburgh lawyers have been paid by the English government to keep Scotland as a helpless, dependent patch of her empire, and since the 'forty-five rebellion Scotsmen, Highlanders particularly, have been used to do a large part of England's dirty work of placing the yoke on innocent races. The latest is the attempt to use Scottish boy soldiers to murder the Irish race. Scotsmen of spirit must revolt against that. Let us rather fight on the side of Ireland

218

for Ireland's independent republic. Our friend McArthur's paper *Liberty* is also devoted to the re-institution of Scottish independence, and Comrade R. Erskine of Mar in his *Guth na Bliadhna* is also wedded to the same cause.

Scotland, however, can only have real independence for all her inhabitants under communism controlled and evolved by workers' committees, as in Russia. . . .

In the autumn we intend to make a "big push" on the Highland question, and to get Scotsmen to rally round communism and work hand-in-hand with our sister race of Ireland against economic as well as political tyranny. Lord Leverhulme must not be allowed by bribery and corruption to use Highlanders to oust Highlanders out of their native land. We must encourage the Highlanders to co-operate communally to cultivate the land with the latest machinery. Only thus can the best results be obtained out of the Highlands and its sturdy inhabitants. The old communal traditions of the clans must be revived and adapted to modern conceptions and conditions. If the Bolshevik notion of world communism through national communism is scientifically correct, then we are justified in utilising our latent Highland and Scottish sentiments and traditions in the mighty task confronting us of transforming capitalism into communism. . . .

Scotch broth

(*The Vanguard*, September 1920)

The poor old *Glasgow Herald* has seemingly got a nasty knock. Our comrade, R. Erskine of Mar . . . at a Sinn Fein demonstration in Trafalgar Square, London, to protest against the virtual imprisonment of Archbishop Mannix, stated that the Scottish Gael is preparing to overthrow "the English government" and to proclaim the independence of Scotland. The *G.H.* stresses the fact that the Lothians were captured and peopled by Saxons, and that Scotland is well represented in the cabinet by Balfour, Bonar Law, Horne, and Geddes. Readers will note that the first article from Comrade Erskine, in our hands before the testy spasm from "Auld Granny" amused the "middle class", lays stress on the Lothian conquest by the Saxons; and readers do not require to be reminded of the great services rendered to Scotland by all the Scotsmen who ever went to the London Parliament! The final angry outburst of the *G.H.* reads thus: "We are discussing serious schemes for removing the local administration of Scotland from Westminster to Edinburgh, and we do not want to have their consideration interrupted by absurd caricatures of their meaning." Someone might send for Graham Moffat: "Granny's" leaders will make his fortune!

By the time this appears we expect to have in being a Scottish Communist Council of Action, and in circulation 100,000 leaflets urging on towards a Scottish Communist Republic. Our vast audiences are catching up the idea already all right; and ideas win in the long run against ridicule and force. Put that in your pipe, "Granny". . . . At the Highland Land League annual conference resolutions were passed in favour of public ownership of the land, economic rent to be paid to the government, of Scottish independence, and of support to the Highland raiders. There was general approval of communism under the control of the industrial workers, the fishermen, and the crofters and other land workers. J. MacLean was asked to second the independence resolution. Comrade McCrae, Highland Labour Party, spoke well for communism. The surprise of the evening was the fine fighting speech of Miss Cameron. A real Gaelic revival as well as a lowland revival must result. . . .

The Irish tragedy: up Scottish revolutionists!

(*The Vanguard*, November 1920)

. . . I hold that the British empire is the greatest menace to the human race. Lloyd George's Caernarvon speech proves it. The best interests of humanity can therefore be served by the break-up of the British empire. The Irish, the Indians and others are playing their part. Why ought not the Scottish?

The corruption of the London communists and the position of the English governing class, then, amply justify the establishment of a Scottish Communist Party as a prelude to a Scottish Communist Republic. Were the SLP and all sound and determined communists to come together at the close of the coal crisis and take the initial step in this matter, we ought to be able to rally Scottish labour so effectively that Scotland would follow Ireland and Scotsmen throughout the world respond to our revolutionary call.

We on the Clyde have a mighty mission to fulfil. We can make Glasgow a Petrograd, a revolutionary storm-centre second to none. A Scottish break-away at this juncture would bring the empire crashing to the ground and free the waiting workers of the world.

This is not the time for the empty conceits of vainglorious demagogues, but the occasion for well-grounded marxians smartly able to seize the upsurging opportunities to rouse and lead our class to victory. English labour is bound to respond to our call if we in Scotland strike out boldly for political conquest. We have no time to waste. Every delay, every hesitation brings the world nearer the perdition Lloyd George and Woodrow Wilson are preparing for us. . . .

Literary note

(*The Vanguard*, November 1920)

Johnston's *History of the Working Classes in Scotland* is a useful book, though like most summaries of complex questions it suffers from over-crowding. It is inclined to be scrappy, and to present short views where long and detailed ones are required by reason of the complex character of the various matters dealt with. The early history of labour in Scotland is not sufficiently detailed, and in one respect at least the author's knowledge of the history of this country would appear to be defective; or at all events considerably wanting in perspective. Johnston has a good deal to say about feudal serfdom, and the shocking social conditions under which labour was carried on under the feudal magnates. He admits, too, that these disgraceful and degrading conditions did not obtain in the Highlands under the clan system; but he signally fails to draw the moral of that surprising fact. The moral he should have drawn, but has failed to point, is this, that in feudalised Scotland the abominations of serfdom obtained because of feudalism, whereas in those parts of the country that escaped feudalism and remained under the Celtic or communistic system these abominations were non-existent. I am not aware that this point has ever been made by any of the writers who have dealt with the history of Scotland, and Johnston's failure to draw the matter out and make the most of it is disappointing, even though, considering the limitations of his historical equipment, it should be inevitable.

The Highland land seizures

(*The Vanguard*, September 1920)

The crofters' agitations for land have been for two generations met in the usual way — the granting of inoperative Acts. Of course, when the government required strong and fearless Highlanders to die for English landlords like the Duke of Northumberland or capitalists like Lord Lever-hulme, promises of land were made to the fisher-crofters, as an earthly paradise was promised the empire's wage-slaves, and a measure of self-government to Ireland and India.

Not one promise has been kept. India has got an "Amritsar", Ireland an "army of anarchy", and Lewis a "Sunlight Soap dictator".

In the Highlands the Board of Agriculture's failure to keep its land promises to what I think were misguided patriots led to the seizures of farms by the desperate ex-service crofters. More of these seizures are likely to take place unless "my friend", Mr Robert Munro (the Highland traitor who got me a three years' sentence for resisting the Conscription Act of the Germans of England) smartens up a bit, or clears out like the other Celtic traitor, Ian MacPherson, the late dictator over the Irish Celts on behalf of the Sassenachs.

The chief farms seized have been Kirkton Farm, Portskerra, Sutherlandshire; the home farm, Raasay Island; and Coll and Gress farms, Lewis.

As the Lewis raids were the most important from a Scottish independence and a world political point of view, it was agreed that Sandy Ross and Peter Marshall proceed to Stornoway during the Glasgow Fair holidays. Sandy alone was able to go, but he managed to see the crofters who had seized Gress Farm.

In the circumstances, I thought it also advisable to go; so off I went on 2 August on my return from Dublin, which city I visited to establish an entente between the Celts of Scotland and the Celts of Ireland, and to further my efforts to prevent Scottish boys being used by England to murder Irish boys.

I found that Lord Leverhulme had succeeded in embittering Stornoway wage-slaves, working out his schemes, against the "raiders" at Coll and Gress by stopping work on roads at the proposed harbour extension from the existing harbour round to Goat Island. The town workers hold the raiders responsible for the loss of wages, for at my meeting in Stornoway on Wednesday, 4 August, apart from drunks who interjected under the protection of the police and an inciting speech made at the close by an important and able personage who obviously was acting "under control" since he guaranteed me protection against violence, I deliberately drew out the feelings of some of the older men, who dared me even to mention the sacred name of Lord Sunlight Soap. I must say, however, that the younger men are more inclined to hold Leverhulme in contempt, especially those who have lived abroad or in the rebellious atmosphere of the Clyde valley.

I visited the Coll raiders, of whom there are thirty (none at Gress). I was only able to meet four, as the others were off at the fishing. The spirit and independence of these men is eloquently indicated in the appended letter signed by two leaders, both of whom I met. . . .

Munro had me carefully watched (and protected) especially going North. Well might he, for this Lewis situation is of world import.

He refused to settle the question, and on request he refused to visit the island, hoping that secret bribery or threats, or social pressure from the suspended wage-slaves of Stornoway, would make the raiders yield. People on the island are afraid to speak their minds fully in private lest the "economic pinch" follow. . . .

The stubborn attitude of the raiders and my visit has spurred him up;

aye, and the Duke of Sutherland and the Marquis of Graham as well since both robbers have been forced to send letters to the press.

The biggest part of the discussion on the Scottish estimates in the Commons on 4 August was taken up with the question of the raids, and Munro had to promise to visit Lewis. . . .

Leverhulme has insisted that he requires Coll and Gress Farms as part of his scheme for dairy farming purposes to supply milk to Stornoway. This excuse is a joke, for I saw on MacBrayne's boats milk cans that had brought milk from Aberdeenshire. If milk is now being brought in, it can surely be brought in afterwards when the population of Lewis has been shepherded into Stornoway as his "lordship's" wage-slaves.

I am convinced that my first impression is correct, that Leverhulme is preparing Lewis and Harris for the navy in case of war with America. The "MacLine" of trawlers (now transferred to Fleetwood) were to sail from Stornoway right north to Iceland and perhaps Greenland, and most of the catches were to be canned at Stornoway. A breed of fishermen would thus be fostered who would know the waters and be handy in case of war. Remember that Britain has forced Denmark to give Iceland independence, and by the use of methods now well known to Leverhulme the inhabitants of Iceland will be induced to take the side of Britain against America. Britain controls Greenland; so that by this chain she would have a continuous sweep right across the north of the Atlantic to Canada.

That America is alive to the situation is seen in her offer to establish a Lewis colony in the United States, to which country the landless and the raiders threaten to go unless Bitter Bobby Munro bucks up.

That other Celtic traitor, Lloyd George, confirmed my suggestion in his reply to Northmuberland and Carson when he asserted that the free ports of Ireland could never be placed at the disposal of any enemy power. Only one "enemy power" has a navy near enough and big enough to menace our Sassenach masters — the United States.

My advice to the Lewis men and to other Highland raiders is — hold fast. Do not bend before Bobby's bounce or beseechings, do not bow down before Baal (soap-bubbles), and do not jazz to America. Play the game of neither English imperialism nor American imperialism. Scottish land must belong to the Scottish race whilst races last, and those who use the land must pay no rent to any man.

Scottish independence means economic as well as political independence, and that can only be assured by the co-operation of all under communism.

I am pleased to state in conclusion that the Clyde workers are prepared to subscribe to help the families of the raiders if the bitter little bounder puts them into prison.

Stray straws: the defeat of the raiders

(*The Vanguard*, November 1920)

. . . As I feared, the government has won the day for Lord Leverhulme in Lewis. T. B. Morrison, KC and MP, took the place of Bitter Bobby in the visit to Stornoway, and had a talk with the raiders. Thereafter their lawyer, Donald Shaw, advised them to give up the two farms at Coll and Gress, and they accepted the advice. We told the Coll leaders that Shaw would give them away — and he has. . . . Perhaps the government may deal generously now with the raiders; perhaps Lord Leverhulme may now proceed with his development scheme; perhaps all may seem well and prosperous in the Lewis. But the day of reckoning is at hand when Highlanders will be called on to die in the war with America. It looks as if the people had sold their sons' very lives for a mess of pottage. . . .

A Scottish Communist Party

(*The Vanguard*, December 1920)

The press report on "A Third International Meeting in Paris" affords the opportunity of letting us publish the fact that we are summoning by advertisement, not by circular, all in Scotland who favour the gist of the "Twenty-one Points" to attend in person or by delegate a conference to form a Scottish Communist Party to represent the marxian communism in Scotland, or a definite series of groups who will co-operate or amalgamate with the most definitely marxian organisation in Scotland, the Socialist Labour Party, which fortunately has its headquarters in Glasgow.

We are of opinion that the SLP will raise no vital objection to the preliminary conditions laid down by the Bolshevik International at Moscow. Until "real delegates" can get a chance to meet our Russian comrades in open and mature conference, the "points" enumerated are but provisional and need cause no heat or undue excitement. The main thing is to get the clearheaded and honest marxian revolutionists into one camp. We in Scotland must not let ourselves play second fiddle to any organisation with headquarters in London, no more than we would ask Dublin to bend to the will of London.

Whatever co-operation may be established between the revolutionary forces in the countries at present composing the "United" Kingdom, that co-operation must be based on the wills of the free national units. . . .

Let attention be paid to point 17. "Each party must change its old name to that of communist party of such and such country, section of the

Third International."

William Gallacher is going the rounds ridiculing the idea of a "Scottish" Communist Party because he has been to Russia and poses as the gramophone of Lenin. Nothing in point 17 precludes the formation of a Scottish party as Scotland is a definite country. The exercise of a little honest thinking will demonstrate that. Now, Scottish marxians are surely not going to accept as an authority on marxism a man such as Gallacher who never was a marxian, but an openly avowed anarchist. Lenin, Trotsky and the Bolsheviki were and are very rigid marxians. Because of their faithful adherence to principles they have won through and are holding out with amazing success.

A real revolutionary party can only be established here on Marx, not on Bakunin, by fully avowed marxists of long years of standing. If Lenin tells us to unite with elements who are anarchists, we must reply by asking the Bolsheviks to unite with the Mensheviks or the Social Revolutionaries. We stand for the marxian method applied to British conditions. The less Russians interfere in the internal affairs of other countries at this juncture the better for the cause of revolution in those countries. Rothstein's activities drove Fairchild out of the BSP, and his approaches to me created a situation that compelled the BSP to gently slip me out. The leadership of the BSP then fell to Lieut. Col. Malone MP, who in 1918 was on the executive of the Reconstruction Society, the body that flooded the country with leaflets poisoning the minds of the people against Russia and the Russian revolution.

To ask me to work with Malone for revolution is a joke. A man like that ought not to be allowed in a revolutionary marxian party. Whatever may be contended against Turati, Kautsky, Hilferding, Hilquit, Longuet and MacDonald ought surely to apply with greater force to men such as Malone. To allow a Malone to lead a revolutionary party after a record such as his is high treason to communism. You might as well appoint Churchill "honorary" president of the Russian republic!

If England is to be led by Malone, then let us marxians in Scotland forge ahead on entirely independent lines.

Scotland is firmer for marxism than any other part of the British empire. Clyde speakers get bigger and better audiences in Scotland than speakers across the borders, with very, very, few exceptions. In other words, Scotland is becoming more self-reliant than ever before and looks hopefully for a lead from men reared and trained on this side of the border.

The preparations to use the Scottish coast and Scottish lads in John Bull's fight with Uncle Sam force on us the policy of complete political separation from England. Hence a Scottish Communist Party. Viewed in

225

the light of all circumstances germane to the crack-up of the British empire and the release of the workers' revolutionary energy, the proposition of a Scottish Communist Party stands foursquare to the impotent cynicism of poets and demagogues and deserters of the cause on the outbreak of war.

Open letter to Lenin
(*The Socialist*, 30 January 1921)

A conference is being held today (Sunday, 30 January) at Leeds to form a united Communist Party as the British section of the Third International. I believe that you have too good a grasp of affairs to be very far deceived by the situation in Britain, and by the pretentions of most of the prominent ones who will be present. A various assortment of personages visited Russia last year, openly, secretly, and "secretly" whilst the authorities were winking the other eye.

From printed reports of statements issued by them in the name of people who did not delegate them we learn that you are asked to believe that large numbers of workers are organised on a workshop basis ready for the signal of revolution, and that a well-organised and disciplined party will be got ready to head the way through the revolution.

You will recognise that it is the business of the British government to deceive you and get you to make false calculations, as it made the Kaiser form wrong estimates and lay plans for the defeat of Germany. You must therefore recognise that anybody or anything coming from Britain should be treated with the utmost caution and scepticism after Russia's treatment by Britain during the last two years and more. British capitalism is not out to recognise or trade with Russian communism, whatever temporary expedients it may resort to. It realises more clearly than any other section of capitalism that a struggle for supremacy has now commenced between capital and labour, and it is determined to crush labour by crushing the Russian republic, and to restore reaction as it is in process of restoring reaction in the defeated countries still called the "central powers".

Only once in four hundred years has England been decisively checked — in the war that gave birth to the United States in the years 1775-86. Today England is gathering her forces together to smash American ambitions as she has just smashed German ambitions. That explains the brutal, bloody and remorseless attempt to crush the spirit of the pluckiest race that has ever stood up to "John Bull, Gentleman", the Irish race; for, if Ireland should side with America in the event of another world war (and it is approaching very near), England must be bottled up on the west.

If that war can be staved off till a German Kaiser and a Russian Tsar are re-established, then Britain will have contact with the whole of Asia and Africa by way of Germany and the other central nations, as well as by Russia and Siberia.

If America presses hard this year whilst British trade is paralysed, and whilst the workers are in no spirit to respond to the patriotic appeals and pressures so skilfully used in the last war, then Britain will sweetly put Earl Curzon aside and meekly send Lloyd George to clasp you to his bosom as some long-lost brother.

A sham Labour government, with our beloved friends MacDonald and Snowden (and ethereal Ethel, too) in it, will be formed, although the real work will be done by the "old gang" under the guise of the Privy Council.

This expedient of itself would not deceive you, since you and your comrades have the exact measure of the leaders of Labour and of the ILP, and that Lloyd George well knows.

He must, therefore, make way for a Communist Party whose "leaders" are controlled by him. Those who are coming together are a heterogeneous mixture of anarchists, sentimentalists, syndicalists, with a sprinkling of marxists. Unity in such a camp is likely to be impossible; but should unity lead to any menace, then the "leaders" will conduct surplus energy through "safe" channels — safe to Lloyd George.

The Parliamentary leader will be, as recently he has been, Lieutenant-Colonel Malone, MP. This gentleman was on the executive committee of the Reconstruction Society, formerly the Anti-Socialist Society, a society that issued millions of leaflets during and after the general election of 1918 poisoning the minds of people against Bolshevism, yourself, Trotsky, and other Russian comrades. After his visit to Russia, Malone addressed meetings about the conditions of Russia, and last year joined the British Socialist Party, after Rothstein's attempt to buy Fairchild and myself brought on Fairchild's retiral from the party and my secret expulsion.

Now *The Communist*, the successor to *The Call* when the BSP was transformed into the Communist Party of Great Britain, has passed into the control and editorship of Mr Meynell, who retired from the directorship of the *Daily Herald* when Lloyd George charged him with bringing jewels to England from Russia to subsidise the *Daily Herald*.

If Lansbury and he thought it good tactics to dissociate the *Daily Herald* from Meynell, why is it that Meynell now assumes editorship of what is recognised as the official organ of the Communist Party of Great Britain? Who is Meynell and what is Meynell, are very appropriate questions. To my knowledge he never was in the SDF or the BSP. He has as much standing in revolutionary circles in Britain as Malone.

It is only in a country such as Britain, ruled by the most unscrupulous and cunning capitalist class that has ever disgraced this earth, that totally unknown, untried, and inexperienced men could be thrust to the front.

On Gallacher's return he preached unity and the sinking of personalities, but he participated in a conference in Glasgow of Scottish groups to form the Communist Labour Party. The object of this was to "dish" the Socialist Labour Party from which, in fact, branches passed over to the CLP, and to have a good show at the Leeds Conference — a Lloyd George caricature of the great Leeds Convention of 1917 after the first Russian revolution. To confuse people, the secretary of the group who formed, and who now compose, the CLP was selected to deceive the unwitting. His name is John MacLean, and he hails from Glasgow as well as myself.

Not content with preaching unity and helping to form a new party in October, Gallacher insisted on sacrificing personality for the sake of the movement. However, what has Gallacher been doing in secret? He has been going round the country and warning socialists that MacLean is suffering from "hallucinations". He wrote to that effect to the SLP when I was arranging a conference to bring my supporters into line with the SLP, and he squirmed when I read his letter in public.

He came to the conference uninvited, and there made similar statements in public in presence of a secret reporter to the Harmsworth papers in Glasgow. Before he went to Russia he, with his colleagues of *The Worker*, burst up comrade Clunie's classes in Fife, where our comrade conducts a number of classes on the principles of marxism.

The man in Britain who is against marxism is against Bolshevism in Russia too. Obscurantism and reaction have ever gone hand in hand.

Gallacher, of course, is going to do the industrial camouflage. He has led you to believe that there is a workshop movement in Scotland. That is a black lie. I have been at work gates all summer and autumn up and down the Clyde valley, and I am positive when I say that victimisation after the premature forty hours strike crushed the workshop movement. Unemployment today has struck terror into the hearts of those at work, as starvation is meant to tame the workless. No industrial movement of a radical character is possible at present outside the ranks of the miners, and that movement has been revived and is being carried on by SLPers.

I am of the belief that the workshop movement in England is as dead as it is in Scotland.

Do not place reliance, then, on the United Communist Party that will be formed today, and do not rely on the workshop movement either.

In Russia, take your advice from neither Quelch nor Fineberg. Take it from Peter Petroff. Petroff is the only Russian who knows the working-class movement intimately in London and Glasgow. Until his imprisonment in 1916 Petroff stayed with me, and worked with MacDougall and me to build up the mass movement that is now beginning to manifest itself in Scotland. Petroff is the only marxist in Russia, then, that has any real comprehension of the situation here, and can fully explain this letter to you. Remember that it was left to me to start the movement in 1917 for the release of Petroff and Tchitcherin, and that it was on Petroff's advice you in Russia made me Consul for Scotland. It was my fidelity to you and the cause of revolution that got me the five years' sentence in 1918.

I am still carrying on, although betrayed, not by the workers, but by so-called "comrades". It is by no accident that Dr Shadwell, after a recent tour over Britain, wrote in a series of articles to the London *Times* that the Clyde was the most revolutionary centre in Britain. The Gallacher gang thrice tried to seize control out of my hands, and failed absolutely. Three thousand five hundred unemployed meet twice a week in the City Hall, so that we may discuss principles and tactics applied to the present situation from a marxian point of view.

As more and more are thrown idle and begin to starve — for the government means them to starve — you can realise that, sooner or later, a mass movement, vaster and bolder than ever before, is bound to show itself. The situation becomes all the more serious, since many wage-slaves here are Irishmen, whose country is being more and more cunningly and cruelly tortured. The rightful racial and class hatred of these men is going to make for an avalanche of opinion and feeling that are bound, sooner or later, to break through the bonds of English capitalism.

Scottish history in the making
(*The Socialist*, 12 May 1921)

Two sensations have stirred Scotland this last week — the murder of a police officer, Inspector Johnston, and the tampering with soup at the communal kitchen, Cowdenbeath. Both these incidents, coming on the heels of the lock-out of the miners, and the display of the forces of the government, should have far-reaching effects on the minds of the working class — more far-reaching than the loss of millions of pounds of wages. Ours is to recognise this fact and make the most of it in driving the people in the right direction communism-wards.

On Wednesday, 14 May, just outside Duke Street Prison, an armed attempt was made to rescue an Irish prisoner, Frank Somers, from a "Black Maria" conveying him from the Central Police Court, Glasgow, to the prison. In the attack the Inspector was killed, and Detective-Sergeant Stirton was wounded in the wrist. The press naturally at once blamed Sinn Feiners, and thus gave the police the excuse to raid all suspected premises and arrest anyone in Scotland. Sinn Feiners may have been the persons responsible for the attack as most people at once would naturally conclude. I think sufficient evidence is forthcoming to prove . . . that the government itself may have been responsible, possibly through Scotland Yard or Dublin Castle agencies working unknown to the Glasgow police authorities.

Let me state my case.

A policeman, Campbell, was killed in Parkhead, Glasgow, early in January 1919, just prior to the forty-hour strike. I then believed he had been killed at the instigation of the government to justify the arming of the police ready for the strike. I further asserted that the murderer would never be found. He has not yet been found, and Bloody Friday proved the accuracy of my publicly expressed suspicions of the motive of the government at least.

Prior to the miners' lock-out on 1 April, 16 alleged Sinn Feiners were tried at the High Court, Edinburgh, and some were sent to Peterhead. English marines drafted into Glasgow got into a "scrap" on Saturday, 16 April, for alleging to the workers living in Kingston, South Side, that they had been sent north not to fight the workers, but a Sinn Fein army. It is evident that their officers may have used the reports of the High Court trial to delude the sailor boys.

Communists, true or false, all over the country, were likewise arrested before 1 April, and sent to prison on a charge of "sedition", with the obvious intent, as I repeatedly told the unemployed, of creating the opinion that an attempt was being prepared to start a revolution. Attempts were made to get me to use strong language, and I refused to play Lloyd George's game and so betray the workers in the present mighty struggle over wages. Even the *Daily Record* on 14 April, in a leading article entitled "Why?" had to write thus: "There is a new note in the public utterances these days of Mr John MacLean and his fellow(?) communist leaders." The others referred to are SLPers like comrades Tom Mitchell, James Clunie and Tom Esterman. The object was to give the soldiers the impression that they were being called out against wild men and madmen, not against the whole wage-earning class.

The government was prepared to spill plenty of blood in Glasgow; in fact, prepared to give us a taste of Paris at the end of the Commune in 1871. To accommodate the wounded Bellahouston Military Hospital was cleared, all but a few beds. That is why it became a national scandal, and the committee has resigned.

My explanation of the situation, and the fact that the forces of the government have been vulgarly displayed in Glasgow, even to the disgust of *The Manchester Guardian*, amidst perfect calm and discipline amongst the starving unemployed, has created the profoundest impression on the working class. Now they know the real meaning of the term "class warfare"; and now they see the need for a new world form of society free from the flaw and penalties of classes.

The government, wild at being outwitted, has determined on success by justification of its "christian manifestation of brotherly love", to use the sweet language of our fighting parsons.

A policeman is killed. The Irish are blamed. Searching and seizure begin. Father McRory, a popular East End young priest, amongst many friends, is arrested. Distracted Irish people rush out along the Gallowgate to rescue him, and are mercilessly clubbed down. Many indiscriminate arrests are made, mostly Scottish workers who happened to be on the spot when the crowds gathered.

More searching and arresting are the order of the day. Of course, a few guns and revolvers of an antiquated or petty type are likely to be found, and these will be flourished to prove the existence of the "spiritualist" Sinn Fein army. Irish people are expected to develop mob riots as well in mild protest against the insulting police arrests. All this is happening when starvation is beginning to play on many miners and others thrown out by the lock-outs. If mobs can be incited, then the government will fill Bellahouston Hospital all right.

We socialists have to be involved too. A raid was made on the premises of the Scottish Labour College, 196 St Vincent Street, at midnight on Wednesday. "Nothing" was found. On Thursday afternoon comrade Tom Mitchell was arrested in his office, 50 Renfrew Street, the excuse being an article by another man, who has also been arrested, appearing in a recent issue of *The Socialist*. My impression is that it is his printing, through the Socialist Labour Press, of the Sinn Fein paper *Dark Rosaleen*, purely a matter of business on Tom Mitchell's part, that has been the revenge motive. Underneath lies the idea to create the impression that a "Bolshevik plot" is still brewing and that we communists are linked up with the Sinn Feiners.

On Monday, 2 May, I threw down my challenge to the government that, give the police what powers it may, I intended to continue speaking in public.

On Tuesday, Sir W. Johnston-Hicks asked the Home Secretary if steps had been taken against me for issuing, last August, a leaflet entitled "All Hail the Scottish Communist Republic",* in which I referred to Scots being used as "bloody tools of the English against our brother Celts of Erin".

*The title was changed later to "All Hail, the Scottish Workers' Republic!"

The Lord Advocate, T.P. Morrison, said he had made enquiries last October, but considered that criminal proceedings were not warranted. My impression is that Morrison was inspired to get the question asked after my Monday challenge, so that I might be involved also in the Sinn Fein fight in Glasgow, on behalf of "our brother Celts of Erin".

On Thursday last I addressed a huge meeting in Barrhead on the Wednesday murder, and advised Irishmen to stand steady and calm. Yet on Thursday night explosives were used to blow up telegraph and telephone poles near Barrhead, and of course the blame was put on the shoulders of Sinn Feiners by the press. Again I suspect, in my mind, the police. The whole situation is wonderfully suspicious when thus knit together and justifies us asking Irishmen and the workers generally to calmly watch the developments.

This is no plea for passive starvation, but for refusal to resort to childish displays of petty force when the government is ready to give us a deluge of blood. Keep Bellahouston Hospital empty, and you are bringing our victory many days nearer. . . .

Speech from the dock, 17 May 1921

(Harry McShane's account in *The Socialist*)

. . . MacLean gave an outline of the lecture which he gave at Airdrie, as at other places. He said that he had given the arguments in other mining districts, although the illustrations sometimes varied. He said that the revolution he advocated was the coming to power of the working class. He was not in favour of fighting with navymen as they were not to blame. He did not believe in exhorting men to violence when they had not the accoutrements of war. He had consistently warned the workers not to run their heads below batons, nor their stomachs against bayonets. The object of the meeting was to encourage the miners, and this was clearly stated by the chairman. He had pointed out that if the workers had spent more money on education instead of on horses they would have got a better return.

He announced at the meeting that he was going to run meetings on different nights in the week in order to have full-time tutors established under the Scottish Labour College in Lanarkshire, Dunbartonshire, Renfrewshire and Greenock. At the meeting he had told the people that in 1914 prices rose, and wages did not rise for twelve months after, therefore from the capitalist's point of view, wages should not go down till next September. He went on to give an illustration about wholesale and retail prices when the Sheriff stopped him.

He said that he deprecated the tremendous cut in miners' wages and

232

brought forward arguments to justify men resisting. He said that the workers ought to follow the example of the Federation of British Industries and form one big union.

The Fiscal, cross-examining, questioned MacLean about what he meant by revolution. MacLean held out both hands, one above the other; he said they represented the two classes in society, the top one being the capitalist class. He then swung his hands round to the reverse position, and said that was revolution.

Speech from the dock, October 1921 (excerpts)

. . . I cannot accept such jumbled statements as mentioned in the fourth charge. . . . I said something on every point as mentioned there, but I said it in my own way and not as mentioned there. After dealing with my own programme for the Town Council, I went on to clear up my position and to specially emphasise the need for one big union as against the Federation of British Industries. I contended that the Federation of British Industries was the power . . . which controlled the coalition government. I argued that the workers should not confine themselves to industrial action, but should take political action as well. Neither political nor industrial action would do separately, and I pointed out in that direction the need for education. I contended people must fight together. They must vote together, they must act industrially together, in unity.

So far as voting was concerned, I pointed out that we were reaching a critical position in Glasgow, that the Labour Party was out to get a majority on the Town Council. I advised the electors to give their votes first to the "reds", failing them the "pinks", but not the "blacks". . . . I added that if Glasgow was captured, Scotland would soon be captured. I for one am out for a Scottish Workers' Republic. I have even issued 100,000 leaflets for a Scottish Communist Republic. I said we must first vote ourselves into political power. I said if we in Scotland made an effort to get a Scottish Communist Republic the British government might then take the initiative against us. I said the danger was that the army, the navy, and the police would be used against us to prevent the establishment of a workers' republic in Scotland.

I then referred to the position of Ireland and said I hoped the workers of Scotland would not allow themselves to be frightened by force. I said we would not use violence; violence would be used against us. That has been discussed by us for 25 years. . . .

I told the workers they would not get anything out of the war. Then came the economic collapse of the world. And the only big city in which the unemployed are organised, where no riots have taken place, is Glasgow. . . .

Election address
(General election, November 1922)

I stand in the Gorbals and before the world as a Bolshevik, alias a Communist, alias a Revolutionist, alias a Marxian. My symbol is the Red Flag, and it I shall always keep floating on high.

For twenty-five years I have been a socialist and have devoted the best of my energy to convert workers to socialism and to teach Marx's writings on wealth production and his interpretation of the course and meaning of historical development during that period.

When war broke out in 1914, I stuck to my Red Flag.

In November 1915, I was dismissed as a schoolteacher by the Govan School Board and the same day I was sentenced to five days in prison or pay £5 for a breach of the Defence of the Realm Act. Being allowed a week to pay the fine, I was free the day after to play a part in the great Clydeside rent strike, the first open display of the class war since the war began. The Govan strikers carried me shoulder high through Glasgow to the Sheriff Court, and at a meeting outside I was instructed to write Asquith, then premier, threatening a continuous strike if rents were not bought back to the pre-war level. Asquith took the hint and I went to Duke Street Prison for five days — on principle. The Rent Restriction Act was passed.

I played an active part in the Clyde shop-steward delegate meeting addressed by Lloyd George and traitor Arthur Henderson in the St Andrew's Hall, on Christmas Day 1915. Lloyd George was beautifully tripped up and fooled. In rage he returned to London and on 8 January 1916 he brought in his Industrial and Military Conscription Bill.

In February I was arrested and taken to Edinburgh Castle as a prisoner of war, was bailed out, and was sentenced to penal servitude for three years at Edinburgh High Court on 12 April 1916. When Jim Connolly saw how things were going in Edinburgh he resolved on the Easter Rebellion in Dublin, the beginning of Ireland's new fight for freedom, a fight that can only end in an Irish workers' republic based on communism.

The February revolution (1917) in Russia forced my release from Peterhead Convict Prison and Perth Penitentiary in June 1917. The November or Bolshevik revolution saw me appointed in January 1918 Russian Consul for Scotland, an honour due to my efforts to get Peter Petroff and Tchitcherin (Russia's Foreign Minister) out of London prisons. I was little more than a month acting as Consul when I was again arrested, and again at the Edinburgh High Court was sentenced to five years' penal

234

servitude. I was released in December 1918, not through the efforts of traitor G.N. Barnes, but by the Cabinet purposely to be used as the Bolshevik bogy against Labour Party candidates, seeing that I was put up as Labour candidate in the 1918 Election for the Gorbals as a challenge to the government.

In 1919 I started a campaign for a united effort to overthrow British capitalism by a General Strike, and at my meetings I made public that I had been drugged in prison through my food like other convicts. The government's reply was the break-up of my family, the blocking my every move through traitors inside the socialist movement, the attempted ruin of my reputation and loss of my tutorship in the Scottish Labour College (founded by me after my dismissal by the Govan School Board) through the dirty work of that communist clown, William Gallacher.

Due to my stand for the unemployed and the miners I got a three months' sentence under the Emergency Powers Act (prepared in 1920 by Lloyd George for the purpose of shutting up real communists) at Airdrie on 17 May 1921. A month after my release I was again arrested. I did eighteen days' hunger strike, before forcible feeding started, as a protest against detention prior to trial. An old brute, Sheriff Boyd, acting for Glasgow's ex-policeman Lord Provost, gave me twelve months. Although getting food through "friends" I found that my food was still being drugged and I gave out a bottle of cocoa and one of tea to William Stewart, Scottish organiser of the ILP, and James Maxton MA, Glasgow organiser of the ILP, showing clear evidence that these drinks had been interfered with. After the election I'm going to carry this devilish prison (and political) practice into the light of day and show John Bull ("Gentleman") up in all his satanic infamy to preserve his right to rob and boss the world.

I feel it necessary to fight him on every occasion. Hence my candidature in the Gorbals. I'll fight till John Bull kills me or I die naturally, but I stand aside for no other man in the working-class movement.

I object to the existing form of society, now known to everyone as capitalist society. Why? Because a few people own the world (outside Russia) and the factories and machinery of wealth production. These are the propertied class, including landlords, capitalists and moneylenders. Most other people have to sell their brain-power or body-power, in short their labour-power, to this class for a return in money called wages. This class is the wage-earning class, or the wage-slave class.

Wages are not based on the money value of the goods produced or services rendered by the slave-class, but on the cost of living. We have seen an unprecedented crash in wages, and still wages are crashing even now to a level for miners and other workers so low that public relief has

235

to be granted to many of them to prevent actual starvation. The next "spring offensive" will be against railwaymen's "Hindenburg line", now that the railways have been melted into four mammoth trusts. By next summer the workers' wages will be so low that they will be less than those given in 1920 to the extent of £700 million per annum; or close on £15 million per week down. The bosses have cruelly seized their chance of unprecedented unemployment to gain their vile end.

Their argument is that the lower wages are, the lower prices will be and the easier sales will become. Thus will trade revive. A lie, I say. United States wage-slaves have a standard of living at least twice that of their fellow-workers in Britain and already the trade boom has started. On 1 October 1922, the United States put on new tariffs of half the price of many imported goods to keep out the sweated goods of Britain and Europe.

We marxians have taught for two generations that the lower wages are compared with the value of the goods produced, the greater the surplus left with the bosses which the workers cannot buy.

Increased production at present would add to this surplus.

But the war has left the people of the world too poor to buy these surplus goods; hence the glut, hence the trade depression, hence unemployment and starvation — a disease peculiar to capitalism.

Robbery of the workers is the root of all the world's troubles, the war with Germany and the coming war with America included.

It is the struggle to get rid of these surplus goods on the world market that has led capitalist countries to steal other people's lands all over the globe. The greediest and dirtiest of all has been John Bull ("Gentleman"). Out of the recent war he has stolen a million and a half square miles of the world. Pressed by Churchill, J.B. spent a hundred million pounds trying to steal Russia from the Bolsheviks and only succeeded in paving the way for the most frightful famine the world has experienced. The drought in South-East Russia could not have wrought the havoc it has done (wiping out a population almost three times that of Scotland) but for the bloody policy of J.B.'s government — Liberals and Tories alike — against Russia. Russia's ruin is the triumph of brutish British capitalism. Mesopotamia has cost another hundred millions and is under the military dictatorship of General Cox.

France has been embittered by Britain's greed against the Germans and by Britain's refusal to help her to get the restoration of the French property destroyed during the war out of the Germans. France therefore has blocked every conference called by Lloyd George, and has helped the Turks against the Greeks (Britain's paid hirelings); and at Mudania France managed to restore the Dardanelles to Turkey and beat Churchill's second rush to seize these straits and Constantinople as an addition to J.B.'s empire. Hence Lloyd George's permanent downfall and Churchill's appendicitis (prison methods). Woodrow Wilson got his knock-out after his folly at the Versailles conference. Assassination is now partly antiquated!

Bonar Law will never play the confidence trick on France, and I calculate France will continue to fight Britain in Europe to prevent a revival of J.B.'s trade on the continent. France's actual or potential ally, the United States, has Japan by the throat and is out to capture the markets in eastern Asia.

The Amritsar massacre and forced belly-crawling in 1919, the imprisonment of Gandhi and thousands of other splendid champions of Indian independence, and Britain's defeat by the Franco-Turkish alliance are conspiring towards not only the political loss of India but the commercial loss of India, too.

The imprisonment of Saglul and other champions of Egyptian independence, and the present open dictatorship of Egypt by Lord Allenby, are making not only for political separation but for trade boycott as well.

The murder of British and Boer workers on the Rand so as to ensure a growing influx of cheaper black wage-slaves will lead to political and economic consequences harmful to J.B.'s trade.

The cruel torture of Ireland has largely ruined Ireland already.

Clearly, then, John Bull's empire is breaking up politically and economically, and the final burst-up will come after war with America unless a world revolution averts the approaching war.

By no accident has Bonar Law, a Canadian of Scottish parentage, of Glasgow business training, and representative of the business Central Division of Glasgow, been appointed Tory premier; and by no accident did he outline his policy in the St Andrew's Hall, Glasgow. He must retain Canada's loyalty to London as a Canadian and as a Scot he must keep the colonies also loyal — colonies largely run by men of Scottish birth or descent.

Against him I stand out as the Scottish workers' supreme champion. I wish a Scottish workers' republic, but Scottish workers to be joined in one big industrial union with their British comrades against industrial capitalism.

I wish Scottish comrades in Canada to establish a Canadian workers' republic independent of John Bull or Uncle Sam ("Gentleman") politically, but linked up with all other American workers in one big industrial union. I wish Scottish comrades in other colonies to do the same.

If we can break up John's blood-soaked empire by separation we shall probably avert a war with America. If not, John must do his own bloody work himself. We must refuse to murder our fellows of this planet at his autocratic bidding.

When all empires are broken up and the workers by political control start to make land and wealth-producing property common property, when of the wealth produced all get sufficient to give them life abundantly with leisure and pleasure and education added thereunto, then all the independent workers' republics will come together into one great League or Parliament of Communist Peoples, as a stage towards the time in the future when inter-marriage will wipe out all national differences and the world will become one.

To get a Scottish workers' republic I shall not go to the London House of Commons, but stay in Scotland helping the unemployed, standing by those at work, educating in the Scottish Labour College, and carrying revolutionary propaganda all over Scotland (and into England too).

I'll support any fight for palliatives honestly started by the workers, until OUR DAY ARRIVES.

If you understand the above fully you'll see that no detailed programme is necessary in this address.

If you cannot agree with me then vote for George Buchanan, the representative of the Labour Party. On no account vote for anyone else.

Yours for the world revolution.

Red flag flutters

(Issued together with November 1922 election address)

To the Gorbals electors I'm issuing the address, a leaflet entitled "All Hail! The Scottish Workers' Republic!" and an article from the November issue of *The Socialist* which I got ready in prison and had written before reading Bonar Law's "Programme Speech" on Thursday, 26 October, in St Andrew's Hall, Glasgow.

I urge readers to buy *The Socialist* and carefully digest my article on the Pacific Ocean Trade Conference sitting whilst Law was speaking. They will then understand that I forestalled Law's single suggestion of an Imperial Trade Conference by my description of the Pacific one.

The silence of the press and Law on the USA's Pacific Conference, whilst urging the British one, is one more proof of my claim that Britain and America are manoeuvring for position before plunging the world into a blood-welter ten times as fiendish as the "great" war.

I agree with Bonar Law when he frankly stated: "In my opinion trade is the most important thing. Now, I have no remedy to give you, but it is the duty of the government to try to help it." Then followed reference to his empire development proposals. I claim that workers need place no faith in empire development as a solution to the trade paralysis of today, the unemployment, and the starvation wages. Britain must have big markets outside the empire, as well as inside.

Where can these markets be obtained? Certainly not in Europe which is plunging deeper into poverty.

Austria is down and out, and closely following her are Germany, Poland, Bohemia, the Balkan States and Greece. The "unconstitutional" and forceful victory of the Fascisti in Italy will lead to imperial ambitions worthy of the Roman empire in its heyday. That signifies class-warfare in Italy and "trouble" in Africa and Asia.

Law says we must regain the confidence of France. I am convinced that France will never again be the dupe of John Bull's old "confidence trick". France will likely continue the obstruction of British trade in Europe until French factories and towns destroyed during the war are restored by Germany.

European possibilities are anything but rosy.

What about Asia and South America? South America is about as shaky as Europe in an economic sense and the USA are bent on capturing what trade is going. The Honolulu Trade Conference just ended shows the USA's plans to capture the trade of the Pacific Ocean.

Britain will have a tight run for trade, it must now be clear. The USA's new tariff (1 October 1922) of 50 per cent on many imports (that is, of 10s on every £1 of goods) must limit the American market for British goods.

The home market depends on the docility of the workers and the situation in Ireland. As long as Lord Carson and John MacLean are alive and free, I fear the prospects of peace are limited.

Law said about the Irish "treaty": "Our word is our bond. . . . Our hearts are moved by the account of horrors which are going on now in parts of Ireland. The people who are suffering have their claim naturally on the Irish government, but we cannot divest ourselves absolutely of responsibility . . ." etc.

At this point in steps Carson with a letter to the press. Most of the letter is a quotation from a writing by a priest deploring the "moral breakdown" in South Ireland.

The heading to the letter characterises the Irish treaty as "the great failure".

Only one vaguely worded sentence need be quoted to prove that Carson, with his die-hards in London, is bent on mischief in Ireland. "It is quite true that the new government must give a fair trial to 'the treaty', and the question of 'how long?' must be one of grave consideration." I'm convinced by that hint that Carson is out for more trouble in Ireland, with economic ruin as a sequel.

So far as I am concerned, I wish it to be understood clearly that there shall be no peace under capitalism, if I can help it.

I mean to fight for the wage-earners by pushing the establishment of one union for all workers so as to prevent further wage-drops and hour extension.

I mean to fight for work for all unemployed or full maintenance at trade-union rates of wages.

I mean to fight for a Scottish workers' republic in which all robbery shall cease. The break-up of every empire, including John Bull's, will make more easy the world revolution from capitalism to communism, and may help to avert a world war which otherwise might come before the workers were ready to take full possession of our planet.

To carry out such work effectively, I have resolved to stay in Scotland, even if the winner in the Gorbals, and so will adopt the Sinn Fein tactics. My battle with Bonar Law will become all the more striking and important. I am looking to Scottish comrades in the colonies taking the cue from me and working for the conversion of these colonies into independent republics. My influence is so great in New Zealand, seemingly, that the government there has excluded my pamphlets. They will simply have to be smuggled in, that's all, for TRUTH MUST PREVAIL.

Explanation of election address
(November 1922)

Readers who have not been in close touch with the various phases of the socialist movement in Britain for the last ten years and have not closely followed my activities since 1914, may wonder at me issuing an election address to the wage-earning class of the British empire. But I am of the opinion, rightly or wrongly, that I am the only standard-bearer of the red flag of marxian communism in the present general election who is fighting untrammelled. No one has done more real work for Russia than I have, by endeavouring to rally all British workers round the mines as a nucleus so that when the clash came British capitalism would have been paralysed by a genuine general strike.

In 1919 whilst in Lancashire I urged an unofficial conference, held in Burnley, of cotton workers to get the cotton trade to rally round Bob Smillie and his fellow miners. At Bradford I urged that the woollen trade of Yorkshire should do the same.

I urged the comrades of these two counties to get into touch with

240

the Clyde Workers' Committee and the general unofficial workers' movement, so that if the paid trade-union leaders funked the issue the rank and file would carry on alone.

When unemployment began to grow bad in the autumn of 1920 I started the Glasgow unemployed movement, and succeeded in getting the use of the City Hall holding 3,500 comfortably. Latterly we had over 4,000 packed into it twice a week, and at least a dozen packed meetings every week in picture houses all over the city.

I predicted that the end of March 1921 would see the capitalists, through the Federation of British Industries, and its willing tool Lloyd George's Cabinet, starting a huge offensive against wages. This I mentioned repeatedly in justification of my attack on John Wheatley and the Labour group in the Glasgow Town Council for their dilatoriness in fighting for the unemployed. . . . *My object was to secure the unemployed so that they wouldn't scab when the fight started.*

My prediction came true. The miners were locked out on 1 April 1921 (All Wage-slave Fool's Day). Betrayed, they fell to ruin and starvation — the greatest betrayal in the annals of Britain. The Clyde dockers were men enough to line up with the miners, but Scotland's Fascisti, White Guards, or National Citizens' Union, provided middle-class scabs to load and unload ships, protected by boys in their teens rigged up as soldiers and sailors.

The Glasgow unemployed did their utmost to get the general strike. The men who betrayed Smillie in 1921 have betrayed the other sections of labour since, and the spring of 1923 will see the offensive against the railwaymen, now that the four big railway trusts have been set a-going.

These industrial traitors are the leaders of the Labour Party and will betray labour politically as they have betrayed labour industrially. . . .

All this time I was anxious about Russia, knowing that the best way to lift pressure off Russia was to engage the capitalist enemy at home.

I haven't got to Russia yet. I'm not going there underground. I must go openly. Lord Curzon, Foreign Minister, has put the bar on my direct request and on my indirect one through Cook's Touring Agency.

In spite of my keen desire to go to Russia, in spite of my equally keen desire to help Lenin and the other comrades I am not prepared to let Moscow dictate to Glasgow. The Communist Party has sold itself to Moscow, with disastrous results both to Russia and to the British revolutionary movement.

After this General Election, I feel sure that a Scottish Communist Party of genuine marxians will spring up, with the object of establishing a Scottish workers' republic, so that Scotland will stand clear of slaughter in the event of war between Britain and America. . . .

241

In any case, the break-up of the British empire is necessary for the real economic development of Russia and the releasing of revolutionary world forces held in check by that bloodiest of bloody brutes, John Bull (Gentleman!).

Scotsmen are found in vast numbers all over John's empire, and these now look to Glasgow for a lead, as Irishmen abroad look to Dublin. Many of these Scotsmen have been in the socialist movement here at home and not a few have imbibed the elements of marxism in my many classes. Bonar Law, as a Scoto-Canadian, has been selected to retain the loyalty of both Scotland and Canada to John's empire. Law received his business training in Glasgow, made his fortune in Glasgow, and represented the Gorbals area I am today contesting, about twenty years ago. G. N. Barnes, one of the many Labour traitors, beat him, and so Law had to be put up for the business Central Division.

I claim, and I think rightly, that I am the clear antithesis to Law. I have survived all the murderously foul attempts of Lloyd George to wipe me out. George is now a past event, and it remains to be seen whether Scotsmen of the slave-class everywhere will rally round me, so that I may checkmate chess-playing Bonar the Brilliant and win both Scotland and the colonies for revolutionary labour and communism.

If the wage-slave class of the Gorbals becomes aware of the significance of the fight, and the mighty influence of my heading the poll on 15 November 1922, all over John's empire, then I feel sure that they will rally to me and their class's real cause as never before have any workers in Scotland.

I ASK ALL SCOTTISH REBELS TO CONCENTRATE ON
GORBALS FOR REVOLUTION.

Municipal election address to the electors of the thirtieth ward
(14 February 1923)
Fellow Workers,

I come before you at this by-election at the request of many members of your ward as a COMMUNIST or RED LABOUR candidate. Pink labourism is of no use to the workers, never will be. Your poverty and misery are more intense today than ever before. Thirteen out of every hundred in Glasgow are getting Parish Council relief, and the number is growing. World developments are bound to make things still worse, even if Britain is lucky enough to avoid another world war.

Mr Bonar Law, at the opening of Parliament yesterday, stated that unemployment was less today by half a million than a year ago. Glasgow at any rate has not benefited, as there are 90,000 workless at the moment — as many as a year ago, if not more. Is Glasgow being specially punished for its fighting attitude during the war?

If it is, it is the business of the workers to reply: and the best reply is voting Red Labour.

As unemployment is a weapon to cow the workers into accepting lower wages and a longer week, it must be clear that the main problem before the workers of Glasgow is unemployment. That was my attitude in October 1920, when I started the present unemployed movement in Glasgow; that is my attitude today.

I propose, if returned, to place before the Corporation a scheme that would absorb all the unemployed of Glasgow. The gist of my proposal is to reclaim all the moorland lying round Glasgow and establish a system of co-operative or collective farming on scientific lines. Out of this vast experiment would arise experience enough to modernise Scottish agriculture.

The cost the first year would be £26,000,000, a sum the government could easily raise on Treasury Bills, and lend to the Corporation free of interest, or at 1 per cent at most. If last year over £100,000,000 were sent abroad as invested capital, why should not this year the above sum be earmarked for Glasgow?

This scheme would involve house-building on the bungalow or cottage principle within village communities scattered all round the area reclaimed. These houses would not only be erected for those working on the land, but also for those employed in the city. An improved system of transit would bring the moorland area within half an hour of the Clyde.

I am in favour of municipalising every industry suitable for local control, as a briefly intermediate system leading on to social ownership; i.e. ownership free from interest-payment.

I wish to see the city extended so as to control the whole Clyde Valley; in other words, its conversion into a provincial council so as to enable the workers more adequately to control all the industries in this very clearly defined area.

The limits imposed by Parliament on the Corporation necessitate a Scottish Parliament. I wish and am striving for one independent of England altogether, for reasons beyond those of Glasgow's immediate interests. I wish a Scottish workers' republic, within which the workers in control can evolve present-day capitalist property into working-class property, as a stage on the road to communal use of all the wealth produced.

My every fight on the Council, my every proposal shall have this larger end in view. . . .

Municipal election address
(used by all candidates in Glasgow, 6 November 1923)
Fellow Citizens,

I come before you as the nominee of the Scottish Workers' Republican Party.

Today the wage-earning class is either partly or wholly idle and living on a starvation insurance or parish allowance, or fully employed at wages well below the 1913 level. Rotten food, under-supplies of food, insufficient clothing, overcrowding in sunless slums, loss of household goods to pawnbrokers, loss and reduction of pensions, worry over debts and the constant fear of eviction form the fate of a growing mass of workers. This is reflected in 1922 in Glasgow in a reduction of births by 1,525 as compared with 1921, an increase of deaths by 2,088, and especially an increase of deaths amongst infants from 3,135 in 1921 to 3,402 in 1922. Impoverished blood, disease, and death — that summarises the situation. The infant death-rate in Kingston in 1922 was 154, in Cathcart 28, i.e. eleven died in Kingston for every two in Cathcart.

The plight of the masses will be worse because of the European tangle of capitalist rivalries and political jealousies, hatreds and ambitions.

Capitalism is smashing itself to death in competition, strife, and bloodshed. In its path to destruction hundreds of millions of helpless people are being crushed by a growing poverty.

The clinging to capitalism, the ownership of the world by a small propertied class, is driving the people of this planet swiftly along the path to perdition.

The hope of humanity and the path to progress lies in the revolt of the wage-earners against the propertied class, the seizure of political power from the propertied class, and the seizure of the land and the means of production from the propertied class.

These seizures of political and economic power constitute the social revolution. The blood-shedding part of the business can safely be left to the Duke of Northumberland and his friends, the British Fascisti.

This great transformation of society, heralded in Russia by the overthrow of the propertied class in 1917, implies the establishment of a workers' republic in every country and of a World Council or Parliament to knit the various republics into one worldwide social organisation.

This great change means that the common people (the workers) will own the world in common, produce wealth in common, possess in common all wealth produced, and by common agreement distribute that wealth to the common advantage. This is a big task for the workers, but one forced on us by the worldwide misery of the masses. There is nothing frightful about the task. When this task is carried through the social stealing of class from class shall end for ever, and with the end of robbery armies and navies no longer shall be required, and social murder or warfare shall vanish for ever. This next form of human society is called communism.

If England is involved in a war against France or any other large world power, our party wishes Scotsmen to stand clear by at once proclaiming a workers' republic in Scotland. That proclamation would imply the establishment of a workers' Parliament in or near Glasgow.

Herein lies the fundamental difference between us Red Labour people and the Pink Labour folk who hide their principles (when they have any) and seek election on petty reforms of a Moderate Party character.

To catch votes many candidates run by the Pinks even exclude all reference to municipalisation and nationalisation.

The collapse of the workers' standard of life through the collapse of the trade unions officered by the pinks, jealous and quarrelling for pelf, position, and power, proves the impotence of all attempts to patch up capitalism, and justifies our party's position that only the social revolution outlined above can lay the foundations for the political and economic security of mankind.

Until developments are ripe for a great mass movement, our party considers it right and proper to take part in the everyday struggle of our class for a sufficient allowance of food, clothing, shelter, education, and leisure, and in the defence of members of our class unjustly treated.

Hence we put forward the following programme at this November election on the clear understanding that nothing we can do in the Town Council will materially alter the general condition of our class:

1. Adequate compensation for the widow and children of Bernard Murdoch, murdered in the Southern Police Station.
2. Release of Thomas Hitman at present lying in Barlinnie Prison under sentence of fifteen months for speaking for the unemployed.
3. Prevention of evictions.
4. Work for the unemployed, organised and executed by the Corporation at an adequate wage; or pressure on the government to provide an allowance adequate to maintain the unemployed.
5. A roomy and well-equipped house for every family.
6. Municipalisation of the milk, bread, clothing, and other supplies able to be handled by the Corporation.
7. No work to be undertaken without the knowledge and consent of the employees' committees.

General election address, Gorbals
(23 November 1923)

Fellow-electors,

I come before you as the nominee of the Scottish Workers' Republican Party at the election to be held on Thursday, 6 December.

My attitude and policy arise out of my view of the world situation and the trend of world events, as do those of Mr Baldwin. He claims that a high tax on foreign goods and a lower one, or none at all, on colonial goods will help the colonies and so revive industry here that the unemployed and the employed alike will get a better chance to live.

That I deny. Nothing Mr Baldwin or any other capitalist politician can do will bring enlarged markets to Britain. His imperial trade preference can but pull the empire more closely together for a bigger and a bloodier war than the last.

Mr Baldwin admits that the European markets are more likely to shrink than expand. Agreed.

Mr Lloyd George and Mr Asquith in the Liberal manifestoes claim that the late Conservative government has lost the Near East market by signing the Treaty of Lausanne in favour of the Turks. Agreed, but with the addition that Mr Lloyd George himself began the ruin.

The Mediterranean trade is likely to be reduced, and Britain may be challenged to hand over Gibraltar to Spain and Malta to Italy, when Italy, France and Spain get into alliance with one another. Already Italy and Spain are embracing one another.

So far as the Far East markets, the markets of the yellow races of Asia, are concerned, last year I tried to impress on you the importance of a trade conference of all countries bordering on the Pacific Ocean called by the United States of America. This conference was to lay the basis of American supremacy in the Far East markets. The struggle for that supremacy is about to begin. This year America has been busy building factories. Next year these factories will turn out floods of goods for the Far East markets. England will be steadily squeezed out. America in September 1922 passed the Fordney Tariff Bill giving power to tax certain European imports as much as 50 per cent of their value.

During the last election Mr Bonar Law proposed the Imperial Trade Conference, which has just ended, as a reply to the above-mentioned Pan-Pacific Conference. Of course, he made no reference to the American one, so that people would miss the meaning of his proposal.

As was clearly indicated at the opening of the Imperial Trade Conference, England's only assured markets were in the colonies. By preference given to goods coming from the colonies it is asserted that the colonies will flourish and trade here will revive. Work will be found for the unemployed. Wages will rise. Baldwin, therefore, seizes his chance to test the electors on the new imperialism.

I see America aspiring to command not only the Asiatic markets but also those of all America as well. I see America's ally, France, pinning down England in Europe and gathering allies and strength to capture the Near East, Mediterranean and African markets. I see England in desperation gathering her imperial resources together for a dying kick in the form of a war with America for supremacy in the Pacific Ocean. Admiral Jellicoe has been in New Zealand preparing the naval defence from Australia round the South Pacific to Cape Horn in South America. Now Singapore has to be a naval base for the fleet to defend India.

As Rosyth was got ready against Germany, so Singapore is being got ready against America in the eternal fight for market supremacy. The war with America is rapidly rushing upon us.

For the wage-earning class there is but one alternative to a capitalist war for markets. The root of all the trouble in society at present is the inevitable robbery of the workers by the propertied class, simply because it is the propertied class. To end that robbery would be to end the social troubles of modern society. The way to end that robbery is the transfer of the land and the means of production and transport from the present possessors to the community. Community ownership is communism. The transfer is a social revolution, not the bloodshed that may or may not accompany the transfer.

Russia could not produce the world revolution. Neither can we in the Gorbals, in Scotland, in Great Britain. Before England is ready I am sure the next war will be on us. I therefore consider that Scotland's wisest policy is to declare for a republic in Scotland, so that the youths of Scotland will not be forced out to die for England's markets.

I accordingly stand out as a Scottish Republican candidate, feeling sure that if Scotland had to elect a Parliament to sit in Glasgow it would vote for a working-class Parliament.

Such a Parliament would have to use the might of the workers to force the land and the means of production in Scotland out of the grasp of the brutal few who control them, and place them at the full disposal of the community. The social revolution is possible sooner in Scotland than in England.

If Baldwin's capitalist policy is to bind the empire closer together to fight American capitalism and incidentally keep the workers enslaved, then the working-class policy ought to be to break up the empire to avert war and enable the workers to triumph in every country and colony. Scottish separation is part of the process of England's imperial disintegration and is a help towards the ultimate triumph of the workers of the world.

My policy of a workers' republic in Scotland debars me from going to John Bull's London Parliament. Last year I told you I would not go, as I could get nothing there. So you sent George Buchanan to get your rents back. Buchanan and his friends have spent a fruitless year and have returned home empty of hand. So, after all, I was right. Had the Labour men stayed in Glasgow and started a Scottish Parliament, as did the genuine Irish in Dublin in 1918, England would have sat up and have made concessions to Scotland just to keep her ramshackle empire intact to bluff other countries. The curious feature in the Gorbals was that the block Irish vote sent Buchanan into the Parliament of the "hated English", whilst the Irish chorus was being sung "Ireland a Nation Once Again"!

It is the Irish vote that prevents Scotland being a nation once again, and prevents us all as slaves getting our freedom. I appeal to Irishmen not to be led any longer by the old nationalist wirepullers, but to think out the situation clearly and calmly. Ireland will only get her republic when Scotland gets hers.

Neither free trade nor protection is of use to the workers. Taxation of land or capital, including the capital levy, is of no use to the workers. No housing or other social reform is really possible whilst industry is paralysed and the earnings of the workers are ever shrinking. The only possible hope of the working class is community ownership of the means of production. The increasing poverty and misery in Gorbals ought to convince the most conservative workers that all the "Woolworth" pottering of the petty politicians of all the "practical" parties (the Labour Party included) has brought no improvement into the life of the citizens of the Gorbals. Your only course now is to back me up for the complete change in the ownership of the world. Every vote cast against me is one cast for world war and the further starvation of the world's workers.

Every vote cast for me is for world peace and eternal economic security for the human family.

12

Letters

Letter to James Clunie from H.M. Prison, Barlinnie
(24 July 1922)
Dear James,

I think it is some considerable time since I received your last to me, but don't imagine you've been swept into the subconscious during the intervening period. I've been wondering how you've been pulling along these "dull industrial days", about your contact with the miners whose plight must be deplorable, your struggles to arouse enthusiasm for next winter's class work (a big task when people's minds are almost exclusively given in serious moments to purely bread and butter questions) and your propaganda work. As I have now only three months to go, at the limit, till my release, I'm looking forward to a long talk on affairs in general and questions in particular you suggested we might profitably discuss. I've heard nothing about Tom [Mitchell] since his visit a long time since, but I expect soon to be writing him. I must have a read of that industrial history book you mention, when I'm in harness again, or off the grass, if you will!

Along with Fourier's book on "The Electron Theory", I'm reading Einstein's popular little book on "The Relativity Theory", as well as Prof. Eddington's on the same subject. This *Relativity* theory is a natural philosophic application of the Hegelian concept, and that's why it has been pushed by Haldane. It seems to me to have emerged fundamentally as a result of Hegel's philosophy, and particularly as a result of problems raised by the electron theory and astronomical theories as to limits to the universe and the position of the solar system in it together with advances and applications of mathematical theories and formulae. Einstein, in his elementary treatise, refers very briefly to the work of others in the spheres of natural science and maths drawn upon by him for his resultant theory of relativity. If you have studied mensuration, algebra, and geometry to any extent you would be able to appreciate to some extent the step forward made by him, and its connection with Marxism, especially, of course, the suggestive hints of Dietzgen for after all; D. simply gives but hints.

Reference to D. reminds me of a report you'll find in this last week's "M.G. Weekly" (July 21) on the third brown cover page, of a conference of philosophers and psychologists on the "Philosophical Aspects of Relativity". The chief combatants in the discussion were Profs. Stout and

Alexander, advocating the older concepts of "idealism" and "realism". It seems to me Dietzgen has given the key to the situation from a relativistic and a Marxian point of view. Whether the professors will be forced out of the old ruts by Einstein's suggestive concepts and by the advance of pscychoanalysis on the materialist basis, is an interesting point that ought to put us on the alert for possible new developments. At home I've Stout's "Psychology" of almost 25 years ago, when I took the Logic Class in Glasgow's 'Varsity, so we may expect him to fight for the old. Only younger men may advance. Einstein is 43 years. . . .

Letter to his daughters

(26 October 1922)

My Dearest Jean & Nan,

I'm sure your mother has told you by this time that I am free again, and I'm sure you'll be very glad to know it. I was so very, very sorry that the wicked men who kept me a prisoner wouldn't let you in to see me, although you had come so far expecting to get in. I've heard wonderful stories how you are both growing so big. I'm just a wee bit afraid that if you don't come home soon again I won't know you. Fancy a father not knowing his own chicks! That's funnier than the stories you read in those comic papers your Aunt Lizzie sends you every week!

And it's not very pleasant for your poor dad to be here writing you in the kitchen without a fire and I won't have one on now perhaps for a good many days, because I'm out most of the day and the evenings about meetings for the town council election and the parliamentary election. Your mother and your Aunt Rose can explain all about these matters to you, and I think you'll both understand better than you did four years ago.

I was amused to read Jean's letter, where she said she was going back *only* to Julius Caesar in history. That's right, Jean. You tell your teacher about Wells' great History of the World and how your father took you back two hundred thousand years before Julius Caesar was born at all. (Your Uncle Bob will show you books written by Julius Caesar describing France, which the Romans called Gaul, and Great Britain which he called Britannia, and Scotland which he called Caledonia.) I must try and send Wells' book through or wait till your next visit to your home.

This afternoon I was at Aunt Lizzie's when Bessie came in and I got her to buy the Children's Encyclopaedia (that's a big word I don't believe your Aunt Rose will be able to say without losing her breath and falling over it) and I'll send all the numbers to you. . . . You'll learn so much that your heads will swell till you'll not be able to get them through the door, and your headmaster will be afraid you'll know more than him and your father put together! Just fancy that, now!

I saw Tom last night, and if he goes on growing as he's doing he'll be able to lift down the moon and walk away with it. What a funny world it would be if no Man in the Moon came out at night to smile at the fairies dancing round the trees on the meadows. Now I'll stop here and I'll write soon again; but you have both to write me a right good letter each, or I'll come thro' and gobble you up like the angry ogre.

Your loving Father.

Letters to James Clunie from Glasgow

(20 April 1923)
Dear James,
. . . Re your MS. I don't like your first two sections, or chapters, as they are too obscure for the young student and the English is sometimes awkward. I intended to give detailed criticism in parallel sheets of paper, but my trouble with the police upset my plans. . . .

The succeeding ones are more concrete, and therefore more clear,

Your method of approach to the specific study of social questions is a good one in preparation of students for a more systematic study of social development and economics.

Unfortunately, I was unable to read the last two or three of your papers, so that I'm not in a position to survey your treatment as a whole. altho' I think bits could be deleted here and there, and other matter added. The style sometimes is fairly loose, and some would say slovenly, altho' on the whole your style is vastly improved.

But I'm thoroughly satisfied your method is evolving along proper lines. . . . Study a good grammar like Nesfield's incessantly for correctness and Blatchford for simple effective style, and you'll evolve quicker yet.

Tell me what you think of the new Scot. W. Repub. Party as outlined in the leaflet. I'm certain London will never lead the Clyde or Scotland, so we must lead ourselves. A separate republic is justifiable as a step to keep Scotland out of future wars involving England; and breaking up the Empire that most of all retards Communism.

A working alliance with Ireland and Russia would give Scotland a great leverage in the period of transition. Think it over. . . .

(23 May 1923)
It was only when I missed the following issue of "The Miner" that I recollected I hadn't replied to yours of 8th inst. But again excuse me, as I'm full up with the by-election. Was out at five back-door meetings this after-

noon. My voice is a "goner", and yet a week has still to go — next Tuesday's polling day.

I enclose samples of two leaflets. My address is every time bringing out sharper and sharper the difference between the pinks and the reds — the dialectic process in the political process, or rather political part of the process. You can show both round amongst comrades as signs of the titanic struggle for supremacy in Glasgow and then in Scotland.

I saw a comrade at the SLC conference in Hamilton (Lanarkshire area) who told me of your first article in "The Miner". On hearing that, I drew the copy from my pocket to show that I was up-to-date, too.

Now, that article was nice, precise, clear and exactly what I'm wishing from you.

You must send on the following issues to keep us abreast of things in Fife.

We are stirring Glasgow, despite the wintry weather, not only in Kingston, but elsewhere as well. We'll pull Glasgow our way by autumn. At least, that's the aim. . . .

(10 July 1923)

I got your welcome letter, press cuttings, and SLC typed report with "The Miner" just as I was leaving for Dublin to see J. Larkin. I was staying in the house of Delia with him and Pete Larkin and Jack Carnie from the Tuesday till the Thursday evening. Pete Larkin has just finished an eight day visit to Glasgow, went home pleased with his reception and 17 meetings (all very large) and will urge Jim to come here for a few days prior to going to Russia. Jim would like to report there on the real state of affairs here.

I hadn't time to read "The Miner", but left it in Larkin's house. Geo. Pollock (ICP) would like to get it for your notes as he's going to write along like lines for the CP of Ireland's paper. . . .

We have just agreed on a constitution for the SWRP and we can now move ahead systematically. We are having monster meetings and as you'll see we are steadily creeping over the city.

The ILP are desperate, as is seen by Dollan's attack on me in "Forward" and by the Commons melodrama of Maxton & Co. If Jim Larkin comes for ten days and later follows with another month's visit you can take it from me that the tide has definitely swung our way. Larkin is re-issuing his "Irish Worker" and we mean to sell it. . . .

(5 October 1923)

. . . So far as the SLC work in Glasgow is concerned I'm at loggerheads with the Committee over their "constitution", one that is tying them up instead of fostering education. I've had to attack them twice at W. Regent St., and I think that will do good. Publicity I find my only safeguard against the opposition parties.

I gave four nights a week and not one class has been started yet. There's business ability for you! The advts. in "Forward" are largely shown, in both Glasgow and Lanarkshire. Had I left my Sunday class to the Committee it, too, would have had a belated start. Happily I got the Ardgowan Picture House and have pushed the advertisement of the class. In the past I used to issue 10,000 leaflets announcing the class. This time the Committee has issued nothing meantime. Fortunately, the manager of the Ardgowan has advertised it in the leaflet I enclose and on the screen this week. He caters for Kinning Park and Kingston, so that a wide area is thus tapped. Latterly I've been getting about 3,000 at W. Regent St., the biggest crowds ever held Sunday after Sunday in Glasgow, and at these I've pushed the class as well as at the Monument every Sunday afternoon. . . .

The SWRP, I expect, will have at least a dozen candidates up in November, and we are using all our speakers as candidates, so as to put on the utmost pressure. . . .

The situation in Germany, where all the propertied parties are joining against the Pink Soc. Dems., will help us tremendously from now right on till the election. I expect a rapid landslide our way sooner or later, if our men have the grit to hold on as we have done this summer. France, Spain and Italy may form a Latin alliance in reply to the Imperial Econ. Conf. now running in London, just as this one is Britain's reply to the USA Pan-Pacific Conf. held on Oct. 25-31 last year. . . .

The size of my Sunday night audience is largely due to the fair interpretation of evolving events in general and in detail. As things are going, a growing number of Glasgow people are quite alive; and should a crisis arise I feel sure the people will come to me for guidance. That is one tremendous advantage of the continuity of meetings and concentration of efforts on Glasgow. . . .

Your old comrade,
John MacLean.

Index

Adamson, William, 194
Addison, Dr, 129, 200
Adler, Friedrich, 15
Aldred, Guy, 20
Alexander, Professor, 250
Allenby, Lord, 237
Anderson, Tom, 138, 211
Ashley, Lord, 120
Asquith, H.H., 35, 85, 176, 234, 246
Avila, John, 191

Bakunin, M., 225
Baldwin, Stanley, 246
Balfour, A.J., 219
Ballantine, 53, 54
Barnes, G.N., 235, 242
Bax, E. Belfort, 76
Beardmore, 103
Bell, Alan, 171
Bell, Richard, 37-8
Bell, Tom, 21-2
Berger, 181
Bernhardi, 76
Bernstein, Eduard, 10
Berwick, Thurso, 22
Blatchford, Robert, 35
Böhm-Bawerk, 33, 34-5
Booth, Charles, 132
Bottomley, Horatio, 168
Boyd, Sheriff, 235
Bramley, Fred, 157-9
Bridges, Robert, 85
Bruce, Robert, 165
Buchanan, George, 238, 248
Burke, Thomas Henry, 171
Burns, Robert, 10, 217
Byrne, L.P., 162
Byrne, Robert, 173

Cadbury, 134
Campbell, J.R., 205
Campbell Bannerman, Henry, 24
Carnie, Jack, 525
Carson, Sir Edward, 103, 239
Cavendish, Lord Frederick, 171
Chamberlain, Austen, 184, 194
Chamberlain, Joseph, 90, 124, 125
    182
Chicherin, G., 15, 229, 234
Childers, Erskine, 172
Churchill, Sir Winston, 142, 161, 188,
    195, 201, 202, 225, 236
Clunie, James, 17, 158, 159, 230, 249-
    50, 251-3
Clynes, J. R., 195, 208

Cole, G.D.H., 22
Connolly, James, 18, 74, 160, 163,
    164, 174, 176, 234
Cowdray, Lord, 183
Cox, General, 236
Croall, 50
Cromer, Lord, 119
Cross, F. J., 132
Cunningham, William, 120
Curzon, Earl, 227, 241

Dalrymple, James, 152, 153
Darcy, M., 173
Darwin, Charles, 76
Debs, Eugene, 163, 181
Denham, 98
De Valera, Eamon, 171, 187, 189
Dietz, D.A., 191
Dietzgen, Joseph, 249, 250
Dollan, P.J., 252
Dorman, 200
Dubb, Henry, 130, 194
Dyer, General, 168, 169

Eddington, Professor A.S., 249
Einstein, Albert, 249, 250
Engels, Friedrich, 124, 243
Erskine, R., 219
Erskine, Stuart, 140, 144n.
Esterman, Tom, 230

Fairchild, E.C., 74, 197, 225, 227
Figgis, Darrell, 162
Fineberg, Joe, 228
Fisher, Lord, 201
Fitzgerald, 179
Fourier, 249
French, Lord, 128, 167, 171

Gallacher, William, 12-13, 18, 21, 71,
    73, 137, 142, 225, 228, 229, 235
Gandhi, Mahatma, 237
Gavin, Pat, 173
Geddes, Alex, 103, 219
George, Henry, 172
Gibbins, 120
Goodsir Smith, Sidney, 22
Gough, General, 103
Graham, Frank, 199
Grayson, Victor, 35, 42
Grey, Sir Edward, 76, 130, 188

Haig, Sir Douglas, 182, 183
Haldane, Lord, 182, 249
Hall, 117

Hardie, James Keir, 10, 24, 42-3, 207
Haywood, William D., 163, 181, 191
Hegel, G.W.F., 249
Henderson, Arthur, 156, 195, 208, 234
Henderson, Hamish, 16, 23
Hendry, David W., 51
Hilferding, R., 225
Hilquit, Morris, 225
Hitman, Thomas, 245
Hobart, 43
Hobhouse, Mrs, 107
Hobson, John A., 120
Hodgskin, 119
Horne, 195, 219
Horthy, 176
Houston, James, 52-4
Huggin, 60
Hughes, J.J., 161
Hunter, Dr James, 18, 86
Hutchinson, Lieut.-Col., 201
Huxley, Thomas, 76
Hyndman, H.M., 10, 35, 38, 71, 72, 74, 92, 215, 216

Jellicoe, Admiral, 128, 247
Johnston, Thomas, 10, 27, 36, 37, 39, 40, 41, 42, 161, 221
Johnston-Hicks, Sir W., 231

Kahn, 138, 193
Kautsky, Karl, 27, 120, 225
Kaye, Arthur, 47
Keane, Dr, 173
Kendall, Walter, 28, 141
Kennedy, Laurence, 173
Kerensky, Alexander, 98, 166, 212
Kirkwood, David, 72, 75, 101
Kitchener, Lord, 128
Krassin, N., 169
Kun, Bela, 176

Labriola, A., 120
Lafargue, 120
Lansbury, George, 204
Larkin, Delia, 161, 252
Larkin, James, 164, 165, 174, 252
Larkin, Peter, 160, 175, 252
Law, Bonar, 24, 152, 155, 161, 213, 219, 237, 238, 240, 242
Law, T.S., 22
Lee, Sheriff, 86, 215
Lenin, V.I., 13, 15, 17, 73, 109, 139, 146, 204, 225, 241
Leverhulme, Lord, 129, 134, 154, 168, 189, 199, 217, 219, 221, 222, 224
Liebknecht, Karl, 15, 16
Lindsay, Dorothy, 132
Litvinoff, Maxim, 99
Lloyd George, David, 82, 85, 87, 96, 101, 109, 128, 144, 154, 155, 161, 167, 169, 175, 176, 179, 180, 181, 182, 183, 185, 194, 195, 201, 202,

215, 220, 222, 227, 228, 234, 235ff., 242, 246
Longuet, Jean, 25
Luxemburg, Rosa, 10, 16

McArthur, 219
McBride, Andrew, 85
McBride, Maud Gonne, 162, 163
McCrae, 220
MacDiarmid, Hugh, 21, 22, 23
MacDonald, J. Ramsay, 24, 156, 194, 225, 227
MacDonnell, Joseph, 161
MacDougall, James D., 11, 14, 28, 71-2, 73, 98, 116, 215, 216, 229
McGinn, Matt, 16
McGrath, Joseph, 161
MacLean, Agnes, 115
MacLean, Daniel, 9
MacLean, Neil, 23
McLoughlin, Sean, 163
MacPhee, Anne, 9
MacPherson, Ian, 163, 222
Macready, General, 179
McRory, Father, 231
McShane, Harry, 21, 73, 143, 232-3
MacSwiney, Lord Mayor, 179
Mallock, 198
Malone, Lieut.-Col., 141, 142, 225, 227
Mann, Tom, 44, 129, 178, 213
Mannix, Archbishop, 219
Markievicz, Countess, 160, 161
Marks, Joe, 191
Marshall, Alfred, 46, 84, 118
Marshall, Peter, 222
Marx, Karl, 9, 10, 28, 33, 34, 35-6, 38, 39, 43, 46, 47-8, 118, 119, 120, 124, 125, 139, 143, 164, 196-7, 199, 200, 202, 225, 234
Maxton, James, 11, 23, 72, 73, 235, 252
Metzen, J.L., 191
Meyers, Frank H., 191
Meynell, Frances, 227
Milner, Lord, 204
Mitchell, Tom, 230, 231, 249
Mitchison, Naomi, 140
Moffat, Graham, 219
Money, Chiozza, 134
Mooney, Tom, 163, 181
Morgari, Ordino, 92
Morrison, T.B., 224, 232
Munro, Robert, 221ff.
Murdoch, Bernard, 245
Murphy, F., 173
Murphy, J.T., 200
Murphy, Matthew, 173

Nicol, Councillor, 209
Northumberland, Duke of, 221

O'Brien, James, 161

O'Brien, William, 161, 162
O'Grady, 202
O'Neil, John, 161
Osborne, W.V., 38, 42, 43
O'Shannon, Cathal, 161, 163, 164
Owen, Robert, 63

Pankhurst, Sylvia, 96, 204
Parnell, C.S., 171
Paton, John, 13
Paton, Dr D. Noel, 132
Pells, Major E.A., 200
Penrhyn, Lord, 31
Petroff, Peter, 15, 72-3, 94, 215, 228-9, 234
Philipps, Sir Owen, 91
Piggott, 159
Plekhanov, G., 120
Pollok, George, 98

Quelch, Harry, 228

Reed, John, 74
Ricardo, David, 118, 119
Rice, Michael, 173
Roberts, 128
Robertson, Dr ("Rob Roy"), 28, 35-6
Rockefeller, 183
Rogers, J.E.T., 120
Ross, Sandy, 209, 210, 222
Rothschild, 96
Rothstein, Theodore, 141, 142, 225, 227
Rowan, James, 191
Rowntree, 132, 134
Rushworth, William, 80
Russell, George (A.E.), 163
Ryan, W.P., 163

Saglul, 237
Sauerback, 46
Schroders, 96
Scott, Professor, 86
Shadwell, Dr, 19, 229
Shammes, Louis, 99
Shaw, Donald, 224
Shaw, Fred, 123
Shaw, G.B., 43
Sheehy-Skeffington, Mrs, 162
Sinclair, Upton, 54

Smilie, Robert, 97-8, 117, 149, 156, 178, 207, 208, 216, 240, 241
Smith, Adam, 118
Smith, Herbert, 156
Snowden, Philip, 227
Somers, Frank, 229
Spence, 209
Spiridonova, M., 15
Stevenson, Chief Constable, 152
Stewart, John, 205, 209
Stewart, William, 235
Stevens, Campbell, 23
Stirling-Maxwell, Sir John, 10, 11
Stirton, Det. Sgt, 229
Stout, Professor, 249, 250
Strathclyde, Lord, 124
Sutherland, 107
Syme, John, 115

Tchitcherin. See Chicherin
Thomas, J.H., 154, 175, 176, 186
Thomson, 119
Trotsky, L., 15, 73, 110, 212, 227
Turati, Filippo, 225
Turner, Bailie A., 152

Usher, Professor Roland G., 105, 106, 120, 183, 195
Ustinoff, 74

Vandervelde, Emile, 92, 94
Vernon, Dr, 199

Wallace, Sir William, 165
Walsh, M., 173
Weir, Lord, 197, 200
Weir, William, 82, 88
West, Henry L., 183
Wheatley, John, 205, 209, 241
White, Governor, 31
Williams, Robert, 154, 155, 178
Wilson, Sir Henry, 168, 169
Wilson, Woodrow, 105, 106, 109, 181, 182, 183, 220, 237

Young, Professor Douglas, 140
Young, James D., 22

Zinoviev, G., 146